Hiking Huntsville

Volume 1

MARCUS WOOLF

MONTVIEW
COMMUNICATIONS
Huntsville, AL

Montview Communications
2606 Bonita Circle
Huntsville, AL 35801
Montviewcommunications@gmail.com
HuntsvilleTrails.com

Although the author and publisher have made every effort to ensure that the information in this book was correct at press time, the author and publisher do not assume and hereby disclaim any liability to any party for any loss, damage, or disruption caused by errors or omissions, whether such errors or omissions result from negligence, accident, or any other cause.

Project Management by Marla Markman, MarlaMarkman.com
Cover and Interior Design by Kelly Cleary, kellymaureencleary@gmail.com

Maps were produced using Caltopo.com as well as openstreetmap.org and ©OpenStreetMap contributors. ©OpenStreetMap data is made available under the Open Database License.

Ordering Information:
Quantity sales. Special discounts are available on quantity purchases by corporations, associations, and others. For details, contact the publisher at the address above.

Publisher's Cataloging-in-Publication Data
Names: Woolf, Marcus, author.
Title: Hiking Huntsville , volume 1 : a guide to 80 trails on Monte Sano Mountain, Huntsville Mountain and Green Mountain / Marcus Woolf.
Series: Hiking Huntsville
Description: Includes index. | Huntsville, AL: Montview Communications, 2022.
Identifiers: LCCN: 2022909456 | ISBN: 979-8-9861788-0-6 (paperback) |
979-8-9861788-1-3 (ebook)
Subjects: LCSH Hiking--Huntsville (Ala.)--Guidebooks. | Huntsville (Ala.)--Guidebooks. | Hiking--Alabama--Guidebooks. | Natural history--Huntsville (Ala.). | Huntsville (Ala.)--History. | BISAC SPORTS & RECREATION / Hiking | TRAVEL / Special Interest / Hikes & Walks
Classification: LCC GV199.42.A2 .W66 v. 1 2022 | DDC 796.5109761--dc23

Printed in the United States of America

For Wendy

CONTENTS

Acknowledgments vii

Preface ix

Introducing the Huntsville Metro Area xi

    Local Hiking Areas...xii

    Climate xiv

    Geography and Geology..xv

    Landscape Highlights xvi

    Flora xvii

    Fauna xviii

    Comfort, Safety and Etiquette xxi

Using This Book xxxiii

Chapter 1: Monte Sano State Park 1

    Section 1: North Plateau Loop 4

        Trail 1: North Plateau Loop 5

    Section 2: Fire Tower Trail, Bog Trail and Bucca Family

                Bike Trail...10

        Trail 2: Fire Tower Trail 11

        Trail 3: Bog Trail 14

        Trail 4: Bucca Family Bike Trail 16

    Section 3: McKay Hollow Trail, Rocky Nightmare Trail

                and South Plateau Loop Trail...............................20

        Trail 5: McKay Hollow Trail 21

        Trail 6: Rocky Nightmare Trail 23

        Trail 7: South Plateau Loop Trail 25

    Section 4: Mountain Mist Trail, Goat Trail, Flat Rock

                Connector Trail and Flat Rock Trail Section.....30

        Trail 8: Mountain Mist Trail....................................... 31

        Trail 9: Goat Trail.. 33

        Trail 10: Flat Rock Connector Trail 36

        Trail 11: Flat Rock Trail 37

Section 5: **Sinks Trail, Stone Cuts Trail, Stone Cuts Bypass, Keith Trail and William Arthur Wells CCC Memorial Trail** 42

Trail 12: Sinks Trail.....................................43

Trail 13: Stone Cuts Trail 45

Trail 14: Stone Cuts Bypass 48

Trail 15: Keith Trail 49

Trail 16: William Arthur Wells CCC Memorial Trail 50

Section 6: **Logan Point Trail, Logan Point Alternate Trail, Flat Rock Connector Trail and Panther Knob Trail** 54

Trail 17: Logan Point Trail 55

Trail 18: Logan Point Alternate Trail 57

Trail 19: Flat Rock Connector......................58

Trail 20: Panther Knob Trail........................59

Chapter 2: **Monte Sano Nature Preserve** 62

Section 1: **Bluff Line Trail, Old Bluff Line Trail, High Trail and Hotel Basin Trail** 66

Trail 21: Bluff Line Trail 67

Trail 22: Old Bluff Line Trail........................69

Trail 23: High Trail 69

Trail 24: Hotel Basin Trail...........................72

Section 2: **Toll Gate Trail and Gaslight Trail** 74

Trail 25: Toll Gate Trail...............................75

Trail 26: Gaslight Trail.................................78

Section 3: **Old Railroad Bed Trail, Belue Trail, Watts Trail, Fagan Springs Trail, Wildflower Trail and Sink Hole Trail** 80

Trail 27: Old Railroad Bed Trail 81

Trail 28: Belue Trail.....................................84

Trail 29: Watts Trail 85

Trail 30: Fagan Springs Trail 86

Trail 31: Wildflower Trail 89

Trail 32: Sink Hole Trail................................93

Section 4: Alms House Trail, Three Caves Loop Trail
**   and Waterline Trail**..96
    Trail 33: Alms House Trail 97
    Trail 34: Three Caves Loop Trail 100
    Trail 35: Waterline Trail.. 102
Section 5: Wagon Trail and Young-Kennedy Trail.................106
    Trail 36: Wagon Trail 107
    Trail 37: Young-Kennedy Trail.................................109
Section 6: Dummy Line Trail and Bankhead Trail.................. 112
    Trail 38: Dummy Line Trail....................................... 113
    Trail 39: Bankhead Trail 115
Section 7: Oak Park Trail, Buzzards Roost Trail
**   and Dallas Branch Trail** 118
    Trail 40: Oak Park Trail... 119
    Trail 41: Buzzards Roost Trail 121
    Trail 42: Dallas Branch Trail.................................... 123

Chapter 3: Monte Sano Preserve and
**   Monte Sano State Park** 125
    Section 1: Trail 43: Cold Spring Trail........................ 126
    Section 2: Arrowhead Trail, Big Cat Hill Bypass and
    **   Natural Well Trail** 132
        Trail 44: Arrowhead Trail and Big Cat Hill Bypass.............. 133
        Trail 45: Natural Well Trail......................................137
    Section 3: Trough Springs Trail and Bushwhacker
    **   Johnston Trail**.. 142
        Trail 46: Trough Springs Trail 143
        Trail 47: Bushwhacker Johnston Trail...................144
    Section 4: Trail 48: Bankhead Parkway...................... 148
    Section 5: Warpath Ridge Trail and Red Lizard Trail 152
        Trail 49: Warpath Ridge... 153
        Trail 50: Red Lizard Trail 155

Chapter 4: Burritt on the Mountain 158

    Trail 51: Rock Bluff Trail 160

    Trail 52: Oak Tree Trail 164

    Trail 53: Discovery Trail 165

    Trail 54: Big Cove Turnpike Trail 168

Chapter 5: Blevins Gap Nature Preserve 172

    Section 1: Jones Valley Loop Trail, Bailey Cove Trail, Walsingham Connector and Walsingham Trail, and Chittamwood Trail 176

    Trail 55: Jones Valley Loop Trail 177

    Trail 56: Bailey Cove Trail 179

    Trail 57: Walsingham Connector and Walsingham Trail 180

    Trail 58: Chittamwood Trail 183

    Section 2: Fanning Trail, Stevenson Trail and Scout Trail 186

    Trail 59: Fanning Trail 187

    Trail 60: Stevenson Trail 190

    Trail 61: Scout Trail 191

    Section 3: Smokerise Trail, Smokerise Connector and Sugar Tree Trail 194

    Trail 62: Smokerise Trail 195

    Trail 63: Smokerise Connector 197

    Trail 64: Sugar Tree Trail 198

    Section 4: Bill and Marion Certain Trail, Lowry Trail, West Bluff Trail and Varnedoe Trail 202

    Trail 65: Bill and Marion Certain Trail 203

    Trail 66: Lowry Trail 206

    Trail 67: West Bluff Trail 207

    Trail 68: Varnedoe Trail 209

Chapter 6: Green Mountain Preserve 214

    Section 1: Alum Hollow Trail, East Plateau Trail, Ranger Trail, Natures Ridge Trail and Gibson Trail 218

    Trail 69: Alum Hollow Trail 219

    Trail 70: East Plateau Trail 222

Trail 71: Ranger Trail...223

Trail 72: Natures Ridge Trail..226

Trail 73: Gibson Trail...227

Section 2: **Talus Trail, Talus Connector and**

Three Sisters Loop Trail 230

Trail 74: Talus Trail 231

Trail 75: Talus Connector 232

Trail 76: Three Sisters Loop 234

Section 3: **West Plateau Trail, Stonefly Trail and**

Oak Bluff Trail 236

Trail 77: West Plateau Trail 237

Trail 78: Stonefly Trail..238

Trail 79: Oak Bluff Trail 240

Chapter 7: Madison County Nature Trail 242

Trail 80: Madison County Nature Trail..............................243

Hikes by Theme..249

History...249

Hikes for Kids 249

Streams, Ponds and Lakes...249

Running Trails 250

Great Views 250

Waterfalls...250

Wildflowers 250

Index... 251

About the Author.. 255

Acknowledgments

I couldn't have made this book without the generosity of many people, especially my wife, Wendy. Her love and support carried me through often-difficult work that lasted more than two years. I would also like to thank my parents, who helped edit the text and provided constant encouragement. A big hug to my friend Andy Somers for advising me on mapmaking, and thanks to authors Karen Somers and James Dziezynski for sharing their wisdom on the process of creating guidebooks. A big shout-out to my longtime friend Brenda Constantino for volunteering to teach me the finer points of Adobe Illustrator. And this book would have never reached its full potential without the guidance and expertise of Marla Markman and the creative hand of Kelly Cleary.

I also received valuable assistance from people at key local organizations, including Melanie Manson of the Land Trust of North Alabama, Katheleen Theriault of the Hays Nature Preserve and Ben Hoksbergen of the University of Alabama in Huntsville. I also got excellent help from local experts on several subjects, including botanist Lynne Weninegar, ecologist Soos Weber, and local trail historian Bruce Martin. Also, thanks to Erin McMahon and Chad Edwards with Huntsville Area Mountain Bike Riders (HAMR) for offering background information on trails and their organization's important work.

I want to give kudos to the city of Huntsville and Mayor Tommy Battle for understanding and appreciating the value of greenways and outdoor recreation. Finally, a big round of applause for the volunteers who work with HAMR, the Land Trust of North Alabama and other local groups to build and maintain our local trails. Without their hard work, hikers wouldn't be able to enjoy fantastic trail systems throughout the Huntsville area.

Preface

When I was 13 years old, my parents informed my brother and me that we were moving from our home in northwest Huntsville to Monte Sano Mountain. To say I was bummed would be putting it mildly. While it took less than 20 minutes to drive from our current house to the top of the mountain, my adolescent mind determined that we were moving to the dark side of the moon.

The mountain was a stranger to me. Our family rarely went there, aside from the occasional picnic in the state park. But that was the case for most people in Huntsville. In those days, the mountain was not a major destination for hiking, biking or pretty much anything else. While the state park offered a few trails, they were not well marked and rarely maintained. With this move, I was being carted off to an alien world. Despite my protests and worries, we moved on a November evening. As we wound our way up Monte Sano in the dark, we ascended into thick fog, and I wondered what lay in my future.

After the move, my parents helped me adjust to my new surroundings by giving me great latitude in how I spent my free time on the mountain. As long as I told them where I was going and I traveled with my best friend, Evan, I could wander wherever I pleased. So on Saturdays, we would shoulder rucksacks and strike off into the woods. Throughout middle school, Evan and I explored the remote mountainsides and deep hollows of Monte Sano, often staying in the forest overnight. We slept on the ground, ate Army C rations, and had encounters with snakes and spiders and cave crickets. We had no guidebooks and no maps and made plenty of mistakes. Sometimes we got lost. But in getting lost, we gained knowledge and confidence, and I became remarkably at ease in the woods. In time, the mountain was no longer a stranger, but another close friend.

Those weekends in the forest sparked my interest in all sorts of outdoor adventures. After college, I moved to California and launched a career as a writer and editor for outdoor magazines. When I moved back to Alabama in 2002, an editor at *Backpacker* magazine taught me how to map and document trails. Before long, I used those skills to write a hiking guidebook for the Atlanta area. That project was a major challenge, and when it was complete, I wasn't sure if I'd ever do another guidebook. But a few years ago, an idea crept into my head.

While hiking Land Trust trails on Monte Sano, I began to encounter more and more people who were new to the area. Often they would ask me for suggestions on trails to explore. During one week in spring, this happened on three separate occasions. With the local population exploding and recreation areas expanding, I realized that folks needed more detailed information on places to hike. During those spring days, I also rediscovered how much I enjoy helping people find their way, especially on a mountain that I love. This book is really an extension of those conversations on the trail; it's another way for me to point people in the right direction and help them enjoy the outdoors.

Whether you've recently moved to the Huntsville area or you're new to hiking, I hope this book can serve as a helpful travel companion. If you're native to the area or an experienced hiker, I hope it will enhance your knowledge of local trails and the history of this special place. And for everyone, my wish is that this book will make the mountains and the other wild places feel more like home.

Introducing the Huntsville Metro Area

Over the past decade, the population of the Huntsville metro area has boomed, and it now includes nearly half a million people. According to the United States Census Bureau, the Huntsville metro area is composed of Madison County and Limestone County and covers more than 1,300 square miles. It includes the major cities of Huntsville, Madison, Athens and Decatur, as well as several smaller neighboring communities. This book focuses on Huntsville and Madison, plus Hazel Green to the north and Gurley and Owens Cross Roads to the east.

The two fastest-growing cities in the metro area are Huntsville and Madison. According to the 2020 census, Huntsville is home to a little more than 215,000 people, making it the most populous city in the state. Between 2010 and 2020, the city population exploded, gaining nearly 35,000 people. In the latest count, the city of Madison also showed significant growth. It recorded a population of 56,933, up from 42,938 in 2010. The census reported that the greater Huntsville metro area has a population of 491,723, projected to rise to 528,141 by 2030.

Of course, these statistics only reflect the area's most recent history. People have occupied this part of the country for more than 10,000 years. By exploring the trails in this book, you'll not only experience the area's wonderful natural features, but also get a sense of its history. For example, the Alum Hollow Trail on Green Mountain will lead you to a rock shelter that served as a dwelling for ancient Native Americans.

Other paths will transport you back in time to Huntsville's pioneer days. The town was settled in 1805 when John Hunt, the city's namesake, moved his family from Tennessee to Big Spring and began farming. The population grew gradually throughout the 1800s, and local trails trace that history. On Monte Sano Mountain, the Old Railroad Bed Trail takes you along the old, rugged route of the now-defunct Monte Sano Railway. In 1888, it was built to carry people from downtown Huntsville to the Hotel Monte Sano. Many trails on the mountain follow old wagon roads and visit pioneer homesites, while others pass stone cabins that the Civilian Conservation Corps built in the 1930s.

Huntsville remained a small Southern town until World War II, when the U.S. Army established Redstone Arsenal. In the 1960s, the city made further strides when NASA created the Marshall Space Flight Center and the U.S. Army Aviation and Missile Command. In Monte Sano State Park, you can hike to a historic fire tower where rocket scientists tracked the telemetry of the Soviet Union's *Sputnik* satellite. While walking the park's North Plateau Loop, you'll pass a planetarium constructed by NASA scientist Wernher von Braun and other members of Huntsville's Von Braun Astronomical Society, which is now known as the Von Braun Astronomical Society.

Whether you're new to this area or you were born here, you'll probably learn something new as you explore the local trails and greenways. While most of us lace up our boots and shoulder a pack to simply enjoy the outdoors, a hike is also an opportunity to explore history. When I read the name of a trail, a street, or a place on the map, it makes me ask, "I wonder why it's named that?" Almost always, the search for an answer makes my hike, and my life, a little more interesting.

LOCAL HIKING AREAS
Monte Sano State Park

As the defense and space industries have fueled growth in the metro area, it has resulted in a much larger population of people who want to hike, bike and run local trails. Fortunately, both governmental and private organizations have greatly expanded the quantity and quality of nearby recreation areas. On the eastern side of Huntsville, Monte Sano State Park has historically been a primary destination for all sorts of trail activities. Over the past decade, the Alabama State Parks Division has improved and expanded the park's facilities, while local groups, such as the Huntsville Area Mountain Bike Riders (HAMR), have constructed and overhauled many trails on the mountain. There are now 35 miles of trails in the state park, and they are now more diverse, easier to navigate, and better maintained.

Land Trust of North Alabama
Nature Preserves

In the 1980s, local builders broached the idea of developing the western slopes of Monte Sano. This led to the formation of the Huntsville Land Trust, which raised enough money to purchase 547 acres on the mountain and prevent the development. Now known as the Land Trust of North Alabama, the organization has protected some 9,000 acres of land in six counties. It has also greatly expanded the number of trails in the Huntsville metro area, from Monte Sano to Madison. Its nine preserves and greenways include more than 70 miles of trails that are maintained regularly by Land Trust volunteers. All of these multiuse trails are open to hikers and mountain bikers, while a couple of preserves also serve horseback riders. While the Land Trust does take donations, it does not require users to pay a fee to enjoy the trails.

Greenways
(See Hiking Huntsville Volume 2)

While Monte Sano State Park and the Land Trust have expanded and improved local trails, city governments have also added areas to walk and ride bikes in a peaceful, natural setting. The cities of Huntsville and Madison operate at least a dozen greenways, which are basically corridors of undeveloped land in urban areas. There are more than 27 miles of local greenways where you can stroll through shaded forests and watch horses grazing in sunny fields. You might see great blue herons soaring above a rushing river or see a hawk perched in a towering oak tree.

While the greenways explore natural landscapes, the trails themselves are paved and mostly level, allowing people of all abilities to access the outdoors. In most cases, there is a buffer zone between the trails and nearby roads, so people can walk, run or ride without worrying about vehicle traffic. Because the greenways are safe and cross easy terrain, they are great places to walk or ride with children.

CLIMATE

The Huntsville metro area climate is classified as "humid, subtropical." It rains frequently in winter, spring and summer, while fall is typically drier. Madison County and Limestone County each receive about 55 inches of rain per year, while the national average is about 30 inches.

Winter is cool in the day and cold at night, with highs in the 50s and lows in the 30s. Occasionally, daytime and nighttime temperatures drop below freezing. During spring, the weather is pleasant, with highs in the 70s and low 80s, and lows in the 50s. When summer arrives, it becomes progressively hotter and more humid, with highs in the 80s and 90s and lows in the upper 60s and 70s. It's still very warm in early September, so the cool, crisp weather of fall shows up later that month or in October. From October through the end of November, highs range from the mid-60s to the mid-70s, and lows range from the low 40s to the low 50s.

Winter

During winter, cold air masses move into the area frequently. Occasionally, mild air from the Gulf of Mexico arrives in the Huntsville area and lingers for several days. When the cold air meets the Gulf air, northern Alabama can experience periods of low clouds and rain. As a result, the region gets about 43 percent of its normal annual precipitation from December through March. Occasionally it snows, though accumulations are typically just a few inches. Over the past 30 to 40 years, there have also been a few significant ice storms. Keep in mind that weather can be erratic in winter, and you might also see days where it's sunny and 65 to 70 degrees. During a three-day period in January of 2022, high temperatures went from the 70s to the 30s, and at least three inches of snow blanketed the Tennessee Valley.

Spring

As spring arrives, warm, moist air moves in and clashes with the cold air, causing the greatest variety of weather during this time of year. You can expect plenty of thunderstorms and other severe weather, including an occasional tornado.

Summer

Day-to-day changes in the summer season are rather small, other than the thunderstorms that provide relief from the heat on about one-third of the days. Temperatures frequently rise to 90 degrees or higher but rarely reach 100 degrees.

Fall

During the fall, the weather is usually dry and pleasant. The air masses are cooler in the lower levels, and the thunderstorm activity of summer decreases sharply. The dry air is very favorable for harvesting cotton and hay crops, important to the economy of the area. A major departure from the relatively dry weather of fall is an occasional rainy spell of one or more days associated with a decaying hurricane drifting northward from the Gulf of Mexico.

GEOGRAPHY AND GEOLOGY

The Huntsville metro area lies within two major physiographic regions: the Highland Rim and the Cumberland Plateau. Portions of Limestone County and western Madison County lie in the Highland Rim, which includes some mountainous terrain but is primarily rolling hills and fertile valleys. Eastern Madison County lies within the Cumberland Plateau, which features more hills and mountains.

The western and eastern sections of the Huntsville area have different landscapes due to different degrees of erosion, says Ben Hoksbergen, a lecturer in the department of history at the University of Alabama in Huntsville. In the western and eastern sections, the underlying bedrock layers are basically the same. But the upper layers that make up the rugged mountains of eastern Madison County have eroded away in western Madison County and beyond.

So why was there more erosion in the west? It's the result of increased fracturing of the bedrock within the radius of the Nashville Dome, an area of tectonic uplift centered on Nashville. As Hoksbergen explains, tectonic plates pushed together along the axis of the Appalachian Mountains, and the bedrock to the west of the mountains buckled. This formed a broad area of structural uplift known as the Cincinnati Arch. The southernmost part of the Cincinnati Arch was the Nashville Dome. As this area was uplifted, the bedrock fractured near the center of the dome, accelerating erosion.

The portion of north Alabama from Huntsville west to The Shoals lies on the outer edge of the Nashville Dome. This area has heavily eroded into rolling hills. But east of Huntsville, the upper layers of the Cumberland Plateau remain and form the more rugged terrain we are familiar with.

Another major feature of the local landscape is the wide and deep Tennessee River, which flows in a northwesterly direction for about 200 miles across north Alabama. The river plays an important role in the region, providing electric power for people throughout the Tennessee Valley and serving as a transportation corridor for a wide range of goods. Plus, it's a hub for recreation, especially boating and fishing.

LANDSCAPE HIGHLIGHTS
Mountainous Terrain

Huntsville sits at the southern end of the Appalachian Mountains. From the ridgetops of Green Mountain to the deep ravines of Monte Sano Mountain, the hiking trails in the Huntsville area explore diverse terrain with impressive natural features. Rising as high as 1,600 feet, these peaks are topped with ridges and rocky outcrops that provide hikers with inspiring views of the Tennessee Valley. Slicing through the hilly terrain are narrow, deep valleys, known as "draws" or "hollows." When you descend into one of these ravines, such as Monte Sano's McKay Hollow, you'll find a quiet, secluded wilderness with towering hardwood trees and tumbling streams.

Waterfalls

Many creeks in the area are much more impressive after seasonal rains. After a good downpour, some of these streams feed waterfalls that plunge from high bluffs and roll down rocky drainages. If you're willing to walk a bit, you can reach hidden falls tucked away in deep pockets of woods. On Monte Sano, the remote Flat Rock Trail leads to a cascade that flows into an isolated draw. On Green Mountain, the Oak Bluff Trail descends to a tumbling creek where water plunges into clear pools.

Rivers and Streams

Alabama is blessed with an abundance of freshwater resources. About one-sixth of the state's surface area is composed of rivers, streams, lakes, reservoirs, ponds, wetlands and estuaries. In the Huntsville area, hiking trails follow a number of creeks, rivers and streams. On Monte Sano Mountain and Green Mountain, mellow creeks flow through the forest, providing kids with places to play on warm days. High in these mountains you'll also find rugged paths that lead to rushing streams and waterfalls that flow after periods of rain.

FLORA
Forests

Most of the trails in the Huntsville area explore forests dominated by hardwoods, such as oak and hickory. North Alabama is home to dozens of oak species, with white oaks, black oaks and southern red oaks being some of the most prevalent. Other common hardwoods include southern shagbark hickory trees, yellow poplars and sweet gum trees. During fall, the leaves of hardwood trees transform and display striking colors. The maples and hickories glow gold and orange, while the oaks form a canopy of rich reddish-brown. As the poplars beam with bright yellows, the sweet gums boast brilliant shades of red. As fall fades, the hardwoods lose their leaves, giving winter hikers clear views of distant mountains and valleys.

Mixed in with the hardwoods are softwoods such as eastern red cedars and a variety of pines, including loblolly, shortleaf and Virginia pines. Throughout the year, these conifers add splashes of deep green to the fields and forests of north Alabama.

As you're exploring the mountains, you'll notice that some sections of the forest are especially dense and choked with brush and smaller, younger trees. These are areas of "succession forest," where the original oaks and hickory trees were cut and cleared for farming and timber. In older forests, where the trees were never cleared or the land has more fully recovered, the trees are taller, stouter and widely spaced, with little or no brush between them.

Wildflowers

With its plentiful water sources, ample rain and diverse geography, Alabama is one of the most biodiverse states in the country, boasting a wide array of native plants and wildflowers. When the wildflowers bloom in spring, they blanket the forests with brilliant colors. During that time, one of the most popular trails in the area is the Wildflower Trail at the base of Monte Sano Mountain. This fairly level path crawls along Fagan Creek, and an impressive array of flowers inhabits the creek bank and nearby slopes. During the first burst of blooms in March, you can see trilliums, Virginia bluebells, anemones, spring beauties and violets. Mid-May brings beautiful Indian pink, fire pink, spiderwort and orchids.

While the creek bottoms are flush with flowers, the higher elevations also have something to offer. The Sinks Trail on Monte Sano leads to a very large colony of Virginia bluebells, which bloom in early to mid-April. If you traverse the crest of Green Mountain in mid-spring, you'll encounter large fields of mayapple. While this appears to be a collection of many individual plants, they are all part of one plant.

***Some less appealing plants, such as poison ivy, poison oak and poison sumac, are included in the "Other Potential Trail Hazards" section.*

FAUNA
Mammals

Alabama is home to 62 native mammals, and you have a good chance of seeing several species while hiking Huntsville-area trails. With regard to larger mammals, you're most likely to encounter white-tailed deer, especially if you're walking in the early morning or early evening. It's common to see a doe and fawns or a single buck dashing through the woods or scampering across mountain roads. In recent years, coyotes have made more appearances, but you're more likely to see one lurking in a residential area than trotting near a hiking trail. In mountainous areas, people have also caught glimpses of bobcats, but sightings are very rare. Not quite as elusive are gray foxes and red foxes. As far as the ultimate North American carnivore—bears—you won't see any in this part of Alabama.

While the larger carnivores are absent or rarely seen, rodents are everywhere. (There are 22 rodent species in Alabama, and most have several litters each year.) If you hear something rustling in the forest, it's most likely a gray squirrel or eastern chipmunk. If the rustling is really loud, it might be an armadillo barreling its way through the woods. In Alabama, eastern cottontail rabbits are abundant, but I honestly see more of them in neighborhood yards than I do in hiking areas. While exploring the woods, you might also see woodchucks, moles and the occasional opossum. Beavers are present in wetland areas, but they use underwater entrances to access their burrows, so it's difficult to spot them.

When it comes to omnivores—creatures that eat both plants and animals—one of the more common species in the area is the raccoon. You might see one in the forest, but they're mostly known for frequenting residential areas, where they forage amongst garbage—thus the nickname "trash pandas."

If you hike at dusk during the spring or summer, you might also see bats darting around as they come out to feed. There are 15 species of these winged creatures in Alabama, and in the Huntsville area you'll primarily see little brown bats and big brown bats.

Birds

With its many mountains, forests, fields and wetlands, the Huntsville area is an excellent place to view birds while hiking. Several species of North American birds migrate to the tropics during winter. Then, during spring, they pass through Alabama as they return to their breeding grounds. These neotropical migrants flock to the hardwood forests of Monte Sano and other area mountains. While walking mountain trails, you might hear the calls of indigo buntings and warblers, or spy some flycatchers and vireos.

Local forests are also home to some impressive permanent avian residents, including red-shouldered hawks and red-tailed hawks. During a hike, it's a real thrill to see one of these beauties soaring overhead. As you visit mountain overlooks and walk along bluffs, you may also see turkey vultures circling as they ride the air currents.

As you explore remote stretches of trail in the mountains and bottomland forests, listen for the call of the barred owl, which resembles a person saying, "Who cooks for you, who cooks for you all." Measuring up to 24 inches long, with a wingspan up to 50 inches, this impressive bird is quite a sight when you see one take flight. While owls mostly feed at night, it's not unusual to see this species out during the daytime.

In the lowlands, while walking near farm fields and forest openings, keep an eye out for barn owls, which are a little smaller than barred owls, measuring 13 to 15 inches long with a wingspan of 31 to 37 inches. Bottomlands, wetlands and riverbanks are also good places to see great blue herons, green herons and belted kingfishers.

Reptiles

There are 50 species of snakes in Alabama. In the Huntsville area, hikers frequently see several species of nonvenomous snakes, like the garter snake, eastern milk snake, black kingsnake, black rat snake, black racer, and the eastern hognose snake, which is often mistaken for the copperhead. Hikers should be aware that three venomous and potentially dangerous species are sometimes seen along local trails. These include the eastern diamondback rattlesnake, the copperhead and the cottonmouth, which mostly inhabits riverbanks, swamps, streams, springs and ponds.

Much less threatening are the several turtle species that inhabit local streams and woodlands. While there are 30 species of turtles in Alabama, hikers will mostly encounter the eastern box turtle, which is primarily a land animal.

Alabama also has at least 30 species of frogs and toads. On summer nights, you'll hear the croaking drone of American bullfrogs rising from swamps, ponds and lakes. In these areas, you might also see green frogs or hear the chirping call of the cricket frog. In marshes and woodlands, listen for the spring peeper, which like the American toad, spends most of its time on land. As you're exploring forests, you might spy a gray treefrog, but you'll need a sharp eye—this chameleon can change to shades of gray, brown and green to camouflage itself.

Amphibians

For great entertainment in spring or summer, visit one of the local creeks or streams to hunt for salamanders. There are more than

40 salamander species in Alabama, and Huntsville-area hikers have observed several, including the marbled salamander, northern slimy salamander, southern zigzag salamander and green salamander. To find these fascinating creatures, head to the Wildflower Trail at the base of Monte Sano. It leads to Fagan Creek, where you can explore the shallow waters and small pools.

***Some wildlife, such as spiders, mosquitoes and other creatures that can sting or bite, are included in the "Other Potential Trail Hazards" section.*

COMFORT, SAFETY AND ETIQUETTE

From short strolls to daylong treks, the trails in the Huntsville area afford a wide range of hiking experiences. You can take a brief walk on a flat, paved greenway path or travel for hours in rugged mountainous terrain. The trips in this book are all day hikes, as overnight camping is not allowed on Monte Sano State Park trails, Land Trust trails and greenway paths. But even a day trip requires some planning. A hike of any type and duration will be more enjoyable if you take the time to consider the route you will take, the environment you will explore and the things you need to carry. Some knowledge and planning can go a long way toward making you safer and more comfortable in the outdoors.

It's important to remember that trail conditions can change, and you might experience or encounter things that differ from what I describe in the book. There has been a tremendous amount of trail building in recent years, so it's possible that trail routes or trail names have changed. You might find that trail signs and blazes (trail markers on trees) have been altered. Also, you might hike a trail during summer, while I have described what you might encounter in winter. For all of these reasons, it's important to prepare properly for your hike, carry a map and other navigational tools, and stay aware of your surroundings as you walk.

WEATHER AND THE ENVIRONMENT

Before you hit the trail, consider the weather you will face and dress appropriately for the full spectrum of weather you might experience. Fall and winter daytime temperatures in the Huntsville area can reach the 60s and 70s, while afternoons can be cooler. Dress in layers so that you can shed or add clothing to regulate your body temperature. Because weather is not totally predictable, it's also a good idea to pack a waterproof shell when traveling in fall or winter to not only keep you dry in rain but also shield you from chilly winds.

Spring is a great time to enjoy blooming wildflowers along the trail, but it's also the season for severe thunderstorms and tornadoes. If you're exploring the mountains, avoid hiking on exposed ridges when lightning is present. Also avoid bodies of water if there's a chance that lightning might strike.

Summers in Alabama are hot and humid, and it's critical to drink plenty of water while hiking. Dehydration can lead to serious illness, including heat cramps, heat exhaustion and heat stroke. Even if you don't become seriously ill, dehydration can make people confused and disoriented and cause them to make poor decisions. This is one way that people get lost in the outdoors. Dehydrated people can also lose their balance and fall, possibly injuring themselves. Be sure to take all the water you'll need on a hike (about one liter or more per hour). Be aware that "potable" (meaning drinkable) water is not available at many trailheads, so pack what you need. Also, don't plan on taking water from streams. Many of the creeks and streams in the area are seasonal and don't run consistently, and drought conditions can leave a creek bone-dry. Even more important, rivers and streams can carry bacteria that will make you seriously sick. If you get into an emergency situation and have to take water from a stream, filter it or boil it to kill bacteria.

Insects such as mosquitoes can be heavy along the trails in summer, so be sure to pack whatever repellent you prefer. An insect repellent with at least 30% DEET or 20% picaridin will also ward off ticks, which are a concern during the spring. It's recommended that you wear long pants during tick season, and you can ward off ticks by treating clothing with permethrin, which is available at sporting goods stores. You should also check your body from time to time to see if ticks have hitched a ride. They tend to latch on to warm, moist areas and frequently hide out where the seams of your clothing meet your skin. At the end of your hike, do a full-body check to make sure you're tick-free.

One thing a lot of people don't think about is sun exposure. Many Huntsville-area trails are shaded by forest, but you can still catch quite a few rays during a day of hiking. Also keep in mind that many greenway paths are more exposed to sun. Before you leave the house, or immediately before you start walking, apply a high-SPF sunscreen. These products are more effective when applied to cool, dry skin. Try to choose a water-resistant sunscreen that will hold up during heavy sweating. If you plan to be out for more than a couple of hours, take the sunscreen with you, because you will probably need to reapply it.

OTHER POTENTIAL TRAIL HAZARDS
Snakes

In all my years of hiking Huntsville trails, I've had very few encounters with venomous snakes, but it has happened. While trail running one summer morning, I rounded a bend and had to suddenly leap over a coiled rattlesnake sunning itself smack dab in the middle of the path. In addition to the eastern diamondback rattlesnake, two other venomous snakes inhabit the area: the copperhead and the cottonmouth. Take some time to browse the internet and learn how to identify these snakes. It's rare to encounter a venomous snake on a trail, as I did. In general, day hikers can avoid them by staying on established paths. If you wander off the trail and enter tall brush or rocky areas with lots of crevices, you're more likely to encounter a snake. If you do leave the trail for a snack break, examine rocks and the surrounding terrain before sitting down. (If you're geocaching, examine hiding spots carefully before reaching in to retrieve a cache.)

If you do come across a venomous snake, slowly back away at least 6 feet and either wait for the snake to leave or go back the way you came. Just don't approach the snake or try to make it go away.

Spiders

Honestly, my only bad spider experience on a trail happened while mountain biking on Monte Sano in the summer. I took a huge web straight to the face, flinched, and flew over the handlebars. Ooof, that hurt. But people rarely get bitten by spiders while day hiking. Still, it's possible to encounter a black widow or brown recluse, two venomous species that inhabit the area. Before you hike, learn to identify these two types of spiders. As with snakes, you're more likely to encounter a spider when you leave the trail to take a break or go exploring. Before you sit on the ground or a rock to have a snack or water break, examine the area to make sure it's free of anything that will sting or bite. When you're ready to hike again, examine anything you've set down—your pack, a jacket, a food bag, etc.—to make sure it's spider-free. If you do get bitten by a venomous spider, exit the trail immediately and go straight to the hospital.

Poisonous Plants

In spring and summer, hikers should be on the lookout for three troublesome plants—poison ivy, poison oak and poison sumac. These plants are covered in an oil that causes rashes and blisters. If you're not familiar with these plants, take a few minutes to research them online and learn to recognize them. In this case, a little knowledge can prevent a whole lot of discomfort.

Poison Ivy: This plant has three leaflets, thus the old saying, "Leaves of three, let it be." It grows as a vine that runs close to the ground or climbs up the sides of trees or other vertical objects. Its three leaflets have jagged teeth on the edges, and there is usually a red spot where the bottom two leaflets join. Also, the stems of the plant appear to be hairy. Poison ivy grows in a wide variety of forested environments and greenways, and it often grows along the edge of trails. In spring and summer, consider wearing long pants if you're heading to areas where poison ivy might be present.

Poison Oak: Like poison ivy, a poison oak plant has three leaflets, but the plant looks more like a shrub. Its leaflets sit at the end of upright stems that can be up to three feet tall. Also, the teeth on the edges of the leaflets are more rounded than those on poison ivy.

Poison Sumac: This plant looks very different from poison ivy or poison oak. It has seven to 15 leaflets that grow in pairs along a stem that is often bright red. Its oblong leaflets have a wavy pattern and smooth edges. The plant grows as a shrub or tree and can be up to 20 feet tall. It typically grows in a swampy area, and during summer it produces a white fruit that can remain on the plant into the fall and winter.

If you're exposed to these plants . . .
If you have a mild rash, wash the affected areas with cold water (and soap, if you have it) as soon as possible. Don't use hot water, as it can open your pores and make things worse. Then head to the drugstore and pick up an anti-itch cream (Extra Strength Benadryl Itch Stopping Cream works well) or hydrocortisone cream. You might even find products made specifically for relief from poison ivy and poison oak. I've also used calamine lotion, and some people say it helps to take antihistamine medicine. Usually, a mild rash will go away in a few weeks. If you get a severe rash, see a physician, who might prescribe a low-dose steroid.

Steep and Slippery Terrain

When it comes to trail hazards, hikers are more likely to suffer a twisted ankle or painful fall than a snakebite. Be especially careful when descending steep, rocky terrain, where a misstep can easily lead to a rolled ankle or even a fall. Consider using trekking poles on a steep path like Monte Sano's McKay Hollow Trail. The poles will improve your balance and reduce impact on your legs, knees and ankles.

Trekking poles can also keep you upright while crossing bodies of water and streambeds. You'll be less likely to fall when you encounter swift water. When creeks and streams aren't flowing, they can still pose problems, however. Sometimes a thin layer of moss or other plant material can cover the rocks at the base of the creek or stream, creating a surface that's as slick as ice.

Preparing for Your Hike

Many people, especially those new to hiking, have a difficult time determining just how far they can walk in a day without wearing themselves out—especially when dealing with summer heat, winter chills and steep trails. Be honest about your physical abilities, particularly when you are considering a long hike over difficult terrain. Most people can do two to three miles in an hour. And remember that heat, cold, rain and the terrain can limit the number of miles you can hike.

Before you set out, try to examine a topographic map of the area to see just how much climbing and descending will be involved. This book includes an estimate of the total elevation gain and loss for each trip—the higher the numbers, the more difficult the hike. Examine maps to become familiar with the area you wish to visit. A little studying will come in handy should you get confused and take a trail that is not part of your planned route.

If you're new to hiking, one thing to consider is time—the time needed to choose a destination and plan your trip, as well as the time needed to gather your gear, reach the trail, and do the hike. Typically, this process takes people longer than they expect. As a result, people arrive at the trailhead later than they planned. In their rush to reach the trail, they might also leave behind essential items. This isn't such a big deal if you're doing a safe, short hike in nice weather when you have sunlight late into the afternoon. But let's say you want to hike several miles during the winter, when darkness falls relatively early. In this situation, you need to ensure that you have adequate time to complete your trip safely.

Footwear and Clothing

Another important step in the planning process is determining the clothing and gear you need. There may be no more important piece of equipment than your footwear. An ill-fitting pair of shoes or boots can quickly ruin a day in the woods. Whether you choose to wear a lightweight pair of low-cut hiking shoes, a midweight pair of boots, or heavy leather boots, get your footwear well in advance of your hike and test it before hitting the trail. You don't want to find out halfway through a long day hike that your shoes don't fit.

For warm-weather day hikes when you're carrying a lightweight pack, low-cut hiking shoes or supportive sandals are fine in most cases. Just be sure that your shoes have the traction, cushioning, support and protection needed for the terrain. For example, extremely rocky trails, like Green Mountain's Ranger Trail or Monte Sano's Toll Gate Trail, might require more ankle support and underfoot protection. In these cases, you might consider wearing hiking boots rather than low-cut shoes.

For cold, wet conditions, people often seek out shoes or boots with a waterproof membrane such as Gore-Tex. That's a good idea, especially if you're going to hike for long periods when it's cold and raining. But keep in mind that, in the South, high levels of humidity limit the ability of waterproof footwear to breathe. Some people prefer to buy a synthetic or leather shoe without a membrane and then add topical waterproofing agents. Also, if you wear shoes while crossing streams, water will flow in through the top and they'll get completely soaked. In this case, a shoe that is not waterproof will dry more quickly.

While they're not as thrilling as a new pair of shoes, socks are also a critical component of your outdoor wardrobe. If you hike in cotton socks, you're taking the expressway to Blister Town, which is not a pleasant place to visit. To prevent blisters, I typically wear merino wool socks, because they pull moisture away from my feet, whereas cotton socks just get soaked. You can also wear a synthetic hiking sock, as these will also wick moisture and help keep your feet dry. Once you become a hiker, you'll actually get excited when someone gets you socks as a gift.

Once you've chosen your socks and footwear, consider the rest of your clothing. For warm-weather hikes, you can wear a T-shirt and shorts made of synthetic materials that pull moisture away from your body and dry quickly. You can also choose clothes that combine synthetic fabrics with small amounts of cotton, which makes them a little softer but still allows them to keep you cool and dry. Just avoid all-cotton clothes, as these will soak up moisture like a sponge and hold onto it, making you feel like you're wearing wet rags. In recent years, companies have also introduced very lightweight wool garments, which could work for you if you don't tend to get hot easily.

In the fall, winter and early spring, the key to staying comfortable on the trail is to regulate your body temperature so that you're not too cold or too hot for long periods. The trick is to dress in layers so that you can add or subtract clothing as needed. In general, opt for synthetic fabrics or wool, or synthetics or wool blended with small amounts of cotton. Again, avoid items made only of cotton, since it doesn't dry easily, and in cold temperatures it can suck heat away from your body. Synthetic fabrics will dry quickest, and in cold weather synthetics and wool won't reduce your body temperature. In recent years, wool clothing has become more popular for cool and cold conditions because modern merino, a fine wool, is much softer and more comfortable than wool of the past.

Equipment

For a quick day hike or trail run, you may not need to carry more than a bottle of water and a light snack. But if you plan to hike a few miles or explore rough or remote terrain, consider packing the following:

Water and Food

When day hiking, plan to carry all the water you will need for the entire day, which will typically be one liter or more per hour of hiking, depending on the weather (you may need more on a hot, humid summer day) and the difficulty of the trail. Do not count on drawing water from streams and springs, because they might not be flowing. If you do draw water from a river or stream, be sure to filter or boil it to kill bacteria.

When hiking for long periods in cold weather, you should bring a stove or other heat source to make a warm drink in case you get wet and chilled. It's also a good idea to carry energy bars that can deliver quick fuel to increase your energy level.

Map and Compass

Even experienced hikers can become disoriented in the outdoors, especially at the end of a long, tiring hike. Whenever possible, you should carry a map to aid in your navigation. I realize that more people are using smartphones to navigate, and there are great apps that allow you to navigate trails when you don't have a cell signal. But it's still good to have a nondigital compass and a paper map, because electronics can lose power. Before you set out on your trip, learn how to use a compass. This book includes compass directions with the trail descriptions to help you stay on course. Equally important, you should learn the basics of reading a map and matching contour lines and other map features to your surroundings. If you don't want to carry a guidebook on your hike, print the map you need on waterproof paper, or print it on regular paper and tuck it into a sealable plastic bag. You can give yourself some peace of mind by learning to use a compass and properly orient your map.

Global Positioning System (GPS) receivers are popular because they make land navigation easier. But, like any tool, a GPS receiver is helpful only if you take time to learn how to use it and understand its limitations. First, remember that batteries can fail, so you should not rely solely on a GPS receiver—always carry a map and compass as well.

First-Aid Kit

You can put together your own first-aid kit or purchase one from a gear store. Modern kits come in a wide range of sizes to accommodate different types of trips and various group sizes. No matter what type of kit you carry, be sure you know how to use its components, and always carry any manual provided with a kit.

For low-risk day hikes, a basic kit is fine. It should include:

- Manual
- Bandages, including gauze and medical tape. Moleskin is very handy for treating hot spots and even preventing blisters. Tincture of benzoin will help moleskin adhere to skin better. Leukotape is also great for preventing hot spots, and it sticks really well.
- Antiseptic to clean wounds
- Drugs, including something to reduce fever (like acetaminophen), something to reduce inflammation (like ibuprofen), electrolyte tablets to overcome dehydration, and antacid tablets
- Prescription medicines
- Cutting tools, like scissors or a razor
- Hydrocortisone cream for skin irritations
- Tweezers
- Duct tape

The number of bandages and the amount of drugs will depend on the size of the group. Many preassembled kits indicate the number of people the kit will serve over a certain period of time. Note that these numbers may be inflated, meaning the kits include twice as much stuff as you'd actually need. But some buffer is built in so you will have enough supplies to handle the unexpected.

Other important items to consider carrying:
- Insect repellent
- Stove/heat source: This allows you to make a hot drink to prevent hypothermia should you get lost or injured.
- Knife or multitool
- Flashlight or headlamp
- Whistle: If you're injured or separated from your hiking partners, use the whistle to signal others, because its sound will travel farther than the sound of your voice.
- Trekking poles: These can stabilize you on uneven or slippery ground and reduce pressure on your legs and knees.
- Gaiters: These keep moisture, mud and trail debris from sneaking into your shoes or boots.
- Cell phone: You can get a cell signal on many Huntsville-area trails, so it's not a bad idea to carry a phone for emergencies. Plus, you can use navigation apps that work even when you don't have cell service. Just remember that batteries die, so consider packing a portable charger, and always carry a paper map for navigation.

Safety Measures

There are many precautions you can take to stay safe while hiking. One of the most important is to let someone know where you are going, particularly if you'll be hiking alone or plan to be gone for several hours. Provide a friend or relative with your itinerary, including the time you plan to return.

Avoid leaving valuables in your vehicle. Trailhead break-ins are not frequent, but they happen.

I love to hike solo, but if you're new to hiking, consider going with a partner or even a group. This not only adds security, but if you get lost, you will feel safer if you are not alone. Plus, in an emergency, it's best if someone can remain with an injured person while someone else goes for help.

The key to not getting lost is to be aware of your surroundings. It's easy to miss a trail junction or accidentally take the wrong path. If your map indicates you should be ascending, and you instead find yourself on a long descent, stop to examine your map and the terrain around you. If you get lost, find a comfortable spot and stay put. A rescue team can find you more easily if you are not wandering.

Trail Etiquette

With more and more people getting out and enjoying our many beautiful trails, it is more important than ever to treat the environment and fellow hikers with proper care and respect.

When you hike, be considerate of those who will follow you. They deserve the same high-quality experience you are seeking. To minimize your impact on the environment, follow these guidelines created by Leave No Trace, a nonprofit organization that educates people about these issues:

- Plan ahead and prepare. Know the regulations and special concerns for the area you'll visit. Schedule your trip to avoid high times of use, and visit in small groups when possible.
- Dispose of waste properly. If you pack it in, pack it out. This means carrying out all trash, leftover food and litter. Deposit solid human waste in catholes dug six to eight inches deep, at least 200 feet from water and trails. Cover and disguise the cathole when finished. Pack out toilet paper and other hygiene products.
- Leave what you find. Examine but do not touch cultural or historic artifacts. Leave rocks, plants and other natural objects as you find them.
- Respect wildlife. Observe wildlife from a distance, and do not follow or approach any animals. Never feed wildlife—feeding damages their health, alters natural behaviors, and exposes them to predators and other dangers. Protect wildlife and your food by storing rations and trash securely.
- Respect other visitors and protect the quality of their experience. Be courteous and yield to others on the trail. Take breaks away from trails and other hikers.

Using This Book

The book is arranged into seven chapters. It includes individual chapters for nature preserves managed by the Land Trust of North Alabama, Monte Sano State Park trails, Burritt on the Mountain and the Madison County Nature Trail. Each trail is numbered, from 1 to 80, so that you can quickly flip through the book to find a specific hike. Each trail description includes a one-way hike that goes in a specific direction. Some areas have numerous paths that can be walked in different sequences and directions, but I have tried to simplify things by making each trail description an exact journey. Each trip consists of capsulized summaries, distance, hiking time, elevation gain and loss, hiking difficulty, location, fees, facilities, driving directions, and highlights. For the actual hike directions, I include waypoints, the mileage mark for each waypoint and GPS waypoints.

Also, trail maps include the distance (in feet or miles) between trail junctions. These numbers will allow you to quickly get an idea of how far you'll travel on any section of a trail. At the end of many trail descriptions, I've included a Trail Facts section to share interesting notes, such as the origins of trail names and the history of areas that the trails explore.

GENERAL TRAIL DESCRIPTION

This brief summary indicates the type of terrain you'll encounter and highlights notable things you'll see along the way. It also calls out any special things you should consider before hiking the trail.

DISTANCE

The first figure listed in this section is an estimate of the one-way hiking distance for each trail. If you're planning to hike the entire length of a trail and then retrace your steps back to the trailhead, just double the hiking distance. The mileage for each trail was calculated using a measuring wheel, GPS unit and mapping software. But keep in mind that mileages in this book may differ from what you see on trail signs or certain maps. All these different sources can often conflict because they've been calculated by different people using different methods over time.

HIKING TIME

This is an estimate of the walking time for the average person for each trip. Estimates are based on my own experiences as well as hiking-time calculator formulas that factor in the terrain and elevation gain and loss. Hiking times do not include rest stops; your actual time on the trail will vary depending on how often and how long you stop. Your hiking time will also depend on other factors, such as your level of fitness, your stride, the weight you carry in a pack, and whether you're walking with kids. For these reasons, consider the hiking time a rough estimate.

ELEVATION GAIN/LOSS

The elevation gain and loss figures are a sum of all the uphill and down-hill segments of a one-way hike on the trail. When the numbers are larger, there will be more changes in elevation, signaling that the trip is more challenging. One of the most strenuous paths, the McKay Hollow Trail, has an elevation gain and loss of +756 feet/-754 feet, meaning you climb a total of 756 feet of elevation and descend for a total of 754 feet of elevation. That's a real thigh-burner that will get your heart pumping. On the other hand, the paved and flat Aldridge Creek Greenway path has an elevation gain and loss of +7 feet/-0 feet, which is an easy stroll.

HIKING DIFFICULTY

Although it's somewhat subjective, the difficulty rating for each trip is based on distance, total elevation gain and type of terrain. The ratings are as follows:

Easy: A relatively short trip with little elevation gain and loss.

Moderate: A trip that requires a few hours of walking and/or includes a few climbs and descents but does not cover a great change in elevation.

Strenuous: This can be a hike of any length that includes very steep sections. Or it can be a long trip covering many miles and requiring several hours. This trip might include steep ascents and descents and great gains and losses in elevation.

LOCATION

This is a specific street address or a general location for the beginning of the trail. For the most part, you can put this information into a mapping app or software to find the parking area and trailhead.

FEES

This includes required fees to access or use the trails. While Monte Sano State Park has an entrance fee, most other areas, including Land Trust of North Alabama trails, do not. At many Land Trust trailheads, you will see boxes where you can deposit a donation. I highly encourage visitors to contribute to the boxes or contribute to the Land Trust online (landtrustnal.org), because the organization does critical work to acquire, preserve and maintain recreation areas, and it often relies on volunteers to build and maintain trails.

FACILITIES

This includes restrooms, water sources, food sources or other structures (such as pavilions) located at a trailhead.

DRIVING DIRECTIONS

These directions begin at major road intersections and end at parking areas for trailheads. While it's probably easiest to use a navigation app, you might lose cell service near some trailheads, so you can carry a printout of these directions as a backup.

HIGHLIGHTS

These are some of the notable things you'll encounter during the hike, whether it's a natural feature such as a waterfall, a bluff view, or an area of historical significance. The highlights could also be things you will experience, such as solitude, easy terrain, or a physical challenge.

WAYPOINT/MILE

Each hike description begins with a waypoint, which is a point of interest along the route. This could be an important trail junction or an interesting feature such as a cave or waterfall. The first waypoint for each trail is the "Trailhead," which is the starting point for the trail. Subsequent way-points are written as hyphenated numbers. These numbers begin with the number I have assigned to the trail (from 1 to 80), a hyphen, and then the number of that specific waypoint. For example, the Trough Springs Trail is the 50th trail in the book, and here is how the listing looks:

Waypoint/Mile

Trailhead (Waypoint 50) (34.7213, -86.5373) The Trough Springs Trail begins at the kiosk on the south side of the Trough Springs parking area.
50-1 (34.7206, -86.5370) (612 ft.) At the four-way junction, the Trough Springs Trail intersects the Natural Well Trail.
50-2 (34.7158, -86.5344) (0.5 mi.) The trail makes a hairpin turn to the north and descends.

GPS COORDINATES/DISTANCE

Each waypoint number is followed by GPS coordinates in parentheses. You can enter these coordinates into a GPS unit or mapping software or app to see the waypoint's exact position. There are several ways to express GPS coordinates, but I have used the Universal Transverse Mercator (UTM) coordinate system expressed in decimal degrees. With this format, the first number is the latitude, and the second number is the longitude. I've used this format because it's simple to plug these numbers into mapping systems like Google Maps and Apple Maps. There are several online sources that offer detailed explanations of the UTM system, but they can honestly get very detailed and down in the weeds. Rather than confuse anyone, I prefer to just recommend that you plug or paste in the numbers provided. For example, for the Trough Springs Trailhead listed above, plug in "34.7213, -86.5373" exactly as written. If you want to input these numbers into a GPS unit, you might have to convert them to another format, such as degrees/minutes/seconds. There are several websites where you can easily convert the format, such as www.fcc.gov/media/radio/dms-decimal.

Following the GPS coordinates is the mileage for that specific way-point. For example, for the Trough Springs listing above, Waypoint 50-2 is 0.5 miles from the beginning of the trail.

TRAIL SECTION DISTANCES

On the maps in the book, you will see black circles at trail junctions. In between trail junctions, next to the trail route, you will see numbers, such as 0.1 mi., 0.2 mi., 0.3 mi., etc. These numbers indicate the distance between two trail junctions. You can use these numbers to quickly calculate how far you've traveled, or how far you need to travel.

TRAIL FACTS

At the end of many trail descriptions, I've included additional facts about the trail, such as background information on the names of trails and historical events related to the hiking area.

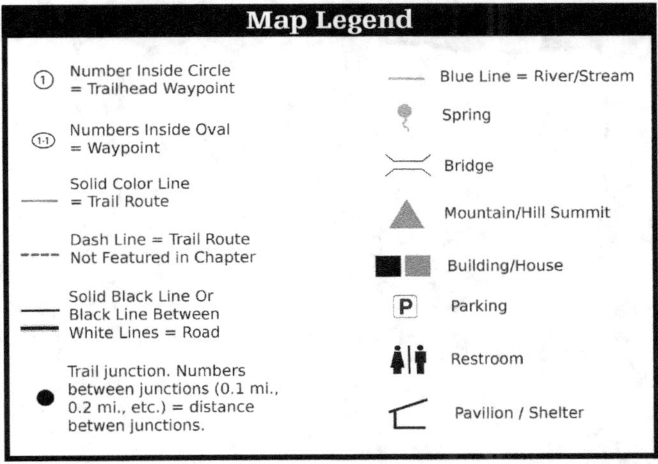

Monte Sano State Park

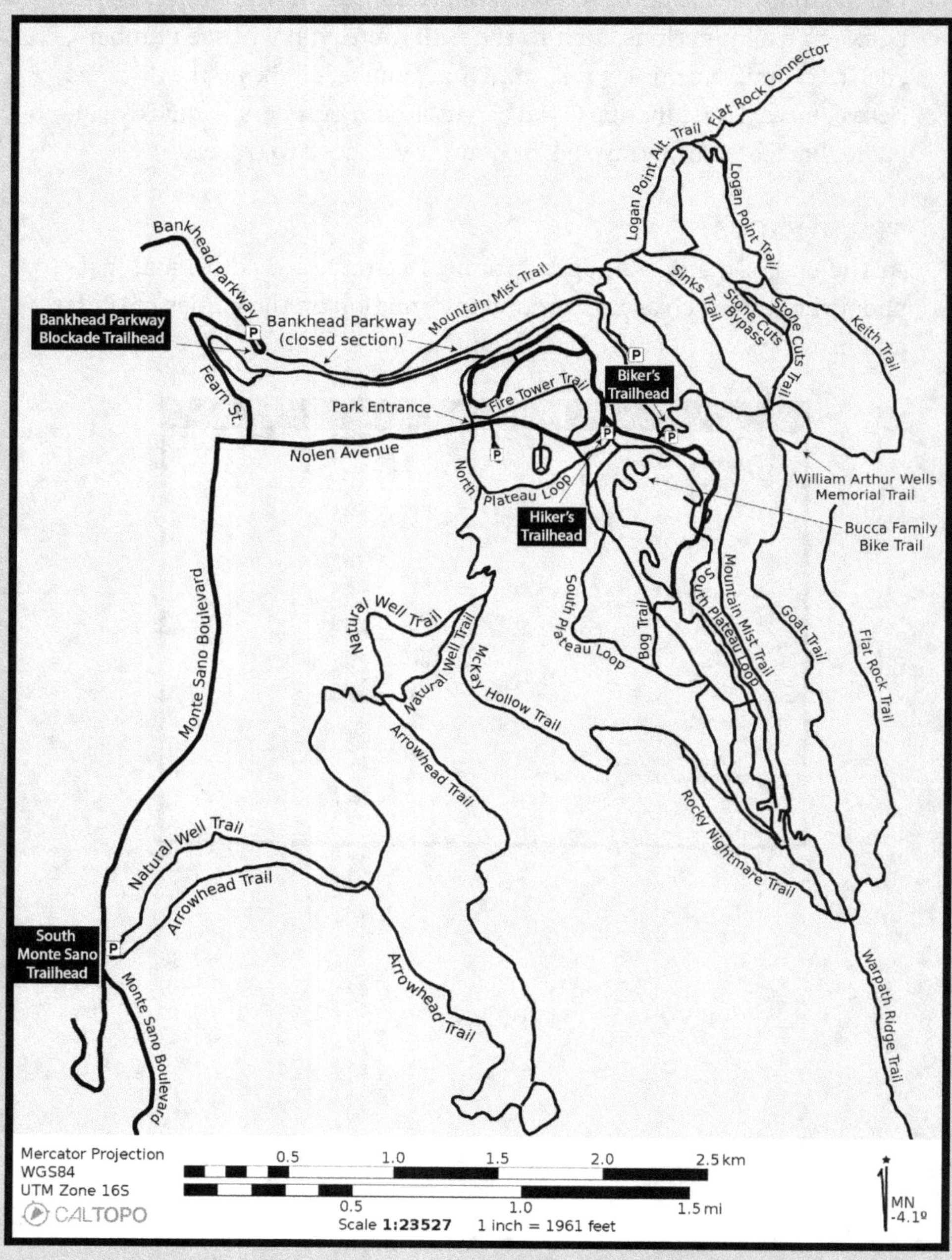

CHAPTER 1

Monte Sano State Park

Covering 2,140 acres, Monte Sano State Park is not only Madison County's largest hiking area but also its oldest. Between 1935 and 1940, the Civilian Conservation Corps constructed the park, which included 11 stone cabins, an amphitheater, a lodge and three hiking trails. Fast-forward some 80 years, and the park now includes at least 25 trails covering more than 35 miles, plus a large picnic area, a playground, an extensive campground, additional cabins, a park store, a beautifully restored lodge, picnic pavilions and more.

It's unusual to have a mountain state park located within a city, and locals are especially lucky to have an extensive trail system only about five miles from downtown Huntsville. Once you decide to go for a hike, you'll drive just minutes to reach a trailhead.

Monte Sano State Park includes four main parking areas where you can access a wide variety of trails for hikers and mountain bikers of varying ability levels. If you're walking with kids or just prefer easier terrain, trails on the mountain plateau (such as the North Plateau Loop) offer a comfortable walk with inspiring views of surrounding valleys. Those seeking a rugged hike into remote woods can explore paths like the McKay Hollow Trail, which dives down steep, craggy slopes to reach secluded streams. In recent years, trail running has become very popular in the park, and serious runners can test their mettle on the paths that make up the Mountain Mist 50K, a grueling race that draws participants from across the country.

In quiet corners of the park, natural attractions will entertain all sorts of outdoor enthusiasts, from birders to photographers to wildflower lovers. If you love chasing waterfalls, you'll find beautiful cascades flowing in hidden coves. Those interested in history will find that the mountain holds intriguing reminders of Huntsville's early days. Along park trails, you'll see where early settlers established homes, where travelers in the 1800s bottled spring water for its "healing" powers, and where rocket scientists climbed a fire tower to watch Sputnik soar overhead.

In Spanish and Italian, Monte Sano means "Mountain of Health." While it's doubtful that the spring water cured the ailments of those early travelers, there's no doubt that the mountain has healing powers. Just walk one of the park's many trails, and you'll be surprised at how it rejuvenates your mind, body and soul.

General Information

Hours: Open 8 a.m. to sunset (trails close 30 minutes before sunset).
Primary trail activities allowed: Hiking, biking
Pets: Leashed pets allowed.
Fees: Adult fee (ages 12+) $5; ages 4-11 $2; seniors (62+) $2; active military $2; kids 3 and under free
Facilities: Restrooms with potable water area available at the picnic area pavilion, the Biker's Trailhead pavilion and the state park store. Snacks and drinks are available for purchase at the park store.
Information: (256) 534-3757; www.alapark.com/parks/ monte-sano-state-park

Driving Directions

Monte Sano State Park Entrance

You can reach Monte Sano State Park by taking Bankhead Parkway on the northwest side of the mountain or by taking Governors Drive on the southwest side of the mountain. On Bankhead Pkwy., you'll travel about three miles of winding mountain roads. If you're not comfortable with that type of travel, take the Governors Dr. route.

Via Bankhead Parkway: From the junction of U.S. 231/431 (Memorial Parkway) and University Drive, travel east on University Dr. 0.3 mi. to where the road becomes Pratt Avenue. Travel 1.6 mi. on Pratt Ave. to the junction with Maysville Road. Continue straight to follow Pratt Ave., which becomes Bankhead Parkway after a few hundred feet. Continue on Bankhead Pkwy. 2.7 mi. and go around the hairpin curve where the road becomes Fearn Street. Follow Fearn St. for 0.7 mi. (going straight at the four-way stop intersection with Monte Sano Boulevard), and then turn left onto Nolen Avenue. Travel 0.7 mi. on Nolen Ave. to the park entrance.

Via Governors Drive: From the junction of U.S. 231/431 (Memorial Parkway) and Governors Drive (U.S. 431), travel east on Governors Dr. for 3.6 mi. Turn left onto Monte Sano Boulevard and travel 2.4 mi. to Nolen Avenue. Turn right onto Nolen Ave. and travel 0.7 mi. to the park entrance.

Picnic Area Parking Lot

From the park entrance, travel a little more than 300 ft. and take the first right into the picnic area parking lot.

Hiker's Trailhead

From the park entrance, travel 0.4 mi. on Nolen Avenue to the Y junction with Bankhead Parkway. Bear right onto Bankhead Pkwy., travel about 170 ft., and turn right into the Hiker's Trailhead parking area.

Biker's Trailhead

From the entrance to Monte Sano State Park, take Nolen Avenue for 0.4 mi. At the Y road junction, bear right onto Bankhead Parkway and travel 0.2 mi. Turn left onto the road that leads to cabins 1–5 and go 138 ft. to the mountain biking parking area next to a pavilion.

Bankhead Parkway Blockade

From the junction of U.S. 231/431 (Memorial Parkway) and University Drive, travel east on University Dr. Go 0.3 mi. to where the road becomes Pratt Avenue. Travel 1.6 mi. on Pratt Ave. to the junction with Maysville Road. Continue straight to follow Pratt Ave., which becomes Bankhead Parkway after a few hundred feet. Go 2.6 mi. and begin to look for a roadside parking space on the left, before you reach the sharp curve where the trailhead is located. If spaces aren't available before the curve, continue around the hairpin curve, where the road becomes Fearn Street. You can usually find more roadside parking a few yards up Fearn St. on the right.

SECTION 1:
North Plateau Loop

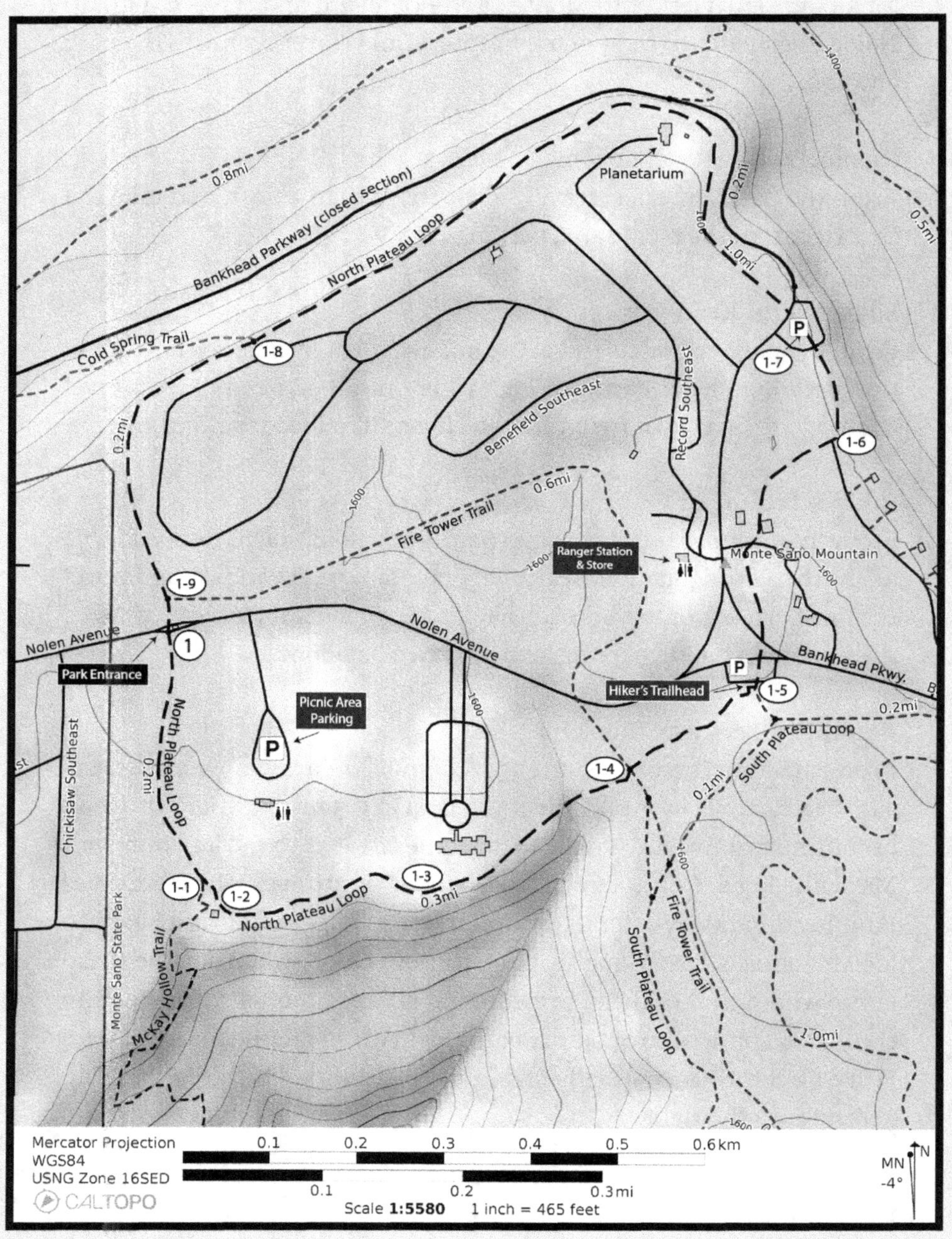

1. North Plateau Loop

Looping through the most visited portion of Monte Sano State Park, this mellow path skirts the picnic area, two overlooks, the rustic Monte Sano Lodge and the park headquarters. On the final leg, it passes the Wernher von Braun Planetarium and crosses a high bluff with views to the north.

Distance: 1.8 mi.

Hiking Time: 30 minutes to 1 hour

Elevation Gain/Loss: +183 ft., -183 ft.

Hiking Difficulty: Easy to moderate

Location: Monte Sano State Park, 5105 Nolen Ave., Huntsville, AL 35801; (256) 534-3757

Facilities: There are restrooms with water at the Biker's Trailhead pavilion. Restrooms and water are also available in the pavilion near the picnic area parking lot. Snacks and drinks are available for purchase at the park store.

Driving Directions: See pages 2-3 and use the directions for Monte Sano State Park entrance and the picnic area parking lot.

Highlights

An Easy Walk: If you're looking for a comfortable stroll, the North Plateau Loop is a great option. As the path loops around the park's northern plateau, it remains mostly level, though you'll make brief, moderate ascents and descents in a couple of places.

A Lot to See Along the Way: This walk also offers plenty of interesting diversions, including the pavilion and rock wall that sit at the edge of the bluff in the picnic area. These are great spots to relax, enjoy a snack, or just soak in the views of McKay Hollow and forested hills to the south.

If you're hiking with kids, the playground is a quick walk from the bluff. Or you can continue east to tour the grounds of the attractive Monte Sano Lodge. After you head north to pass through the heart of the north plateau, you're greeted by another overlook offering excellent views of forested ridges and knolls to the east.

The path soon climbs to pass beneath the planetarium, which is one of the largest astronomical observatories in the South. Then you finish with a walk along the quiet, high bluffs on the northern edge of the plateau.

An overlook along the North Plateau Loop offers excellent views of mountains to the east.

Inspiring Views: The two overlooks along the loop provide some of the best views on the mountain. From the picnic area bluff, you'll gaze over a large tract of undisturbed forest that stretches to the horizon. In the foreground, McKay Hollow runs deep, and thick forest forms a great green trough. On each flank, a ridge slopes toward the floor of the hollow. On the far horizon, Green Mountain stretches like a pale blue wall. At the northeastern overlook (near the top of Bankhead Parkway), you get a bird's-eye view of a prominent ridge that fills the foreground. A classic mountain saddle sits between the Logan Point knoll and a narrow ridge. Beyond the ridge and to the east, low hills and a green valley stretch as far as you can see.

Waypoint/Mile

Trailhead (Waypoint 1) (34.7443, -86.5185) The following hike description begins near the park entrance on Nolen Avenue. Face the park entrance hut as if you're about to enter the park, and turn right to enter the woods on the south side of Nolen Ave. From here, the trail runs south and skirts the west side of the disc golf course.

1-1 (34.7417, -86.5183) (0.19 mi.) The trail intersects with the McKay Hollow Trail, which is slightly to the right and crosses a stream. Walk about 200 feet toward the nearest corner of the pavilion to reach Waypoint 1-2.

1-2 (34.7413, -86.5178) (0.24 mi.) The trail continues east along the rock wall of the overlook.

At 0.3 mi., look left to see the outdoor amphitheater, which the Civilian Conservation Corps (CCC) built in the 1930s.

1-3 (34.7416, -86.5152) (0.39 mi.) The path traverses the rear grounds of the restored Monte Sano Lodge. Constructed in 1939 by the CCC, the lodge burned in 1947 and remained a crumbled ruin for more than 50 years. In 2002, restoration of the lodge began, and the building is now used to host business meetings, weddings, and other gatherings.

1-4 (34.7429, -86.5129) (0.5 mi.) At the four-way junction, the Fire Tower Trail intersects and runs left (northwest) and right (southeast). To continue on the North Plateau Loop, continue straight, traveling northeast.

1-5 (34.7437, -86.5113) (0.6 mi.) The path reaches the main trailhead kiosk in the hikers parking lot. To continue on the North Plateau Loop Trail, turn left and travel north to cross the parking lot. Then cross the road and walk toward the ranger offices ahead on the right. At 0.8 mi., you'll see to the left a pavilion used by large groups. Walk another 460 ft. to reach Waypoint 1-6.

1-6 (34.7464, -86.5104) (0.9 mi.) The path reaches the end of the road used to access park cabins. Cross the paved road, turn left and travel north, skirting the edge of the bluff. After walking a little less than 500 ft., you'll reach the overlook.

1-7 (34.7477, -86.5107) (0.99 mi.) As you reach the overlook parking area, you'll see to the right an interpretive sign detailing some of the local bird species. During nice weather, this overlook is a popular destination, as walkers, runners and bikers can access it via a closed section of Bankhead Parkway (Trail 48, see page 148).

A rushing stream flows beside the North Plateau Loop.

Continue to the far side of the overlook parking area. At 1.2 mi., the North Plateau Loop passes within a few yards of the rear of the planetarium. You'll soon reach a quieter section of the trail as you follow the edge of a bluff.

1-8 (34.7475, -86.5176) (1.5 mi.) Cold Spring Trail intersects on the right and descends moderately to steeply to the west.

1-9 (34.7446, -86.5186) (1.8 mi.) The Fire Tower Trail intersects on the left. To complete the loop, continue straight and travel south for about 100 ft., crossing Nolen Avenue, passing the entrance hut and ending at your starting point on the south side of the road.

Trail Facts

An Old Road: The North Plateau Loop was originally a carriage road built for guests of the Hotel Monte Sano. Operating from 1888 to 1896, the hotel also served as a health spa and offered a variety of diversions to help people enjoy the clean mountain air. This included carriage rides along the rim of the mountain's north and south plateaus.

Planetarium: In 1954, Wernher von Braun, Ernst Stuhlinger and other members of the Rocket City Astronomical Association (now the Von Braun Astronomical Society) began constructing the planetarium atop Monte Sano. The society paid $1 to lease 13.5 acres of land within the state park. To view the heavens, the observatory employs a 16-inch Celestron reflecting telescope and a 21-inch mirror. A projector displays images of stars onto the observatory dome, which is made from a dummy fuel tank that was built to test the Saturn V rocket. Now more than 60 years old, the planetarium still hosts regular stargazing events. Visit www.vbas.org for details.

Monte Sano Lodge: The CCC constructed the lodge in the 1930s, but within a few years, a fire destroyed the structure. "Supposedly, a preacher at First Baptist Church did a Sunday morning sermon about this den of iniquity on the top of the mountain, and coincidentally that evening the lodge caught fire and burned down," says local historian Bruce Martin. The lodge remained a stone ruin until it was rebuilt in 2002, and it now serves as an excellent venue for weddings, business meetings and other gatherings.

SECTION 2:
Fire Tower Trail, Bog Trail and Bucca Family Bike Trail

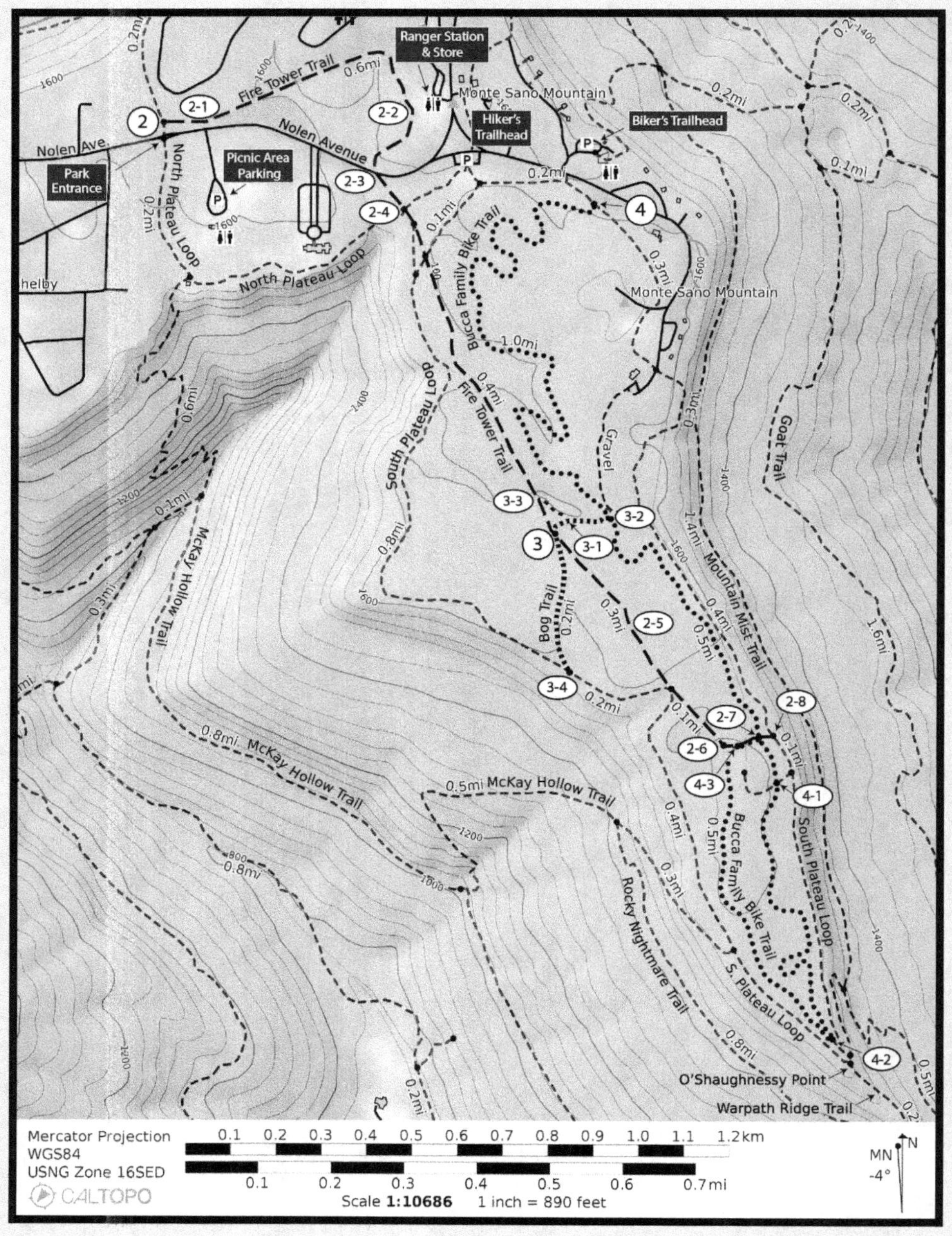

2. Fire Tower Trail

Running through the heart of the park's southern plateau, the Fire Tower Trail explores Monte Sano's intriguing history. From the site of a historic railroad, you pass a Japanese tea garden, a pioneer home site and a massive fire tower built in the 1940s.

Distance: 1.5 mi.
Hiking Time: 45 minutes to 1 hour
Elevation Gain/Loss: +108 ft., -136 ft.
Hiking Difficulty: Easy
Location: Monte Sano State Park, 5105 Nolen Ave., Huntsville AL, 35801; (256) 534-3757
Facilities: Restrooms and water are available in the pavilion near the picnic area parking lot. Snacks and drinks are available for purchase at the park store.
Driving Directions: See pages 2-3 and use the directions for Monte Sano State Park entrance and the picnic area parking lot.

Highlights

A Family Friendly Walk: The Fire Tower Trail gains and loses little elevation over 1.5 mi., making it a level, comfortable path for people of all ages. As you walk, you can investigate many interesting features, from the railroad tracks to the Japanese tea garden and the massive fire tower.

Monte Sano Railway: The short railroad track near the beginning of the Fire Tower Trail marks part of the route of the Monte Sano Railway. Built in 1888, the train carried people from the downtown Huntsville Opera House to the Hotel Monte Sano. For much of the way, the train followed the same route that Bankhead Parkway now covers. The train would climb nearly 1,000 ft. as it made the 8-mi. trip up the mountain, which took 20 minutes. You can see more remnants of the railroad and learn more about its history by hiking the Old Railroad Bed Trail in the Land Trust's Monte Sano Nature Preserve (see page 80).

North Alabama Japanese Garden: With its striking teahouse, beautiful azaleas and Japanese maple trees, Monte Sano's Japanese tea garden is one of the most serene spots on the mountain. This is the perfect place to decompress. Plus, it offers a picturesque backdrop for nature photography. In 1988, Robert Black, who grew up on the mountain, began building the garden after he closed his garden center. According to a WAFF 48 report, Black had several Japanese plants left over, and he worked with a state park ranger to find a suitable creek on Monte Sano where he could plant them. At that time, few people visited the land that holds the garden. Thanks to the efforts of Black and the state park, an overlooked plot of land is now a jewel in the park.

Waypoint/Mile

Trailhead (Waypoint 2) (34.7446, -86.5186) To reach the trailhead, begin at the main parking lot for the picnic area. Proceed to Nolen Avenue and turn left to walk west along the side of the road. Immediately beyond the park entrance building, turn right to cross Nolen Ave. Enter the North Plateau Loop trail and walk north about 100 ft. to the junction with the Fire Tower Trail, which intersects on the right.

2-1 (34.7447, -86.5177) (285 ft.) The path runs level as it hugs the edge of the woods beside Nolen Avenue. You'll soon pass a short section of railroad track marking the former route of the Monte Sano Railway (see Highlights, above). At 0.2 mi., the path to the North Alabama Japanese Garden intersects on the right. In 1988, Robert Black began building the garden as a hobby. In the garden, you'll find a traditional teahouse as well as healthy populations of native azaleas and Japanese maples. At 0.26 mi., you'll see to the left a path that leads to the park campground.

2-2 (34.7450, -86.5126) (0.4 mi.) After passing a stand of bamboo, the trail skirts the Japanese garden and heads south.

2-3 (34.7450, -86.5126) (0.5 mi.) Cross Nolen Avenue, bear left and take the Fire Tower Trail southeast.

2-4 (34.7436, -86.5135) (0.6 mi.) The Fire Tower Trail intersects with the North Plateau Loop Trail. Continue straight, traveling southeast, and cross a small stream bordered by moss-covered rocks. If the stream is running, this is a peaceful spot to relax and enjoy the sounds of the burbling water.

At 0.64 mi., a connector trail intersects on the right and stretches 354 ft. to meet the South Plateau Loop. After walking another 267 ft., you'll cross the South Plateau Loop. Continue straight to travel south on the Fire Tower Trail. At 1.1 mi., the Fire Tower Trail crosses the Bog Trail, which descends to the left (northeast) and also heads to the right (south). Go straight, traveling southeast, to continue on the Fire Tower Trail.

2-5 (34.7343, -86.5072) (1.3 mi.) Historical signs mark the former sites of the Fearn Home, built in 1835, and the James O'Shaughnessy home, built in 1890. You'll notice that the path is very wide here, as this was the road to the O'Shaughnessy home. Otherwise, there is little evidence that a home was here, save for a few foundation stones. However, several signs describe the former homes as well as the lives of the Fearns and O'Shaughnessys, who were prominent members of the community.

The trail is wide as it crosses fairly level ground, and the South Plateau Loop trail intersects at 1.4 mi. After another 94 ft., the South Plateau Loop meets the Fire Tower Trail again.

2-6 (34.7319, -86.5051) (1.5 mi.) At the Y junction, bear left to continue on the Fire Tower Trail, heading east.

2-7 (34.7320, -86.5043) (1.54 mi.) After walking about 250 ft., you'll reach a junction with the Bucca Family Bike Trail. From here you can continue on the Fire Tower Trail another 115 ft. to reach its endpoint at a junction with the North Plateau Loop at **Waypoint 2-8** (34.7322, -86.5040) (1.59 mi.). Or you can turn right to visit the base of the Fire Tower.

To visit the base of the Fire Tower: Turn right at Waypoint 31-7 and travel southeast on the Bucca Family Bike Trail. Go 0.1 mi., traversing a gentle slope, to reach the gravel path that leads to the Fire Tower. At Waypoint 4-1, turn right onto the gravel path and ascend to the Fire Tower. You'll walk about 370 ft. to reach the base of the tower. Originally built as a wood structure in the

The fire tower atop Monte Sano rises 100 feet.

1940s, the tower was upgraded to a metal frame in the 1960s. Note that the tower is closed, and the stairs are not accessible.

Trail Facts

Monte Sano Railway: The railroad operated for less than 10 years. In 1896, the Hotel Monte Sano failed to open, so the train didn't operate. Due to the lost revenue, the Monte Sano Railroad Company failed to make its payments to the Baldwin Locomotive Works in Philadelphia. Though the hotel reopened in 1897, the railroad never operated again. "On a court order it was sold to the creditors," Montesano.org reports. "In 1896 the crossties and rails were sold, and the balance of the equipment was scrapped."

Fire Tower: On Oct. 4, 1957, the Soviet Union launched Sputnik, the first artificial satellite. It circled the Earth once every hour and 36 minutes, and people with binoculars could view Sputnik before sunrise and after sunset. According to a historical marker, members of NASA climbed Monte Sano's 100-foot-tall fire tower to view the satellite and record its telemetry. Technically, NASA didn't exist until the following year, so the people who climbed the tower would have worked for the National Advisory Committee for Aeronautics (NACA), the precursor to NASA.

3. Bog Trail

This short path makes for an interesting side trip if you're traveling the Fire Tower Trail, South Plateau Loop or Bucca Family Bike Trail. The main highlight of the trail is a small pond that serves as a good spot for wildlife watching and nature photography.

Distance: 0.3 mi. to 0.5 mi.
Hiking Time: 10 to 15 minutes
Elevation Gain/Loss: +60 ft., -28 ft.
Hiking Difficulty: Easy
Location: Monte Sano State Park, 5105 Nolen Ave., Huntsville, AL 35801; (256) 534-3757
Facilities: There are restrooms with water at the Biker's Trailhead

pavilion. Restrooms and water are available in the pavilion near the picnic area parking lot. Snacks and drinks are available for purchase at the park store.

Driving Directions: See pages 2-3 and use the directions for the Monte Sano State Park entrance and the Biker's Trailhead.

Highlights

The Bog: This small body of water is the site of a natural "perched pond," meaning the pond covers stone that's impervious to water. In 1886, the Hotel Monte Sano had a landscape architect enhance the pond to serve as a tourist attraction. Horse-drawn dredges were used to scoop out material and increase the depth of the water. The architect's men built a fence around the pond, added ducks and geese, and planted what they considered water lilies, but were actually American lotus. In Southern streams and ponds, you'll see this plant, which boasts large lily pads. For decades, this Monte Sano bog was known as the Lily Pond.

Waypoint/Mile

Trailhead (Waypoint 3) (34.7363, -86.5093) To reach the Bog Trail, begin at the Hiker's Trailhead on Nolen Avenue. Take the wide South Plateau Loop Trail, following white blazes and heading southeast. Walk 137 ft. and turn right onto the South Plateau Loop Trail. Walk southwest for 0.1 mi. to the junction with the Fire Tower Trail. Turn left onto the Fire Tower Trail and travel south 0.4 mi. to the junction with the Bog Trail, which is marked with orange blazes. From the trailhead, you have two options:

Option 1: Explore the Bog

From **Waypoint 3,** turn left and travel east to head toward the bog.

3-1 (34.7366, -86.5088) (158 feet from Waypoint 3) After a brief and gradual descent, you'll approach the edge of the bog and see a path on the left. In this spot, you'll also see the first interpretive signs for an outdoor classroom. If you turn left and follow this trail, you can browse the classroom interpretive signs, though many are old and faded. The area hasn't been used as a classroom for more than 20 years. After about

330 feet, the path connects with the Fire Tower Trail at **Waypoint 3-3** (34.7371, -86.509). From Waypoint 3-1, you can also continue straight to explore the eastern side of the bog.

3-2 (34.7320, -86.5043) (475 ft. from Waypoint 3) The Bog Trail intersects with the Bucca Family Bike Trail. To return to the Hiker's Trailhead, you can retrace your steps and take the Fire Tower Trail back. For a little longer walk, turn left onto the Bucca Family Bike Trail and follow it for 1.0 mi. to the South Plateau Loop. Then turn left onto the South Plateau Loop and travel about 0.2 mi. to the Hiker's Trailhead.

Option 2: Head to the South Plateau Loop

From **Waypoint 3,** turn right and descend a path that has eroded due to draining water. This 0.2-mi. stretch of trail isn't particularly interesting, but it does allow you to quickly jump over to the South Plateau Loop Trail if you would like to explore that path.

3-4 (34.7334, -86.5090) (0.2 mi. from Waypoint 3) The Bog Trail meets the South Plateau Loop at a T junction. If you turn right onto the South Plateau Loop and head northwest, you can walk a little less than a mile to return to the Hiker's Trailhead.

Trail Facts

A Romantic Escape: The people who altered the pond area also built a gazebo there. Hotel guests could pay the desk clerk a couple of extra bucks to rent the gazebo for a romantic evening escape. The hotel also provided blankets and pillows. But it's doubtful that a summer evening in the gazebo would have been comfortable, much less romantic, considering you'd spend much of your time swatting mosquitoes.

4. Bucca Family Bike Trail

I've included this path because it's open to hikers, but it's primarily a path for beginner bikers and families biking with kids. The single-track path is mostly flat and free of rocks and other obstacles, making it ideal for riders of all ability levels.

Distance: 2.7 mi.
Hiking Time: 1 hour
Elevation Gain/Loss: +217 ft., -213 ft.
Hiking Difficulty: Easy
Biking Difficulty: Easy
Location: Monte Sano State Park, 5105 Nolen Ave., Huntsville, AL 35801; (256) 534-3757
Facilities: There are restrooms with water at the Biker's Trailhead pavilion. Restrooms and water are also available in the pavilion near the picnic area parking lot. Snacks and drinks are available for purchase at the park store.
Driving Directions: See pages 2-3 and use the directions for the Monte Sano State Park entrance and the Biker's Trailhead.

Highlights

Beginner-Friendly Hiking and Biking: If you're headed to the state park for a family outing, be sure to bring your bikes. Kids and riders of all ability levels will enjoy the easygoing Bucca Family Bike Trail. Designed specifically for beginning riders, the path is mostly free of the roots, rocks and other obstacles you'll encounter on Monte Sano's more technical trails. Also, the trail covers ground that's fairly flat, so you can control your speed easily and avoid tough climbs and tricky descents.

Access to Great Views: From the southern end of the Bucca Family Bike Trail, you can quickly reach one of the best views in the park. O'Shaughnessy Point, at the tip of the plateau, provides a towering view of McKay Hollow and the western side of Monte Sano. A picturesque cedar tree frames your view as you look left to peer down into Big Cove, where small fields and neighborhoods share space.

Waypoint/Mile

Trailhead (Waypoint 4) (34.7430, -86.5083) To reach the trailhead, begin at the Biker's Trailhead parking area off the main park road (Bankhead Parkway). Head toward Bankhead Pkwy., traveling southwest. Go about 200 ft., and then turn left onto Bankhead Pkwy. Cross the road and take the path immediately on the left, which heads into the woods. Go about 60 ft., and then turn left onto the South Plateau Loop, traveling southeast. After walking about 260 ft., turn right onto the Bucca Family Bike Trail and follow the dark pink blazes.

The Bucca Family Bike Trail soon winds its way across the plateau. The single-track path drops and rises gently and makes a series of turns that are easy to negotiate on a bike. In a few spots (such as at 0.8 mi.), you'll encounter tighter turns that require a bit more skill, but it's still beginner-level stuff. The path stays mostly in the center of the plateau; you don't really have any impressive views, but the hardwood forest is open and inviting.

3-2 (34.7367, -86.5079) (1.1 mi.) The Bucca Family Bike Trail intersects a gravel road and the Bog Trail. To continue on the Bucca trail, turn right and take the second trail, following the dark pink blazes. If you don't wish to continue on the Bucca trail, you can take the gravel road to loop back to your starting point. Just turn left onto the gravel road, follow it for 0.2 mi., and then take a paved road for about 200 ft. to reach the South Plateau Loop. Turn left onto the South Plateau Loop, travel northwest 0.3 mi., and then turn right onto the path that leads to Bankhead Parkway and the Biker's Trailhead.

At 1.3 mi., the Bucca trail parallels the South Plateau Loop and runs through dense forest with pines, sweet gum and plenty of undergrowth. If you travel the path in winter, you can look left and just make out the distant ridges to the northeast. At 1.6 mi., after you cross a powerline break, look up and to the right for a view of the fire tower.

2-7 (34.7320, -86.5043) (1.6 mi.) You reach a four-way junction with the Fire Tower Trail. Continue straight, traveling southeast on the Bucca Family Bike Trail.

4-1 (34.7312, -86.5038) (1.7 mi.) Cross the gravel road that leads to the fire tower. To visit the base of the fire tower, turn right onto the gravel road and ascend for 0.1 mi.

4-2 (34.7260, -86.5025) (2.2 mi.) The South Plateau Loop intersects on the left. To continue on the Bucca Family Bike Trail, make a hairpin turn to the right to travel northwest. But, before you make the turn, consider making the short trip to enjoy the awesome view at O' Shaughnessy Point. Instead of making the sharp turn to the northwest, take the short path that heads west toward the bluff. Go about 60 ft. and then turn left onto the South Plateau Loop. Travel southeast 125 ft. and you'll see the O'Shaughnessy Point rock outcrop on the right.

4-3 (34.7320, -86.5048) (2.7 mi.) The Bucca Family Bike Trail meets the Fire Tower Trail. Turn right and travel east 170 ft. to meet the Bucca Family Bike Trail at Waypoint 2-7. To return to the beginning of the Bucca Family Bike Trail, turn left and travel north for 1.5 mi.

Trail Facts

Building the Bucca Trail: It's hard to believe now, but for decades there were almost no mountain bikers on Monte Sano. Then, in 2005, Monte Sano State Park hired a new manager who embraced mountain biking. That year, members of the Huntsville chapter of the Southern Off-Road Bicycle Association (SORBA) began to design, build and maintain Monte Sano bike paths. SORBA member Matt Bucca created the Bucca Family Bike Trail, which was completed in 2012 and played a key role in growing mountain biking in Huntsville. "That's what really began to change things," said former SORBA president Mary Anne Swanstrom. "That opened things up for families and people who wanted to try the sport."

SECTION 3:
McKay Hollow Trail, Rocky Nightmare Trail and South Plateau Loop Trail

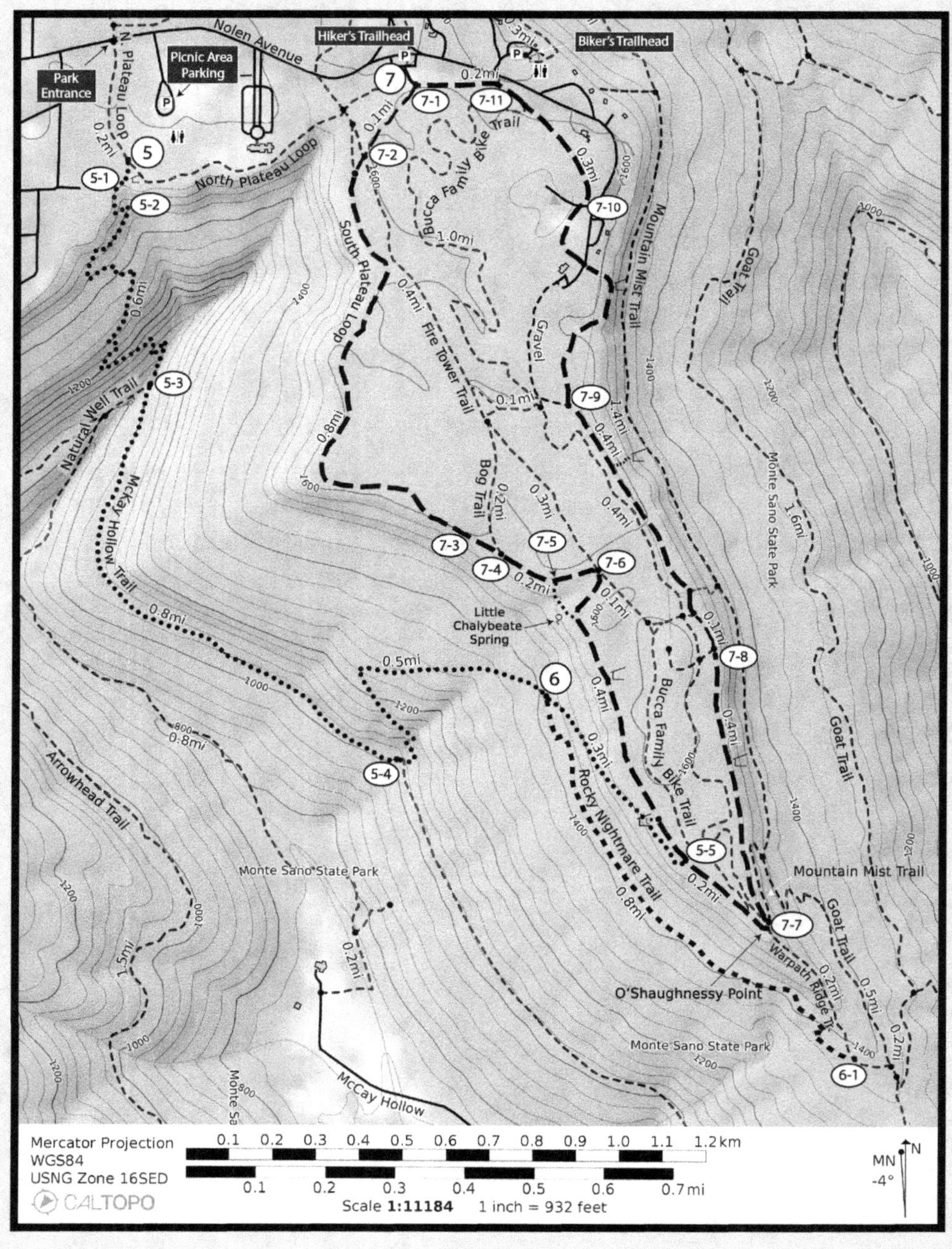

5. McKay Hollow Trail

The McKay Hollow Trail is one of the most challenging hikes on Monte Sano, but it's also one of the most rewarding. After a visit to the tranquil Blue Spring Falls, you'll descend more than 500 feet on a steep, rocky path to reach McKay Hollow, one of the most remote areas of the park. After crossing a spring-fed creek, you'll have an easy stroll across a low plateau that courses through the hollow. At mile 1.5, take a quick break and grab a snack, because the final leg is a real thigh-burner. You'll climb for almost a mile and gain more than 580 feet of elevation to reach the top of the mountain's southern plateau.

Distance: 2.4 mi.
Hiking Time: 1.5 to 2 hours
Elevation Gain/Loss: +756 ft./-754 ft.
Hiking Difficulty: Strenuous
Location: Monte Sano State Park, 5105 Nolen Ave., Huntsville, AL 35801; (256) 534-3757
Facilities: Restrooms and potable water are available in the pavilion near the picnic area parking lot. Snacks and drinks are available for purchase at the park store.
Driving Directions: See pages 2-3 and use the information for the Monte Sano State Park entrance and the picnic area parking lot.

Highlights

Blue Spring Falls: If you can do this hike a day or so after a good rain, you'll see tendrils of water slip over the lip of the crescent bluff to drop about 15 feet and splash onto a long stone shelf. From this curved platform, the water spills down a tongue of boulders and scree.

Wild and Remote Areas: At about the half-mile mark, where the McKay Hollow Trail dives into the ravine, it feels like a rugged, remote path far away from civilization. The terrain resembles a Western wilderness, as boulders and twisted cedars hug the steep slope. To the right, a towering ridge looms over the deep ravine, giving hikers the sense that they're delving deep into a big wilderness. At the base of the hollow, you're hundreds of feet and a far distance from the activity in the park's picnic area. When Big Spring Creek is running, the hollow is filled with the echoes of rushing water and wind.

Epic Views: After you climb up from the base of Blue Spring Falls, you'll walk the edge of the bluff and enjoy excellent views of the mountain's eastern ridge. From here, you can also see down the length of the forested McKay Hollow. At 0.17 mi., a rock outcrop offers good views to the south, and at 0.45 mi., you can pause to enjoy another outcrop with good views before descending into the hollow. At the southern end of the trail, at the top of the plateau, you can walk a short distance to O' Shaughnessy Point and one of the most spectacular vistas on the mountain.

Waypoint/Mile

Trailhead (Waypoint 5) (34.7417, -86.5183) The McKay Hollow Trail begins in the park picnic area, near the pavilion that sits on the edge of the overlook. To reach the trailhead, begin at the southwestern corner of the park's main parking lot. Walk south on the wide gravel path

marked with white blazes. About 170 ft. before you reach the pavilion at the overlook, bear right and cross a small creek to reach a brown post that marks the junction of the McKay Hollow Trail and the South Plateau Loop. From here, the McKay Hollow Trail, marked with yellow blazes, moves toward the bluff.

5-1 (34.7412, -86.5182) (166 ft.) A brown post with a McKay Hollow Trail sign sits beside the creek at the edge of the bluff. Bear right to cross the creek bed, and descend to the southwest.

The path traverses the face of the bluff and descends gradually. At first, the trail is rocky, but it soon becomes a narrow dirt path.

5-2 (34.7409, -86.5183) (411 ft.) The trail

makes a sharp right turn and heads south toward a yellow sign marked, "Warning Difficult Trail."

5-3 (34.7371, -86.5179) (0.75 mi.) At the trail junction, the McKay Hollow Trail goes to the left (south) and crosses the narrow Blue Spring Creek. At this same point, the Natural Well Trail goes straight (southwest). There's also a sign informing travelers that the terrain between this point and the park picnic area is steep and not open to bikes.

5-4 (34.7289, -86.5115) (1.59 mi.) The trail turns left to the northeast and ascends the steep slope.

6 (34.7304, -86.5077) (2.1 mi.) The Rocky Nightmare Trail intersects on the right. To continue on the McKay Hollow Trail, go straight and head southeast. The path climbs steadily out of the hollow and reaches a shelter at 2.3 mi.—the perfect spot to catch your breath after the long ascent.

5-5 (34.7270, -86.5041) (2.4 mi.) The McKay Hollow Trail ends at the intersection with the South Plateau Loop Trail.

Trail Facts

Original Trail Name: When the Civilian Conservation Corps built the park, it created three trails, including the Walnut Bottoms Trail running through McKay Hollow. It was named for the plethora of walnut trees that thrived in the bottomland. But in the 1990s, the path was renamed the McKay Hollow Trail. Supposedly, the hollow is named for a family that once lived in the ravine.

6. Rocky Nightmare Trail

Don't let the name frighten you. Sure, this path has rocky sections that challenge mountain bikers and trail runners. But for hikers, it's a comfortable walk through an attractive hardwood forest. If you walk it during winter, you'll enjoy occasional views of distant mountain ridges.

Distance: 0.8 mi.
Hiking Time: 25 to 30 minutes
Elevation Gain/Loss: +106 ft., -131 ft.
Hiking Difficulty: Easy to moderate

Location: Monte Sano State Park, 5105 Nolen Ave., Huntsville, AL 35801; (256) 534-3757
Facilities: At the picnic area, there are restrooms and potable water in the pavilion near the parking lot. At the Hiker's Trailhead, there are no facilities and no sources of potable water. Snacks and drinks are available for purchase at the park store.
Driving Directions: See pages 2-3 and use the information for the Monte Sano State Park entrance and either the picnic area parking lot or the Hiker's Trailhead.

Highlights

Nightmare-Free Hiking: For the most part, this is a mellow trail with just a couple of rocky areas and few changes in elevation. It's wise to wear durable, stable hiking shoes or boots, as you will encounter fields of rubble.

Quiet Woods: At the southern end of the plateau, you're in one of the remoter and quieter areas of the park. Pretty much all you'll hear is your shoes shushing through the leaves blanketing the ground. Also, you won't encounter many other folks here, because the Rocky Nightmare Trail is not as well known or as popular as the other trails it parallels—the McKay Hollow Trail and the South Plateau Loop.

Waypoint/Mile

Trailhead (Waypoint 6) (34.7304, -86.5076) There are two ways to access the beginning of the Rocky Nightmare Trail. If you're up for a challenging hike, begin in the state park picnic area and follow the McKay Hollow Trail for 2.1 mi. to the beginning of the Rocky Nightmare Trail at Waypoint 6. For an easier walk, begin at the Hiker's Trailhead and follow the South Plateau Loop for 1.6 mi. to the southern end of the McKay Hollow Trail at Waypoint 5-5. Then turn right onto the McKay Hollow Trail and travel 0.3 mi. to the beginning of the Rocky Nightmare Trail at Waypoint 6.

From Waypoint 6, the trail enters hardwood forest with widely spaced trees and little undergrowth. At 0.3 mi., the path traverses one of the few rocky sections, where the hiking isn't especially difficult, but you'll need to step carefully to avoid twisting an ankle.

6-1 (34.7228, -86.4999) (0.8 mi.) The Rocky Nightmare Trail ends at the junction with the Warpath Ridge Trail. Rather than retracing your steps, consider turning left to hike north on the Warpath Ridge Trail. As you approach the top of the plateau, you'll traverse a knife-edge ridge where the land falls away dramatically to the east and west.

Trail Facts

The "Rocky Nightmare" Name: The Southern Off-Road Bicycle Association originally built this path as part of a training course for the International Mountain Bicycling Association. After the trail lay dormant for 10 years, members of the Huntsville Area Mountain Bike Riders (HAMR) decided to finally finish the route. "We knew the trail had several very rocky sections, but at the time all the leaves had fallen in that area," says a HAMR spokesperson. "The day before we began construction, a few of our trail crew members used backpack blowers to blow off the trail, and we had an 'oh no' moment, as it was WAY rockier than we anticipated. It was a nightmare, as the work was super slow and strenuous with all of the rocks."

7. South Plateau Loop Trail

Measuring 3.4 mi., the South Plateau Loop is one of the longest trails in Monte Sano State Park. But the path is mostly level, as it follows the edge of the plateau, so it's perfect for hikers of all ability levels. The loop also boasts several interesting features, including excellent bluff views and rustic rest shelters. Plus, the trail runs near popular waypoints like the Joe B. Shirley Fire Tower and O'Shaughnessy Point.

Distance: 3.4 mi.
Hiking Time: 1.5 to 2 hours
Elevation Gain/Loss: +166 ft., -179 ft.
Hiking Difficulty: Easy to moderate (due to distance)
Location: Monte Sano State Park, 5105 Nolen Ave., Huntsville, AL 35801; (256) 534-3757
Facilities: At the Hiker's Trailhead, there are no facilities and

no sources of potable water. Snacks and drinks are available for purchase at the park store. At the park picnic area, there are restrooms and potable water in the pavilion near the parking lot. There are also restrooms with water at the Biker's Trailhead pavilion.

Driving Directions: See pages 2-3 and use the information for the Monte Sano State Park entrance and the Hiker's Trailhead.

Highlights

Bluff Views: The South Plateau Loop offers one of the most beautiful treks on the mountain. The western side of the loop delivers a steady stream of excellent views across the vast ravine known as McKay Hollow. On the eastern side of the loop, the bluff provides expansive views of the lowlands to the east, including Mills Hollow, and smaller mountains dotting the area.

Some Monte Sano shelters date back to the 1930s.

Rustic Shelters: Along the western and eastern sides of the loop, shelters perched at the edge of bluffs provide welcome shade and panoramic views. Most of these structures feature a shingled roof, stone or wooden benches, and no walls. On the eastern side of the loop, a couple of shelters are several yards off the main trail and tucked into the woods, providing a bit more solitude.

Joe B. Shirley Fire Tower: At 2.2 mi., you'll meet a path that leads directly to the 100-foot-tall fire tower. The tower has been decommissioned for decades and its ladder and metal cab are no longer accessible. But it's an impressive structure with an interesting history. (See page 14 for more info.)

O'Shaughnessy Point: Named for James O' Shaughnessy, who built a house on the Monte Sano plateau in 1890, this outcrop lies just before the 1.8-mi. mark of the South Plateau Loop. The high perch offers an inspiring view of McKay Hollow as well as the mountain's western ridge and rural lowlands to the south. On the large landing at the edge of the bluff, there's enough room for the whole family to pose for a photo. If you want to rest your legs or enjoy lunch, take a seat on the wood bench overlooking the point.

Waypoint/Mile

Trailhead (Waypoint 7) (34.7438, -86.5113) Begin your hike at the Hiker's Trailhead parking lot trailhead kiosk. Enter the woods beyond the kiosk and travel southeast following the white blazes. Enter the wide path that heads southeast and follow the white blazes.

7-1 (34.7435, -86.5110) (137 ft.) At the trail junction, the South Plateau Loop Trail goes left (east) and right (southwest). The following hike description begins by going right.

7-2 (34.7419, -86.5124) (0.1 mi.) The South Plateau Loop crosses the Fire Tower Trail, which runs northwest and southeast. To stay on the South Plateau Loop, continue straight, traveling southwest.

At 0.19 mi., a path on the right runs about 370 ft. to meet the Fire Tower Trail. Continue straight and travel south on the South Plateau Loop. At 0.89 mi., you'll reach a rock outcrop with good views.

7-3 (34.7339, -86.5097) (0.94 mi.) A shelter sits on the right side of the trail.

7-4 (34.7334, -86.5089) (1.0 mi.) The Bog Trail intersects on the left and ascends to the north.

7-5 (34.7329, -86.5074) (1.09 mi.) An unmarked side trail intersects on the right. If you take this path, you'll descend stepped stones for 180 ft. and reach a stream fed by Little Chalybeate Spring. The Hotel Monte Sano created the steps so guests (many of whom were ill) could retrieve the spring water, which was supposed to have medicinal benefits. At one time, there was a springhouse near the stream, and an attendant would fill bottles of water for people to take with them.

After it drops 180 ft. to the stream, the trail continues for about another 250 ft. It passes beneath pines as it climbs back to the South Plateau Loop. If you want to skip this path, continue straight at Waypoint 7-5 and head northeast.

7-6 (34.7332, -86.5065) (1.1 mi.) At the junction with the Fire Tower Trail, turn right and travel southeast. Walk 96 ft. to the next trail junction and turn right to follow the South Plateau Loop Trail, which bends to the southwest. (If you continue straight at Waypoint 7-6, you'll follow the Fire Tower Trail.)

Walk another 0.2 mi. to reach a shelter that sits in the shade of trees on the right side of the trail. At 1.5 mi., a sign on the right directs you to a rest shelter and the McKay Hollow Trail, which descends into the valley immediately to your right.

5-5 (34.7270, -86.5041) (1.6 mi.) The McKay Hollow Trail intersects on the right. Continue straight, heading southeast. In another 0.1 mi., the Bucca Family Bike Trail intersects on the left.

7-7 (34.7254, -86.5021) (1.8 mi.) The Warpath Ridge Trail intersects on the right and runs level as it travels southeast along a ridge crest. Turn left and travel north to continue on the South Plateau Loop.

In 47 ft., you'll reach the junction with the Mountain Mist Trail, which descends to the north. Continue straight on the South Plateau Loop. In 96 ft., you'll see a path on the left that connects to the Bucca Family Bike Trail. From this point, continue straight, traveling northwest. At 2.0 mi., a path on the right leads to a shelter that sits about 25 ft. off the trail.

7-8 (34.7314, -86.5037) (2.2 mi.) The path on the left leads to the base of the fire tower.

At 2.3 mi., the Fire Tower Trail intersects on the left and heads west. Continue straight on the South Plateau Loop. After another 200 ft., you'll encounter a steep connector trail that measures 338 ft. and leads east to the Mountain Mist Trail.

At 2.5 mi., a path on the right side of the trail (northeast) leads to a shelter that's about 160 ft. from the South Plateau Loop Trail and sits tucked away on the side of the bluff.

7-9 (34.7365, -86.5073) (2.6 mi.) At the trail junction, turn right to travel northeast to continue on the South Plateau Loop.

At 2.8 mi., a trail shelter sits on the right (east) side of the trail. Go another 0.1 mi. and cross a paved road to travel northwest on the South Plateau Loop.

7-10 (34.7410, -86.5068) (3.0 mi.) Cross a gravel road and travel northeast, following the white blazes.

After another 0.2 mi., the Bucca Family Bike Trail intersects on the left. Continue straight, traveling northwest.

7-11 (34.7434, -86.5089) (3.3 mi.) On the right, a connector path leads to Bankhead Parkway and the road leading to the Biker's Trailhead. Continue west for another 0.1 mi. to return to Waypoint 7-1. From there, you'll turn right and travel north to return to the trailhead and Hiker's Trailhead parking lot.

Trail Facts

Shelters: In the 1930s, the Civilian Conservation Corps built the shelters, using materials on the mountain. To this day, you can see some of the original support posts made from Monte Sano cedar trees. In some of the shelters, you'll see a sign for the Young Adult Conservation Corps (YACC). Operating from 1977 to 1982, the YACC was a federally funded program that provided people ages 16 to 23 year-round employment in jobs related to conservation. Members of the YACC refurbished the roofs of the shelters, outfitting them with more modern materials.

Little Chalybeate Spring: Chalybeate spring water contains salts of iron, magnesium, manganese and calcium. So it tastes as bad as you can imagine. Nevertheless, chalybeate waters have been praised for their healing properties since the 17th century. (You know the old saying—if it tastes bad, it must be good for you.) Serving as a sanitorium, the Hotel Monte Sano not only encouraged guests to visit Chalybeate Spring, but also placed a bottle of the stuff in each guest's room every day.

Stone Steps to the Spring: The steps leading to the spring were intentionally made of sandstone. Unlike limestone, sandstone is porous, so slippery algae and moss won't grow on the surface. Also, the rough texture of sandstone provides added traction. Originally, cedar rails were also placed on each side of the steps to help people descend the steep slope.

SECTION 4:
Mountain Mist Trail, Goat Trail, Flat Rock Connector Trail and Flat Rock Trail Section

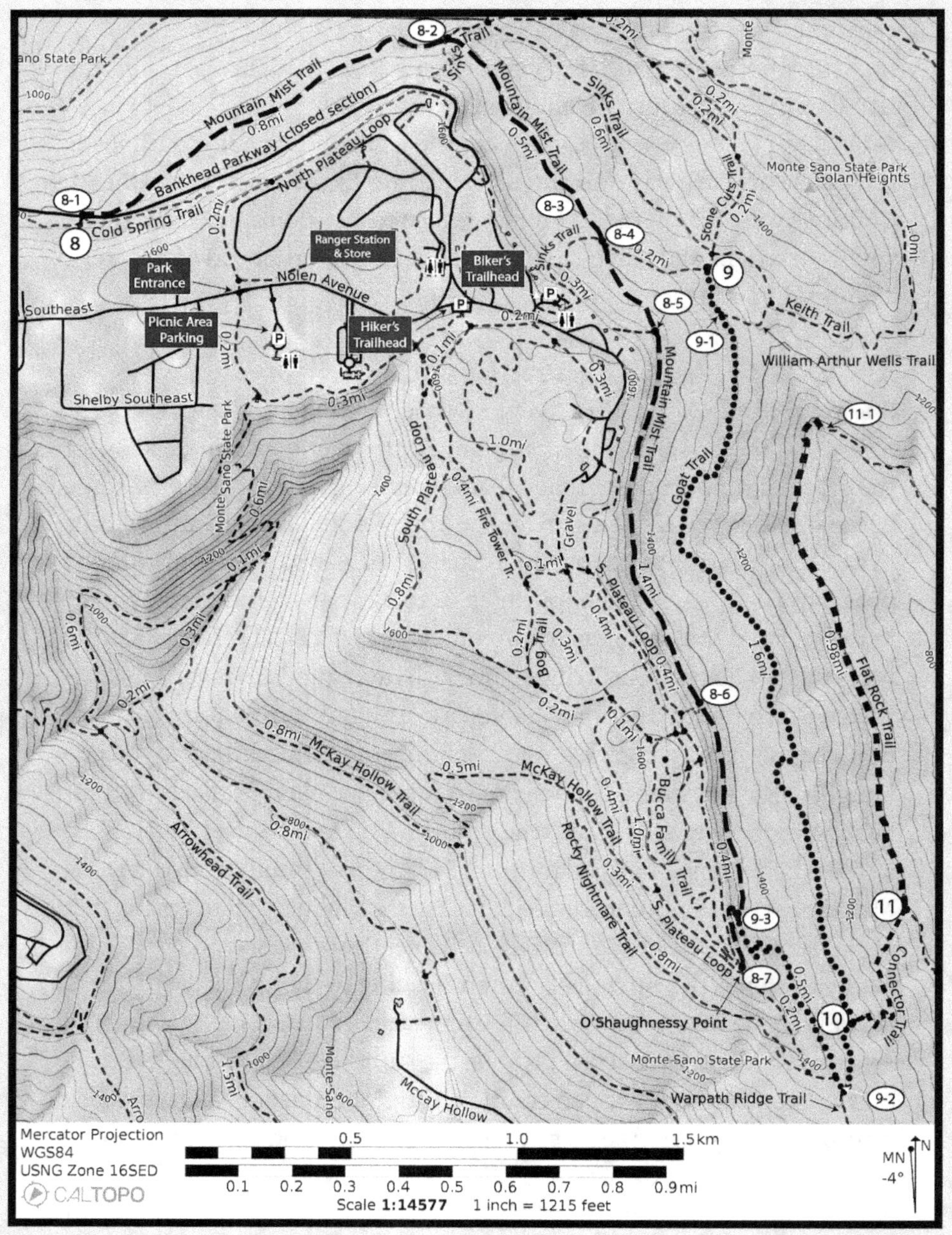

8. Mountain Mist Trail

Iconic would be a good way to describe this trail. It explores classic Monte Sano terrain, with an open forest of towering trees and high bluffs. Portions of the trail follow the route of the grueling Mountain Mist 50K, one of the country's most highly regarded trail-running races. After a little more than 2.5 mi., you'll pass Goat Rock, a rock formation formerly frequented by the mountain's renowned small herd of wild goats.

Distance: 2.8 mi.

Hiking Time: 1.5 to 2 hours

Elevation Gain/Loss: +354 ft., -481 ft.

Hiking Difficulty: Moderate to strenuous

Location: Monte Sano State Park, 5105 Nolen Ave., Huntsville, AL 35801; (256) 534-3757

Facilities: There are no facilities or sources of potable water at the trailhead.

Driving Directions: For the closest access to the Mountain Mist Trail, park near the closed section of Bankhead Parkway. See page 3 and use the information for the Bankhead Parkway Blockade.

Highlights

Serene Woods: From the moment the trail leaves Bankhead to its final ascent of the plateau, the Mountain Mist Trail leads you through some of the most tranquil woods on the mountain. Granted, if you visit on a weekend, or a time when the trails are teeming with bikers, it might not feel so sublime. But hit this trail on a weekday, and you'll love it. The first mile feels like real wilderness, as the ravine shelters you from any sense that a city lies nearby. As you climb the eastern side of the plateau, the forest floor is open and inviting, while high bluffs and skyscraper trees add a bit of grandeur to the trail.

Goat Rock: A little more than 2 mi. into the hike, you'll reach Goat Rock, a large rock overhang with a bench beneath it. The top of this rock used to be a hangout spot for a herd of goats that roamed the mountain trails. The goats have disappeared in recent years, and this rock shelter is now primarily known as a good spot to rest and enjoy some shade.

A Classic Trail-Running Route: The trail's favorable terrain makes it a popular trail-running route for people of all ability levels. For the most part, the surface is packed earth. While you need to stay alert to avoid stumbling, you'll face few major obstacles. Also, there are few steep climbs. In the first mile, the trail is pretty level, and the ascent to the top of the plateau is gradual. From the end of the Mountain Mist Trail, a variety of mellow trails will return you to your starting point.

Waypoint/Mile

Trailhead (Waypoint 8) (34.7462, -86.5240) The Mountain Mist Trail technically begins on the south side of the closed section of Bankhead Parkway, at the junction with the Cold Spring Trail. From this point, descend and go 110 ft. to reach the opposite side of Bankhead Pkwy.

8-1 (34.7466, -86.5238) (110 ft.) On the north side of Bankhead Parkway, begin a gradual descent on the double-track path.

8-2 (34.7514, -86.5119) (0.8 mi.) The Mountain Mist Trail crosses the Sinks Trail, which ascends to the left toward Logan Point and rises steeply on the right to meet the North Plateau Loop. To continue on the Mountain Mist Trail, go straight and turn to the south. The path soon drops gradually though the ravine with mature hardwoods and rolling terrain.

8-3 (34.7469, -86.5078) (1.2 mi.) On the right side of the trail, you'll see an old stone structure. This was part of a water tank that the Civilian Conservation Corps built to store water for the construction and operation of Monte Sano State Park. When the tank was full, it held 16,000 gallons. Beside the tank, in a separate small building, there was a 65-horsepower diesel pump.

8-4 (34.7514, -86.5119) (1.3 mi.) The Mountain Mist Trail crosses the Sinks Trail again. To the right, the Sinks Trail climbs 0.3 mi. to the Biker's Trailhead. To the left, the Sinks Trail dives toward the base of the ravine. Stay alert in this area, as bikers might be moving swiftly down the steep Sinks Trail. To continue on the Mountain Mist Trail, go straight and soon begin a steady climb out of the ravine.

8-5 (34.7434, -86.5050) (1.5 mi.) On the right, a steep path measuring 516 ft. climbs the bluff and ends at the rear of cabin 7.

8-6 (34.7329, -86.5037) (2.2 mi.) On the right, a connector trail measuring 338 ft. makes a very steep climb to meet the South Plateau Loop. Also to the right and a few yards up the slope is Goat Rock, where a bench sits beneath a large rock overhang.

From Waypoint 8-6, the path becomes more level, never drifting far from 1,480 ft. of elevation. To the right are towering limestone bluffs, and a few massive trees lord over the forest.

9-3 (34.7270, -86.5022) (2.7 mi.) The Goat Trail intersects on the left and goes south. To continue on the Mountain Mist Trail, take a sharp turn to the right and begin a moderate ascent toward the top of the bluff.

8-7 (34.7258, -86.5020) (2.8 mi.): The Mountain Mist Trail ends at the junction with the South Plateau Loop.

Trail Facts

The Mountain Mist Trail Name: Often, from late fall to winter, thick fog blankets the trails on Monte Sano Mountain. The white veil that falls across the woods inspired the name of the Mountain Mist Trail.

The Notorious Mountain Mist Trail 50K: Attracting some 500 runners from all over the country, the Mountain Mist Trail 50K is one of the oldest and most well-known trail-running competitions in the Southeast. During this grueling contest, runners negotiate rough and rocky trails in Monte Sano State Park and other properties managed by the Land Trust of North Alabama. The route includes some ridiculously steep terrain, such as the "Suicide Drop" into McKay Hollow.

9. Goat Trail

With a name like Goat Trail, you might expect this path to feature the kind of steep and rocky terrain that only a goat could negotiate. But it's an easy to moderate trail that explores the less-visited eastern slope of the mountain. Its name is derived from a herd of goats that once frequented this part of the mountain. While the goats are long gone, the trail still has its attractions, including some nice views and plenty of peace and quiet.

Distance: 2.6 mi.
Hiking Time: 1.5 to 2 hours
Elevation Gain/Loss: +610 ft., -413 ft.
Hiking Difficulty: Moderate
Location: Monte Sano State Park, 5105 Nolen Ave., Huntsville, AL 35801; (256) 534-3757
Facilities: There are restrooms with water at the Biker's Trailhead pavilion. Restrooms and potable water are available in the pavilion near the picnic area parking lot. Snacks and drinks are available for purchase at the park store.
Driving Directions: See pages 2-3 and use the directions for the Monte Sano State Park entrance and the Biker's Trailhead.

Highlights

Winter Views: Fewer people hike in winter, but it's really a great time to hit certain trails, as you'll have better views of the surrounding landscape. That's especially true with the Goat Trail. One of my favorite spots is near the 0.2-mi. mark, where you can see three to four layers of forested ridges stretching to the horizon.

Solitude: The Goat Trail visits one of the quieter parts of the state park, especially where it reaches the southern end of the plateau. It's also peaceful near the extreme southern end of the trail, where it turns north to wind through the boulder-strewn cedar grove.

Part of a Good Loop Hike: Combine the Sinks Trail, Goat Trail and Mountain Mist Trail for a moderate (and occasionally challenging) 4.5-mi. loop.

Waypoint/Mile

Trailhead (Waypoint 9) (34.7454, -86.5033) For the most direct route to the Goat Trail, begin at the Biker's Trailhead. Follow the Sinks Trail for 0.5 mi. to its junction with the Goat Trail. At the trailhead, you'll see three benches. Take the path that runs beside the sign that reads "William Arthur Wells CCC Memorial Trail." This is actually the beginning of the Goat Trail, which runs level to the south.

9-1 (34.7439, -86.5029) (476 ft.): The William Arthur Wells CCC

Memorial Trail intersects on the left and soon drops dramatically to the southeast. Continue straight traveling southeast to take the Goat Trail.

The initial stretch is perhaps the most scenic part of the Goat Trail, especially in winter. When the trees lose their leaves, you'll have a broad view of distant ridges, stretching from the northeast (on your left) to the southeast (on your right). At 0.4 mi., Chestnut Knob (1,610 ft.) dominates your view to the southeast. Then, 0.2 mi. farther down the path, the woods become dense, and the rocky ground is littered with fallen trees. But at 0.7 mi., the surroundings are more interesting as a classic mountain saddle appears, and Chestnut Knob and an unnamed peak flank a short ridge.

At 1.3 mi., moss-covered boulders are strewn about the rolling terrain. After another 0.1 mi., the nearby mountains are close companions on your walk.

10 (34.7242, -86.4984) (1.8 mi.): The Goat Trail-Flat Rock Connector path intersects on the left and descends. Continue straight to cross a wood footbridge at 1.95 mi.

9-2 (34.7223, -86.4988) (2.0 mi.) The Warpath Ridge Trail intersects on the left. To continue on the Goat Trail, go straight and climb gradually to the northwest. After another 95 ft., the Warpath Ridge Trail once again intersects on the left and goes west. Continue straight, traveling northwest on the Goat Trail.

At 2.2 mi., you'll enter a more exotic landscape where bright-green moss blankets the pale-gray boulders. Age-old cedars with thick, twisted trunks cast shade over the trail. But soon, you return to the mixed hardwoods as switchbacks take you up a long slope.

9-3 (34.7226, -86.4990) (2.6 mi.) The Goat Trail ends at a Y junction with the Mountain Mist Trail. If you turn right onto the Mountain Mist Trail and travel north, you can walk 1.4 mi. to loop back to the Sinks Trail. Or you can go left to travel northwest and ascend the Mountain Mist Trail to reach the top of the ridge. From there, you can take an easy trail back to Bankhead Parkway near the Biker's Trailhead. Just travel north on the South Plateau Loop for 1.5 mi., and then turn right onto a short connector trail that meets Bankhead Pkwy.

Trail Facts

The Mysterious Goats: The Monte Sano goats are something of a mystery. No one is exactly sure where they came from or when they arrived on the mountain, but it's generally believed that they escaped from a local farm. In the 1990s, people often saw them on top of Goat Rock. If approaching hikers got too close, the goats would scamper down the hill and shelter under the rock overhang. Eventually, officials tried to rid the park of the goats, and the animals migrated to the more remote Golan Heights region, about 1 mi. away in the northeastern part of the park. However, in the past few years the goats have disappeared entirely.

10. Flat Rock Connector Trail

This short path connects the Goat Trail to one of the best sections of the Flat Rock Trail. At the end of this connector path, you can walk a little less than a mile to reach a remote creek and impressive waterfall.

Distance: 0.12 mi.
Hiking Time: 5 minutes
Elevation Gain/Loss: +3 ft., -103 ft.
Hiking Difficulty: Easy
Location: Monte Sano State Park, 5105 Nolen Ave., Huntsville, AL 35801; (256) 534-3757
Facilities: At the Hiker's Trailhead, there are no facilities and no sources of potable water. At the Biker's Trailhead pavilion, there are restrooms with water. Restrooms and potable water are available in the pavilion near the picnic area parking lot. Snacks

and drinks are available for purchase at the park store.
Driving Directions: See pages 2-3 and use directions for the Monte Sano State Park entrance and either the Hiker's Trailhead or the Biker's Trailhead.

Highlights

Access to a Waterfall: The connector trail itself isn't especially noteworthy, but it allows you to extend your walk on the Goat Trail to include a visit to a tumbling stream and nearby falls.

Waypoint/Mile

Trailhead (Waypoint 10) (34.7241, -86.4981) There are several ways to reach the Flat Rock Connector. From the Hiker's Trailhead, you can connect the eastern side of the South Plateau Loop with the Mountain Mist and Goat trails for a 2.5-mi. trip to the connector. From the Biker's Trailhead, you can connect the Sinks and Goat trails for a 2.3-mi. hike to the connector.

At the junction of the Goat Trail and the Flat Rock Connector, descend the leaf-covered path heading east. Be aware that there are no blazes on the trail. Also, this route sees relatively little traffic, so the path is not well-defined in areas.

The walk begins with a moderate descent. You'll make your way down for 0.17 mi. and then follow a level stretch of trail across the slope. At 0.26 mi., pay close attention to make out the path, which might be obscured by leaves and fallen trees.

11 (34.7273, -86.4966) (0.12 mi.) The Flat Rock Connector meets the Flat Rock Trail, which runs northwest and southeast. To hike to the attractive streambed and waterfall, turn left and travel north on the Flat Rock Trail for 1.8 mi.

11. Flat Rock Trail Section

If you're willing to walk a few miles, you'll get a big payoff by hiking this trail. Measuring a little less than a mile, this section of the Flat Rock Trail leads to a remote creek drainage with a nearby waterfall. After periods of heavy rain, an impressive flow of water tumbles down the creek. Not far from the creek is a set of falls with curtains of water cascading down rocky ledges.

Distance: 0.98 mi.
Hiking Time: 30 minutes
Elevation Gain/Loss: +151 ft., -166 ft.
Hiking Difficulty: Moderate
Location: Monte Sano State Park, 5105 Nolen Ave., Huntsville, AL 35801; (256) 534-3757**Facilities:** At the Hiker's Trailhead, there are no facilities and no sources of potable water. At the Biker's Trailhead pavilion, there are restrooms with water. Restrooms and potable water are available in the pavilion near the picnic area parking lot. Snacks and drinks are available for purchase at the park store.
Driving Directions: See pages 2-3 and use directions for the Monte Sano State Park entrance and either the Hiker's Trailhead or the Biker's Trailhead.

Highlights

Secluded Stream and Waterfall: This stretch of forest sees relatively little traffic, so it's the perfect place to enjoy some solitude and the calming waters of a wilderness stream. Reaching the creek requires a long out-and-back hike, so it doesn't appeal to the masses. Also, many people simply aren't familiar with the Flat Rock Trail. While it's one of the area's longest paths and skirts much of Monte Sano, it crosses a patchwork of private and public land—so several sections aren't maintained, and it's easy to get off course. As a result, there's a good chance you'll see few other hikers.

When you reach the creek, cross it and head upstream, walking along the base of the bluff, to find a beautiful set of falls. If you visit them on a bright day, you'll see sunlight flash across the water that emerges from the high bluff and cascades down a series of stone ledges.

Waypoint/Mile

Trailhead (Waypoint 11) (34.7273, -86.4966) There are several ways to reach the Flat Rock Connector and the beginning of this section of Flat Rock Trail. From the Hiker's Trailhead, you can connect the eastern side of the South Plateau Loop with the Mountain Mist and Goat trails for a 2.5-mi. trip to the connector. From the Biker's Trailhead, you can connect the Sinks and Goat trails for a 2.3-mi. hike to the connector. After you descend the Flat Rock Connector and reach the junction with the Flat Rock Trail, turn left and travel north on the single-track path, descending slightly.

A waterfall sits tucked away in the forest near the Flat Rock Trail.

The trail begins in an open forest of sweet gum trees, oaks and maples, and a thick bed of leaves covers the ground. Soon, you'll find that the leaf-covered path is difficult to see, and it's sometimes hard to discern the trail from natural drainages. You might also have to pick your way through downed limbs.

At 0.3 mi., the trail is fairly level and passes through an inviting stretch of forest with mature, widely spaced trees and rocky bluffs. Ahead, the trail alternates between a double-track and single-track path as it moves through more sweet gum trees and other stout hardwoods. **11-1** (34.7408, -86.4996) (0.98 mi.) The Flat Rock Trail meets the stream. You can cross it and ascend the opposite slope to find good places to hang out. To find the falls, cross the creek and head upstream on the right side of the creek bed, traveling northwest, for a little less than 200 ft. The waterfall is on the right.

Trail Facts

Tricky Navigation: The Flat Rock Trail is the longest trail on Monte Sano. Beginning near the Bankhead Trailhead and ending near Dug Hill Road, it stretches more than 8 mi. But some sections cross private property, and many portions of the trail are not maintained, so it's difficult to navigate. From the creek described in this hike, it's possible to continue hiking east on the Flat Rock Trail. However, you'll find that the actual path eventually disappears, and you could find yourself somewhat lost on a very remote stretch of the mountain. For this reason, I have only included a couple of sections of the Flat Rock Trail in this book. If you do attempt to hike the entire thing, you should load the route into a GPS and use the device in addition to a paper map.

SECTION 5:
Sinks Trail, Stone Cuts Trail, Stone Cuts Bypass, Keith Trail and William Arthur Wells CCC Memorial Trail

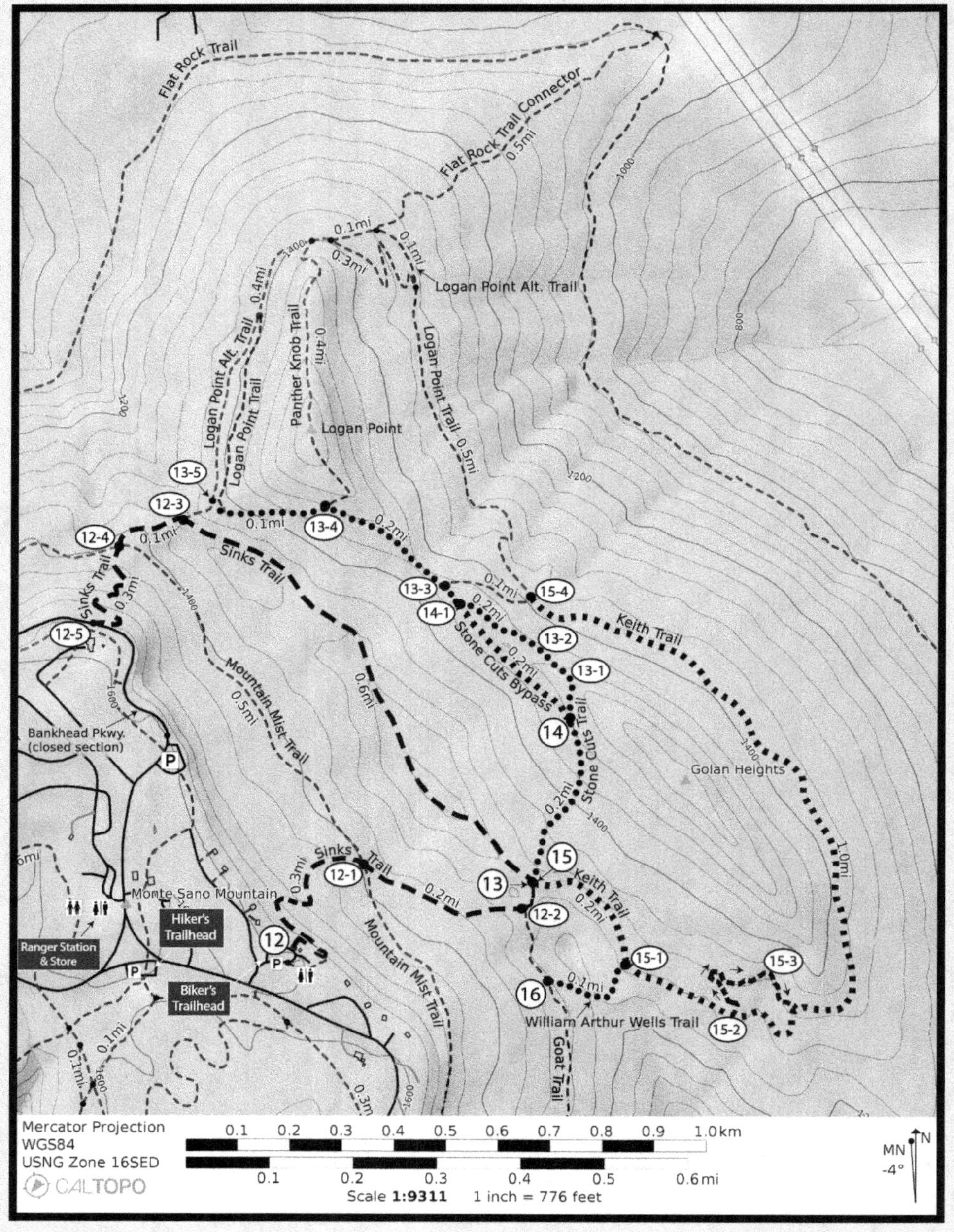

12. Sinks Trail

With steep sections at each end, the Sinks Trail is one of the more challenging paths on the mountain. However, it rewards hikers with a ramble through the "sinks," where draining water has formed large depressions and rolling terrain. The landscape is not only unusual, but also a prime spot to find a wide variety of wildflowers.

Distance: 1.5 mi.

Hiking Time: 1 hour

Elevation Gain/Loss: +379 ft., -433 ft.

Hiking Difficulty: Moderate to strenuous

Location: Monte Sano State Park, 5105 Nolen Ave., Huntsville, AL 35801; (256) 534-3757

Facilities: The pavilion at the Biker's Trailhead has restrooms with water. Restrooms and potable water are available in the pavilion near the picnic area parking lot. Snacks and drinks are available for purchase at the park store.

Driving Directions: See pages 2-3 and use the directions for the Monte Sano State Park entrance and the Biker's Trailhead.

Highlights

A Challenging Hike: From the Biker's Trailhead, the Sinks Trail drops more than 350 vertical ft. over just 0.7 mi. (That's steep.) At the other end of the trail, there's another thigh-burner, as you gain 135 ft. of elevation in the last 0.2 mi. There are a few level sections where you'll roll along easily, but this path has plenty to challenge anyone looking to burn some calories.

The Sinks: At about the half-mile mark, the trail cuts through the base of a deep ravine. In the open hardwoods, you have a clear view of a forest floor that rolls like waves. Deep streambeds carve the land, running between hillocks and depressions that form small grassy coves, little hideaways and a stone amphitheater. All the water from surrounding hills rolls into the sinks, so the soil is rich. During spring, wildflowers thrive here, and bluebells carpet the ground.

Waypoint/Mile

Trailhead (Waypoint 12) (34.7443, -86.5081) The exact starting point for this trail has shifted over the years, but the following description begins on the northeast side of the Biker's Trailhead parking area. Enter the path next to the Sinks Trail marker and immediately curve toward to the southeast. At 240 ft., take a sharp left turn to leave the top of the bluff and descend a single-track path. Follow the red blazes as you move northwest along a steep slope.

12-1 (34.7459, -86.5067) (0.3 mi.) The Sinks Trail crosses the Mountain Mist Trail and makes a moderate to steep descent to the southeast. If you're hiking, be on the lookout for bikers, as this section includes a bike jump and is a popular place to ride fast.

12-2 (34.7449, -86.5034) (0.53 mi.) This wide, flat trail junction is known as the Three Benches area (named for the seating here). To the right, you'll see the beginning of the Goat Trail and a sign for the William Arthur Wells CCC Memorial Trail. (See page 50 for details on this path dedicated to WWII veteran William Wells.) From this junction, the Sinks Trail bends to the north. After you continue down it for a little more than 200 ft., you'll reach a junction with the Keith Trail and Stone Cuts Trail.

13 (34.7455, -86.5030) (0.57 mi.) At this junction, the first path on the right is the Keith Trail, which runs east. The second path on the right is the Stone Cuts Trail, which makes a moderate ascent to the north. To continue on the Sinks Trail, take the path that makes an obvious bend to the left and descends to the northwest.

At 0.6 mi., the small path on the right (to the north) descends into a sink, where stone walls surrounding the depression form a natural amphitheater. It's one of the most attractive areas of the sinks and worth the quick side trip. At 0.8 mi., the path runs through an especially pretty area where streambeds crisscross the rolling landscape.

12-3 (34.7520, -86.5104) (1.2 mi.) At the trail junction, the Logan Point Trail (marked with orange blazes) goes to the right and ascends to the northeast. The Sinks Trail goes left and climbs gradually to the southwest.

12-4 (34.7515, -86.5119) (1.3 mi.) The Sinks Trail crosses the Mountain

Mist Trail at a four-way intersection. To the right, the Mountain Mist Trail heads southwest and descends gradually. To the left, it begins a gentle drop to the east. To continue on the Sinks Trail, go straight and take the single-track path that heads south and immediately begins a moderate to steep climb.

During your steep ascent, stop at 1.4 mi. to catch your breath. Here you'll find a nice rock perch with views of the valley to the north. From here, switchbacks take you through the final stretch.

12-5 (34.7501, -86.5123) (1.6 mi.) The Sinks Trail ends on the north side of Bankhead Parkway.

Trail Facts

Natural Sinks: The sinks are an example of Monte Sano's "karst" topography. Much of Monte Sano consists of limestone rock. When rainwater hits a bed of limestone, it becomes mildly acidic and begins to dissolve the surface. Over time, this creates sinkholes, as well as caves and cuts (see the next entry on the Stone Cuts Trail).

13. Stone Cuts Trail

The Stone Cuts Trail is one of the most popular routes on Monte Sano, as a relatively short path leads to a fascinating hallway of stone and rocky tunnels. On their way to the Stone Cuts, hikers negotiate a steep descent as well as a steep climb when they return to the trailhead. But a wide range of people successfully complete this trip, including hikers with kids.

Distance: 0.8 mi.

Hiking Time: 30 to 40 minutes

Elevation Gain/Loss: +290 ft., -211 ft.

Hiking Difficulty: Moderate

Location: Monte Sano State Park, 5105 Nolen Ave., Huntsville, AL 35801; (256) 534-3757

Facilities: The pavilion at the Biker's Trailhead has restrooms with water. Restrooms and potable water are available in the pavilion near the picnic area parking lot. Snacks and drinks are available for purchase at the park store.

Driving Directions: See pages 2-3 and use the directions for the Monte Sano State Park entrance and the Biker's Trailhead.

Highlights

Stone Cuts: One of the most popular paths on the mountain, the Stone Cuts Trail explores a narrow stone passageway with tunnels and tight squeezes. The trail covers moderate terrain and requires a bit of scrambling, but it's not really dangerous. So, it's a good place to entertain older kids. For the most direct access to the Stone Cuts, begin at the Biker's Trailhead and follow the Sinks Trail to the Stone Cuts Trail. Just be aware that the Sinks Trail is steep, so you'll face a challenging descent at the beginning of your hike and a steep climb at the end of your journey.

Waypoint/Mile

Trailhead (Waypoint 13) (34.7455, -86.5030) To reach the trailhead, begin at the Biker's Trailhead and follow the Sinks Trail 0.57 mi. to the junction with the Stone Cuts Trail. Several trails meet at this junction, and it can be confusing, but the trail signs will point you in the right direction. Enter the Stone Cuts Trail and follow the white blazes, ascending to the north.

14 (34.7483, -86.5023) (0.23 mi.) At the Y junction, go right and climb to the north to continue on the Stone Cuts Trail. If you go left, you'll enter the Stone Cuts Bypass, which stretches 0.2 mi. to rejoin the Stone Cuts Trail at Waypoint 14-1. This is a good option for anyone who doesn't wish to scramble through the rugged passageways of the main Stone Cuts Trail. If you continue on the Stone Cuts Trail, you'll travel another 328 ft. to reach Waypoint 13-1.

13-1 (34.7490, -86.5022) (0.28 mi.) At the top of the ridge, turn left and go northwest along the spine of the ridge.

13-2 (34.7497, -86.5029) (0.3 mi.) The trail reaches the entrance to the first stone hallway. A flat-topped boulder provides a good place to enjoy winter views to the north.

Descend the narrow path surrounded by stone walls covered in moss and lichen. Along the way, you'll duck into dark corridors and squeeze through narrow hallways. One of my favorite spots is a long stone tunnel where shafts of light cut across the darkness.

14-1 (34.7503, -86.5047) (0.4 mi.) After emerging from a tunnel to reenter the light, the path intersects with the Stone Cuts Bypass Trail. This path goes left and crosses easy terrain as it heads southeast. If you want to do a shorter trip, go ahead and take the Stone Cuts Bypass back to the Sinks Trail. To continue on the Stone Cuts Trail, bear right and go northwest, following the crest of the ridge.

13-3 (34.7507, -86.5050) (0.5 mi.) The Logan Point Trail intersects on the right and descends to the northeast. Continue straight, traveling west on the Stone Cuts Trail.

Hikers pass through narrow, rocky corridors on the Stone Cuts Trail.

13-4 (34.7521, -86.5076) (0.6 mi.) The Panther Knob Trail intersects on the right and rises steeply to the northeast. The Stone Cuts Trail bends to the left and descends. This section is rocky, with lots of roots. Plus, it can get muddy and slippery after it rains, so watch your step.

13-5 (34.7521, -86.5098) (0.8 mi.) The Stone Cuts Trail ends at the junction with the Logan Point Trail and the Logan Point Alternate Trail. From here, you have a few options to return to the Biker's Trailhead:

1. Retrace your steps: **1.3-mi. return trip**

2. Take the Logan Point Trail to the closest Sinks Trail junction (Waypoint 12-3) and follow the Sinks Trail back: **1.2-mi. return trip**

3. Take the Logan Point Trail and the Sinks Trail to the Mountain Mist Trail at Waypoint 12-4. Then take the Mountain Mist Trail to the Sinks Trail at Waypoint 12-1. From here, take the Sinks Trail back to the Biker's Trailhead: **0.9-mi. return trip**

Trail Facts

How the Stone Cuts Formed: Much of Monte Sano Mountain consists of limestone that's around 300 million years old. The Stone Cuts area is an example of the mountain's "karst" topography, where limestone has eroded to form fissures and other landforms like sinkholes. When rain reaches the ground, it becomes acidic and can erode the calcareous rock like limestone. If there are cracks in the rock, this weathering process can enlarge fractures in the stone. This action created the passageways of the Stone Cuts.

14. Stone Cuts Bypass

This short and fairly level path is a good option for hikers who prefer to avoid the rugged terrain of the main Stone Cuts Trail. Also, people who hike the main Stone Cuts Trail can use the bypass as a quick and easy way to return to the Sinks Trail.

Distance: 0.2 mi.
Hiking Time: 5 minutes
Elevation Gain/Loss: +30 ft., -53 ft.
Hiking Difficulty: Easy
Location: Monte Sano State Park, 5105 Nolen Ave., Huntsville, AL 35801; (256) 534-3757
Facilities: The pavilion at the Biker's Trailhead has restrooms with water. Restrooms and potable water are available in the pavilion near the picnic area parking lot. Snacks and drinks are available for purchase at the park store.
Driving Directions: See pages 2-3 and use the directions for the Monte Sano State Park entrance and the Biker's Trailhead.

Highlights

A Quick Way Back: The Stone Cuts Bypass never gains or loses more than about 20 ft. of elevation, making it pretty level. If you've taken your time while exploring the Stone Cuts, the bypass will help you shave off some time for your return to the parking area.

Waypoint/Mile

Trailhead (Waypoint 14) (34.7483, -86.5023) The Stone Cuts Bypass Trail begins 0.23 mi. from the start of the Stone Cuts Trail, which is Waypoint 13. To follow the Stone Cuts Bypass, turn left and head northwest.

14-1 (34.7503, -86.5047) (0.2 mi.) The Stone Cuts Bypass ends at the intersection with the Stone Cuts Trail atop the ridge.

15. Keith Trail

Winding through the eastern edge of the state park, the Keith Trail visits one of the more secluded sections of the trail system. High ridges and rock bluffs surround the trail, heightening the feeling that you're deep in an isolated wilderness.

Distance: 1.3 mi.

Hiking Time: 30 to 40 minutes

Elevation Gain/Loss: +301 ft., -207 ft.

Hiking Difficulty: Moderate

Location: Monte Sano State Park, 5105 Nolen Ave., Huntsville, AL 35801; (256) 534-3757

Facilities: The pavilion at the Biker's Trailhead has restrooms with water. Restrooms and potable water are available in the pavilion near the picnic area parking lot. Snacks and drinks are available for purchase at the park store.

Driving Directions: See pages 2-3 and use the directions for the Monte Sano State Park entrance and the Biker's Trailhead.

Highlights

Winding Stream: If you can, hike this path in winter after it rains. You'll be rewarded at the half-mile mark, where the path crosses a tumbling stream. When the trees are stripped of their leaves, you can see the creek moving like a great snake. It twists through the forest, stretching as far as the eye can see, and disappears in the distance.

Waypoint/Mile

Trailhead (Waypoint 15) (34.7455, -86.5030): To reach the trailhead, begin at the Biker's Trailhead. Follow the Sinks Trail 0.57 mi. to the junction of the Sinks Trail, Stone Cuts Trail and Keith Trail. The first path on the right is the Keith Trail, which runs east and immediately rollercoasters. At 0.1 mi., to your right the opposite ridge dominates the skyline.

15-1 (34.7440, -86.5013) (0.1 mi.) The William Arthur Wells CCC Memorial Trail intersects on the right and descends gradually to the southwest. The path dives to cross a small drainage and then moves up the slope gradually.

15-2 (34.7431, -86.4990) (0.33 mi.) The trail splits and goes in two different directions. An older track bears right and goes southeast, while a newer course goes left and climbs to the northeast. To follow the description below, go left and climb.

15-3 (34.7438, -86.4980) (0.49 mi.) The pass crosses one of the larger streambeds in this corner of the park. After a good rain, a healthy cascade of water pours down the drainage. Not far ahead, the trail swings to the north to crawl up the slope.

At 0.7 mi., the green fields and homes along Dug Hill Road are just visible in the cove below. Here, on the east side of the ridge, it's very quiet, and civilization seems far away.

15-4 (34.7505, -86.5032) (1.3 mi.) The Keith Trail intersects with Logan Point Trail, which goes left (west) to ascend, and goes right (northwest) and descends. To return to the beginning of the Keith Trail, turn left onto the Stone Cuts Trail and travel southeast about 0.6 mi.

16. William Arthur Wells CCC Memorial Trail

Named in honor of World War II veteran William Arthur Wells, this path (once called the Chestnut Trail) connects the Goat Trail and Keith Trail. While the trail is short, it does have steep sections where it drops into a drainage and climbs back out. (For more on William Wells, see Highlights and Trail Facts.)

Distance: 0.12 mi.
Hiking Time: 5 minutes
Elevation Gain/Loss: +39 ft., -58 ft.
Hiking Difficulty: Easy to moderate
Location: Monte Sano State Park, 5105 Nolen Ave., Huntsville, AL 35801; (256) 534-3757
Facilities: The pavilion at the Biker's Trailhead has restrooms with water. Restrooms and potable water are available in the pavilion near the picnic area parking lot. Snacks and drinks are available for purchase at the park store.
Driving Directions: See pages 2-3 and use the directions for the Monte Sano State Park entrance and the Biker's Trailhead.

Highlights

War Veteran Memorial: At the age of 17, William Arthur Wells (known as Arthur) joined the Civilian Conservation Corps. His service included a stint on Monte Sano Mountain, helping to develop the state park. Wells was 19 when he left the CCC in 1941 to join the Navy. During World War II, he served as an electrician's mate aboard the destroyer USS *Hoel*. On October 25, 1944, the Japanese sank the *Hoel* during the Battle of the Leyte Gulf, and Wells was lost at sea. He was 21 years old.

In 2007, Arthur's brother Robert and three investment partners purchased 40 acres of land on Monte Sano. Robert gifted the land to the state park, making only one stipulation—that the park dedicate a trail to his dear departed brother. On April 14, 2018, Arthur's service and sacrifice were honored as the Chestnut Trail on Monte Sano was renamed the William Arthur Wells CCC Memorial Trail. At the age of 81, Robert attended the trail dedication ceremony.

Waypoint/Mile

Trailhead (Waypoint 16) (34.7437, -86.5029) For the most direct route to the William Arthur Wells Trail, begin at the Biker's Trailhead. Follow the Sinks Trail for 0.5 mi. to its junction with the Goat Trail. (You'll see three benches at the junction.) Travel south on the level path that runs beside a sign marked William Arthur Wells CCC Memorial Trail. After walking 476 ft., turn left onto the William Arthur Wells CCC Memorial Trail, which drops down and heads southeast. After a little more than 300 ft., the path begins a steady moderate climb.

15-1 (34.7440, -86.5013) (0.12 mi.) The William Arthur Wells Trail ends at the intersection with the Keith Trail.

Trail Facts

The USS *Hoel* and the Battle of Leyte Gulf: When the USS *Hoel* was sunk, 253 people onboard died, and only 86 survived. The destroyer was one of seven American warships lost during the battle at sea, which lasted from Oct. 23 to Oct. 26, 1944. However, the Allied forces would eventually win what is considered one of the largest naval battles of World War II. When the fight was over, the American and Australian forces had decimated the Japanese fleet and allowed the U.S. Sixth Army to secure the island of Leyte. For the Japanese, the defeat at Leyte caused them to lose their hold on the Philippines and eventually lose the war.

SECTION 6:
Logan Point Trail, Logan Point Alternate Trail, Flat Rock Connector Trail and Panther Knob Trail

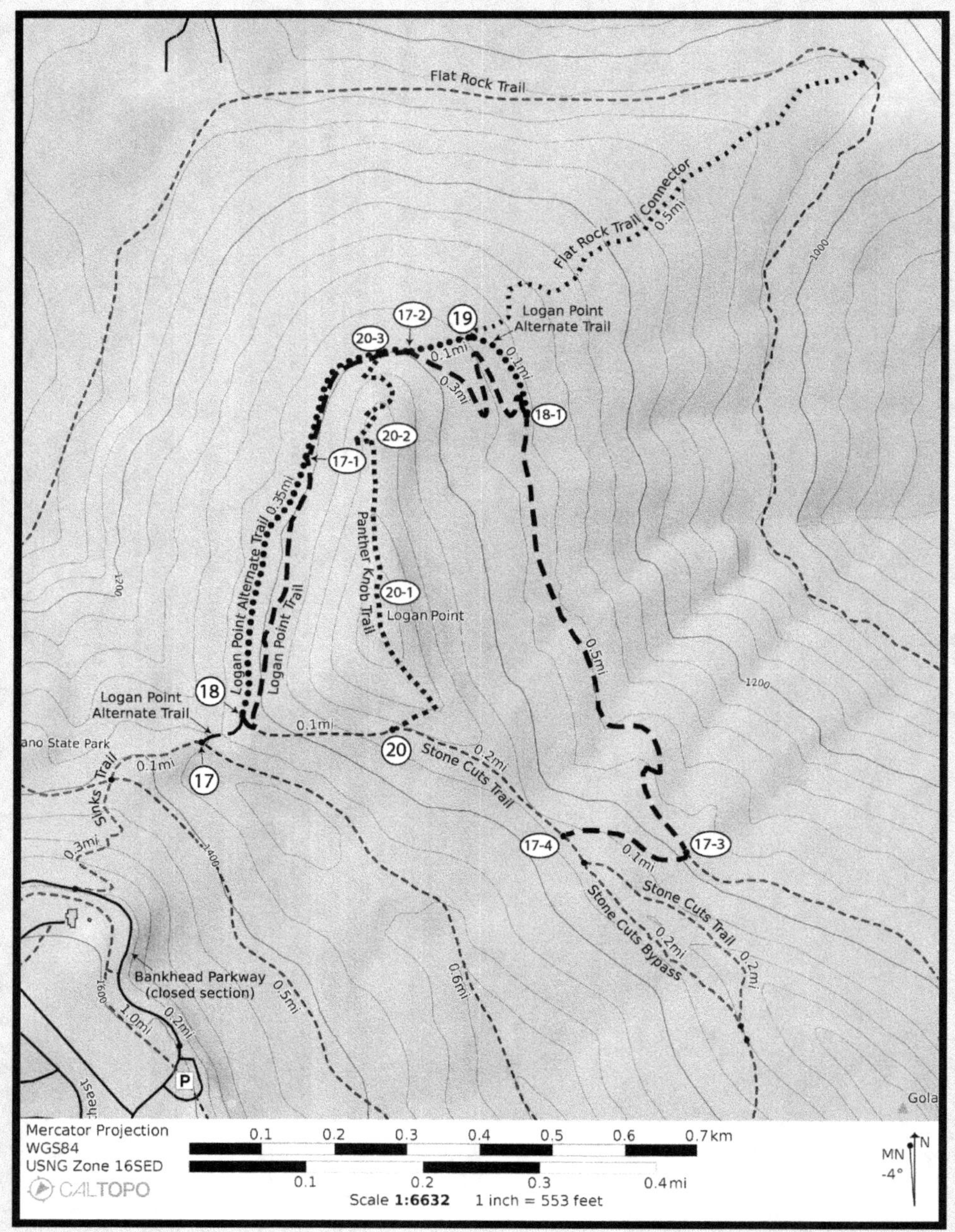

17. Logan Point Trail

Contrary to what its name implies, this trail doesn't actually visit the top of Logan Point, and it doesn't offer any great views. It does, however, lead to the Panther Knob Trail, which will take you to the Logan Point summit at 1,579 ft. The Logan Point Trail also traverses the extreme eastern edge of the state park, so it's a good choice for hikers who want to explore some of the mountain's remotest areas.

Distance: 1.4 mi.
Hiking Time: 30 to 45 minutes
Elevation Gain/Loss: +200 ft., -105 ft.
Hiking Difficulty: Moderate
Location: Monte Sano State Park, 5105 Nolen Ave., Huntsville, AL 35801; (256) 534-3757
Facilities: There are no facilities or sources of potable water at the Bankhead Parkway Blockade Trailhead.
Driving Directions: See page 3 and use the directions for the Bankhead Parkway Blockade.

Highlights

Access to the Logan Point Summit: From the beginning of the Logan Point Trail, you'll walk less than half a mile to reach the Panther Knob Trail.

Waypoint/Mile

Trailhead (Waypoint 17) (34.7519, -86.5104) From the Bankhead Parkway Blockade parking area, there are two ways to reach the Logan Point Trail:

1. Bankhead Parkway, Mountain Mist Trail and Sinks Trail (1.2 mi.): From the parking area, walk 0.3 mi. on the closed section of Bankhead Parkway and turn left onto the Mountain Mist Trail. Follow the Mountain Mist Trail 0.8 mi., and then turn left onto the Sinks Trail. Travel northeast on the Sinks Trail for 0.1 mi., and then turn left onto the Logan Point Trail. Ascend, traveling northeast, following the orange blazes.

2. Bankhead Parkway and Sinks Trail (1.4 mi.): From the parking area, walk 1 mi. on the closed section of Bankhead Parkway, and then turn left onto the Sinks Trail. Follow the Sinks Trail 0.4 mi., and then turn left onto the Logan Point Trail. Ascend, traveling northeast, and following the orange blazes.

18 (34.7520, -86.5098) (0.1 mi.) The Logan Point Trail intersects with the Logan Point Alternate Trail. To continue on the Logan Point Trail, bend to the right at the wide junction. Almost immediately, you'll bend back to the left and take a narrow path that climbs gradually to the north.

The Logan Point Trail remains a narrow path of packed earth as it rolls gently along the low flank of the slope.

Author Marcus Woolf maps and measures the Logan Point Trail.

17-1 (34.75560, -86.50887) (0.3 mi.) The Logan Point Trail drops to meet the Logan Point Alternate Trail. Turn right to continue on the Logan Point Trail, which shares a path with the Alternate Trail.

20-3 (34.7569, -86.5078) (0.45 mi.) The Panther Knob Trail intersects on the right side of the trail and ascends to the southwest. To continue on the Logan Point Trail, go straight and travel east on the level path.

17-2 (34.7569, -86.5078) (0.48 mi.) The Logan Point Alternate Trail goes left and descends to the northeast. To continue on the Logan Point Trail, bear right and head southeast. The trail soon creeps down the northeast slope of Logan Point.

18-1 (34.7563, -86.5056) (0.75 mi.) The path drops down to a Y junction where the Logan Point Alternate Trail goes left and soon ascends. Bear right to travel south on the Logan Point Trail. For the next 0.3 mi., the walking is mellow and it's very quiet here on the extreme eastern side of the state park. Off your left shoulder, small breaks in the foliage reveal Highway 72 far below.

At 1.1 mi., switchbacks take you up the slope, and after another 0.1 mi., you reach the first of three wooden bridges that are 10 to 15 ft. long.

17-3 (34.7505, -86.5031) (1.26 mi.) The Keith Trail intersects on the left. Turn right to follow the Logan Point Trail, which climbs to meet the Stone Cuts Trail in 0.1 mi. Not far ahead, you'll pass massive twin oaks that are too big to put your arms around.

17-4 (34.7507, -86.5050) (1.4 mi.) The Logan Point Trail ends at the junction with the Stone Cuts Trail. For the most direct route back to the beginning of the Logan Point Trail (and Bankhead Parkway), turn right onto the Stone Cuts Trail. Follow it for 0.3 mi. to reach the junction with the Logan Point Trail. From this point, you can descend the Logan Point Trail to return to Waypoint 17, and then take either the Sinks Trail or Mountain Mist Trail to the paved Bankhead path.

18. Logan Point Alternate Trail

While the Logan Point Trail rolls and twists along the lower slopes of Logan Point, this alternate trail is more level as it crosses the western side of the hill. Near its end, the Alternate Trail makes a rocky descent, but it's only about 0.1 mi.

Distance: 0.53 mi.
Hiking Time: 3 to 5 minutes
Elevation Gain/Loss: +21 ft., -66 ft.
Hiking Difficulty: Easy to moderate
Location: Monte Sano State Park, 5105 Nolen Ave., Huntsville, AL 35801; (256) 534-3757
Facilities: There are no facilities or sources of potable water at the Bankhead Parkway Blockade Trailhead.
Driving Directions: See page 3 and use the directions for the Bankhead Parkway Blockade.

Waypoint/Mile

Trailhead (Waypoint 18) (34.7570, -86.5075) The Logan Point Alternate Trail lies 200 ft. from the beginning of the Logan Point Trail. For directions to the start of the Logan Point Trail, see page 55 and use directions to the Trailhead (Waypoint 17). From Waypoint 17, follow the Logan Point Trail and ascend gradually for 200 ft. At a wide junction, bear left and follow the Logan Point Alternate Trail, which climbs gradually to the north.

From Waypoint 18, the Logan Point Alternate Trail makes a long, easy run, remaining fairly level as it circles around Logan Point, which looms above on the right.

17-1 (34.75560, -86.50887) (0.24 mi.) The Logan Point Trail intersects on the right. Continue straight on the level path to follow the Logan Point Alternate Trail, which shares a path with the Logan Point Trail.

20-3 (34.7569, -86.5078) (0.35 mi.) The Panther Knob Trail intersects on the right side of the trail and ascends to the southwest. To continue on the Logan Point Alternate Trail, go straight and travel east on the level path.

17-2 (34.7569, -86.5078) (0.38 mi.) The Logan Point Alternate Trail goes left and makes a moderate, rocky descent to the northeast, following a drainage.

19 (34.7571, -86.5064) (0.43 mi.) The Flat Rock Connector Trail intersects on the left and descends gradually. The Logan Point Alternate Trail bends to the right and descends gradually to the southeast.

18-1 (34.7563, -86.5056) (0.53 mi.) The Logan Point Alternate Trail ends at the junction with the Logan Point Trail, which is marked with orange blazes. If you go straight, you'll follow the Logan Point Trail south to its junction with the Keith Trail (in 0.5 mi.) and the Stone Cuts Trail (in 0.6 mi.). If you take a sharp turn to the right, you'll follow the Logan Point trail northwest for 0.3 mi. to its junction with the Logan Point Alternate Trail at Waypoint 17-2.

19. Flat Rock Connector Trail

This short trail makes a moderate descent to the Flat Rock Trail and ends at the level, rocky landscape that inspired the "Flat Rock" name. Be aware that portions of this route cross or run near private property, and a sign says that the trail is closed during hunting season, from October 1 to January 31. Also, at the time of publication, this trail was not blazed and was difficult to follow, though pink ribbons on trees marked the route. Due to the private-property issue and the difficulty in navigating the route, I recommend that you avoid this trail. However, I have mentioned it in the book because people hiking in the state park night encounter the trail and be curious about it.

Location: Monte Sano State Park, 5105 Nolen Ave., Huntsville, AL 35801; (256) 534-3757

Facilities: There are no facilities or sources of potable water at the Bankhead Parkway Blockade Trailhead.

Driving Directions: See page 3 and use the directions for the Bankhead Parkway Blockade.

20. Panther Knob Trail

A short, steep climb leads to the summit of Logan Point, one of the must-visit spots on Monte Sano. After topping out at 1,580 ft., the path descends the northern side of the point. On the way down, it twists through narrow hallways of stone and a jumble of mossy boulders.

Distance: 0.48 mi.

Hiking Time: 20 minutes

Elevation Gain/Loss: +157 ft., -246 ft.

Hiking Difficulty: Moderate

Location: Monte Sano State Park, 5105 Nolen Ave., Huntsville, AL 35801; (256) 534-3757

Facilities: There are no facilities or water at the Bankhead Parkway Blockade Trailhead. The pavilion at the Biker's Trailhead has restrooms with water. Restrooms and water are available in the pavilion near the picnic area parking lot. Snacks and drinks are available for purchase at the park store.

Driving Directions: There are two access points for the trail. See page 3 and use directions for the Bankhead Parkway Blockade, or see pages 2-3 and use directions for the Monte Sano State Park entrance and the Biker's Trailhead.

Highlights

Logan Point Summit: At the knoblike summit of Logan Point, slip off your pack and take a seat on the large rock outcrop. From your high perch, enjoy a lofty view of the lowlands to the east. If you visit mid-week, you might have this scenic lunch spot to yourself. High on this hill, far removed from the heart of the park, you'll hear nothing but the wind passing over the peak.

Waypoint/Mile

Trailhead (Waypoint 20) (34.7521, -86.5076) The Panther Knob Trail begins 0.6 mi. from the start of the Stone Cuts Trail and is marked with blue blazes. For the most direct route to the beginning of the Panther Knob Trail, begin at the Biker's Trailhead in the state park. Or, for a slightly longer hike, begin at the trailhead on the closed section of Bankhead Parkway.

Option 1 to Reach Trailhead

Biker's Trailhead to Panther Knob Trailhead (1.1 mi.): Follow the Sinks Trail 0.57 mi. to the Stone Cuts Trail. Travel 0.6 mi. on the Stone Cuts Trail to the junction with the Panther Knob Trail, which intersects on the right and rises steeply to the northeast.

Option 2 to Reach Trailhead

Bankhead Parkway Blockade to Panther Knob Trailhead. For this option, choose one of two routes:

Route 1 (1.4 mi.): Combine the Bankhead Parkway, Mountain Mist, Sinks, Logan Point and Stone Cuts trails. From the Bankhead Parkway Blockade parking area, walk 0.3 mi. on the paved Bankhead path and turn left onto the Mountain Mist Trail. Follow the Mountain Mist Trail 0.8 mi., and then turn left onto the Sinks Trail. Travel northeast on the Sinks Trail for 0.1 mi., and then turn left onto the Logan Point Trail. Go 0.1 mi., turn right onto the Stone Cuts Trail, and travel east 0.1 mi. to the junction with the Panther Knob Trail, which is on the left.

Route 2 (1.6 mi.): Combine the Bankhead Parkway, Sinks, Logan Point and Stone Cuts trails. From the Bankhead Parkway Blockade parking area, walk 1 mi. on the paved Bankhead path, and then turn left onto the Sinks Trail. Follow the Sinks Trail 0.4 mi., and then turn left onto the Logan Point Trail. Ascend for 0.1 mi. and turn right onto the Stone Cuts Trail. Travel east 0.1 mi. to the junction with the Panther Knob Trail, which is on the left.

From the trailhead at Waypoint 20, follow the blue blazes and begin climbing the steep path, winding among boulders, oak trees and small cedars. When you've walked 240 ft., take a sharp turn to the left and ascend to the northwest. At 0.11 mi., you'll reach the top of Logan Point.

Enjoying winter views on the Logan Point summit

20-1 (34.7537, -86.5078) (0.16 mi.) Just beyond the high point of the knob, boulders on the right provide a good spot to sit and enjoy the view.

20-2 (34.7557, -86.5077) (0.3 mi.) The trail turns left and drops through a cut in the boulders.

20-3 (34.7570, -86.5078) (0.48 mi.) The Panther Knob Trail ends at the T junction with the Logan Point Trail and Logan Point Alternate Trail, which run left (southwest) and right (northeast).

Trail Facts

Where's Panther Knob? While this path is named the Panther Knob Trail, it's not actually located on Panther Knob. At some point, the name Panther Knob was attributed to Logan Point—hence the name of this trail. But the real Panther Knob is about 1.8 mi. to the northwest (straight-line distance) on Chapman Mountain. Panther Knob is now part of a residential area, and Hawks Way and Talon Circle form a crescent below the summit.

Monte Sano Nature Preserve

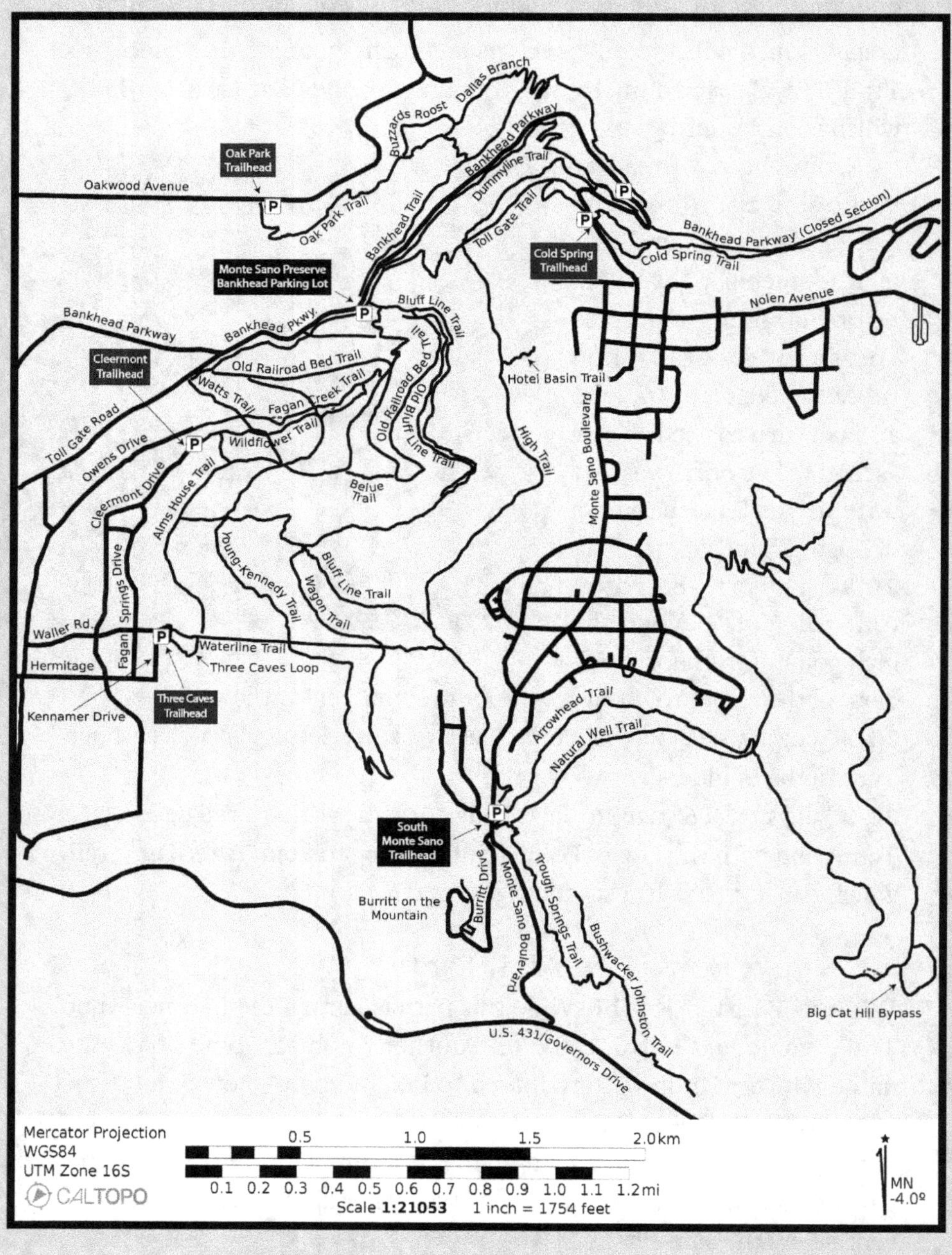

CHAPTER 2

Monte Sano Nature Preserve

One of the remarkable aspects of the Huntsville and Madison area is the impressive amount of recreation land and the great number of trails within or near the city limits. A great example of this is the Monte Sano Nature Preserve. Located only about two miles from downtown Huntsville, the preserve covers more than 1,100 acres, making it one of the largest urban land preserves in the country.

Established in 1987, the Monte Sano Nature Preserve includes more than 23 miles of public trails for hiking, biking, trail running, birding and many other outdoor pursuits. On any given day, you'll see wild-flower enthusiasts, outdoor photographers, dog walkers and folks getting their kids outdoors.

There are six trailheads located throughout this large preserve, which occupies portions of most slopes on Monte Sano Mountain. The multiple access points allow people to explore a wide variety of terrain and ecosystems. Along the low creek bottoms, you can stroll through a lush landscape that bursts with color as wildflowers bloom in spring. Higher on the mountain, waterfalls tumble from rocky bluffs, and paths wind through rugged stone hallways. On hilltops and high plateaus, rock outcrops offer lofty views of neighboring mountains and valleys.

Several trails also allow you to step back in time. On the Old Railroad Bed Trail, you'll follow the route of a train that chugged its way up the mountain in the 1800s. At Three Caves, you'll get a bird's-eye view of a quarry where limestone was extracted in the 1940s and 1950s to build roads and bridges in the area. Whether you're a history buff, a dedicated hiker, or someone who just wants to stroll in the fresh air, the Monte Sano Nature Preserve has just what you need, and you don't have to go far to reach it.

General Information

Hours: Open dawn to dusk.

Primary trail activities allowed: Hiking, biking

Pets: Leashed pets allowed.

Fees: There are no required fees to use the trails, but many trailheads have a donation box near the information kiosk in the parking area.

Facilities: Some Land Trust trailheads include restrooms or portable toilets, but several have no facilities or sources of potable water. Be sure to check the Facilities description for each trail.

Information: (256) 534-5263; www.landtrustnal.org/properties/monte-sano-preserve/; questions@landtrustnal.org

Driving Directions

South Monte Sano Trailhead

From the intersection of California Street and Governors Drive (U.S. 431), head southeast on Governors Dr. for 2.6 mi. Turn left onto Monte Sano Boulevard. Travel 0.8 mi. and turn right into the gravel parking area for the South Monte Sano Trailhead. If parking isn't available, you can park on the opposite (west) side of Monte Sano Blvd.

Three Caves Trailhead

From the intersection of Governors Drive and California Street, drive north on California St. 0.5 mi. and then turn right onto Hermitage Avenue. Travel east on Hermitage Ave. 1.1 mi., and then turn left onto Kennamer Drive. Travel 0.2 mi., and then turn right at Waller Road to enter the trailhead parking area.

Cleermont Trailhead

From the intersection of Governors Drive and California Street, drive north on California St. 0.6 mi. and then turn right onto Hermitage Avenue. Travel east on Hermitage Ave. 0.9 mi., and then turn left onto Cleermont Drive. Travel 0.9 mi., and near the end of Cleermont Dr. you'll see a parking area on the left.

Bankhead Trailhead

From the intersection of U.S 231/431 (Memorial Parkway) and University Drive, travel northeast on University Dr. 0.3 mi., and then continue straight to travel east on Pratt Avenue. Travel 1.8 mi. on Pratt Ave., passing through the Five Points district, to the intersection with Maysville Road. Go straight, traveling east, to take Pratt Ave., which becomes Bankhead Parkway. Travel 1.4 mi. to the Monte Sano Preserve Bankhead parking lot, which is on the right.

Oak Park Trailhead

From the intersection of U.S 231/431 (Memorial Parkway) and Oakwood Avenue, travel east on Oakwood Ave. for 1.5 mi. and then turn right into the Oak Park parking area.

Cold Spring Trailhead

From the intersection of U.S 231/431 (Memorial Parkway) and University Drive, travel northeast on University Dr. for 0.3 mi., and then continue straight to travel east on Pratt Avenue. Travel 1.8 mi. on Pratt Ave., passing through the Five Points district, to the intersection with Maysville Road. Go straight, traveling east, to take Pratt Ave., which becomes Bankhead Parkway after a few hundred feet. Go 2.6 mi. to the hairpin curve, where the road becomes Fearn Street. Travel approximately 0.4 mi. on Fearn St. to the small parking area on the left with room for a few cars. The trailhead is 130 ft. farther up the road on the left.

Bankhead Parkway Blockade

From the junction of U.S 231/431 (Memorial Parkway) and University Drive, travel east on University Dr. Go 0.3 mi. to where the road becomes Pratt Avenue. Travel 1.6 mi. on Pratt Ave. to the junction with Maysville Road. Continue straight to follow Pratt Ave., which becomes Bankhead Parkway after a few hundred feet. Go 2.6 mi. and begin to look for a roadside parking space on the left, before you reach the sharp curve where the trailhead is located. If spaces aren't available before the curve, continue around the hairpin curve, where the road becomes Fearn Street. You can usually find more roadside parking a few yards up Fearn St., on the right.

SECTION 1:
Bluff Line Trail, Old Bluff Line Trail, High Trail and Hotel Basin Trail

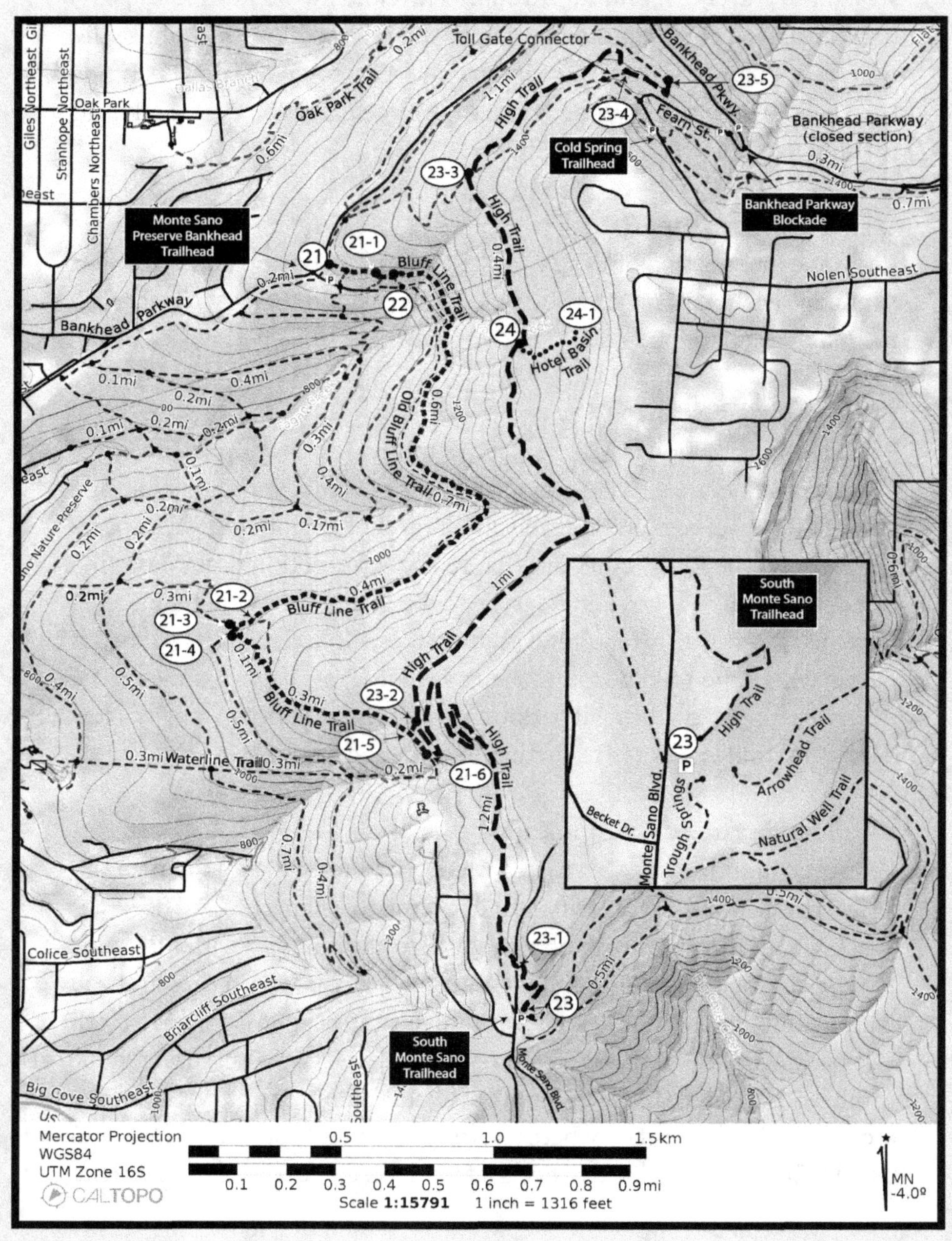

21. Bluff Line Trail

It's a tale of two trails. For the first 1.5 mi., the Bluff Line Trail is a mellow path that ambles through a shaded hardwood forest and crosses the occasional stream. You can do any portion of this first section as a comfortable out-and-back trip. Over the last half mile, the Bluff Line Trail is more challenging. It's more exposed to sun and climbs steadily—sometimes steeply—to end at the junction with the Waterline Trail.

Distance: 2 mi.

Hiking Time: 1 hour

Elevation Gain/Loss: +352 ft., -87 ft.

Hiking Difficulty: Moderate

Location: Land Trust of North Alabama Monte Sano Nature Preserve, 2442 Bankhead Pkwy. NE, Huntsville, AL 35801

Facilities: The Monte Sano Preserve Bankhead Trailhead area has a portable toilet and a pavilion with picnic tables, but no source of potable water.

Driving Directions: See page 65 and use the directions for the Bankhead Trailhead.

Highlights

Beautiful, Shaded Forest with Streams: A perfect path for a warm day, the Bluff Line Trail runs through a forest of mature trees that offer ample shade. The first 0.8 mi. is especially beautiful, as the path crosses Fagan Creek and other small streams that typically flow in spring and other rainy periods.

Options for Easy and Moderate Hikes: For the first 1.5 mi., the Bluff Line Trail gains very little elevation, making it a great option for families with kids and others seeking easy terrain. Hikers seeking more of a challenge can continue on for another half mile, where the path gains another 200 ft. of elevation. At the end of the Bluff Line Trail, you can take the High Trail and Toll Gate Trail for a 2.5-mile loop that returns you to the Bankhead Trailhead parking area.

Waypoint/Mile

Trailhead (Waypoint 21) (34.7441, -86.5443) To reach the beginning of the Bluff Line Trail, begin at the northwest end of the Monte Sano Preserve Bankhead parking lot. When you enter the parking area, this is the first trailhead on the left, near Bankhead Parkway. A sign indicates that this path leads to the Toll Gate, High, Panther's Knob, Bluff Line and Railroad Bed trails. Ascend this trail and walk 160 ft. to a four-way trail junction. At the four-way junction, enter the Bluff Line Trail and head east.

After 211 ft., a path on the right descends 160 ft. to meet an old section of the Bluff Line Trail. Continue straight on the Bluff Line Trail.

21-1 (34.7438, -86.5426) (544 ft., 0.1 mi.) On the right, a connector trail drops steeply at first and soon descends moderately, eventually leading to the parking area. Continue straight to follow the Bluff Line Trail.

After another 90 ft., bear left at the Y junction. (If you take the path on the right, you'll descend the Old Railroad Bed Trail.) Continue on to cross a powerline break that's about 70 ft. wide. At 0.3 mi., a 33-ft. wood footbridge carries you across Fagan Creek.

21-2 (34.7333, -86.5470) (1.4 mi.) At a wide, clear area, the Bluff Line Trail continues straight and continues heading west. To the left, you'll see a rocky drainage, which was part of an old Bluff Line Trail route. From Waypoint 21-2, go another 270 ft. to where the Bluff Line Trail intersects with the Wagon Trail (Waypoint 21-3).

21-3 (34.7331, -86.5478) (1.48 mi.) At the junction with the Wagon Trail, turn left and travel south 30 ft. to reach a junction where the Bluff Line Trail intersects on the left.

21-4 (34.7330, -86.5478) (1.49 mi.) Turn left to follow the Bluff Line Trail, which snakes its way uphill.

After ascending gradually for 0.15 mi., a connector trail intersects on the left. Keep heading straight and travel southeast.

21-5 (34.7297, -86.5412) (1.9 mi.) The Bluff Line Trail splits. If you turn left and travel northeast, you'll ascend the Bluff Line Trail for 118 feet and meet the High Trail. If you continue straight and travel southeast, you'll go another 240 feet to meet the Waterline Trail.

21-6 (34.7291, -86.5408) (2 mi.) The Bluff Line Trail ends at the junction with the Waterline trail.

22. Old Bluff Line Trail

***As this book was being completed, the Land Trust announced that it was closing the Old Bluff Line Trail route. Be sure to avoid walking on any closed trail sections.*

23. High Trail

Stretching more than 3 miles, this is one of the longer trails in the Monte Sano Preserve. Beginning on the southwest side of Monte Sano Mountain, the path crosses Monte Sano Boulevard and then traverses the upper western slope of the mountain. For most of the way, there are few major changes in elevation, making this a mostly comfortable walk in quiet, shaded woods. At 2.2 mi.., a short side trail leads to the ruins of baths operated by the Hotel Monte Sano in the 1800s. (See page 81 for more information on the Hotel Monte Sano.) At 2.6 mi., the trail makes a final gradual ascent to end about 0.2 mi. west of the Bankhead Parkway Blockade. While this isn't a difficult hike, it is a lengthy walk, so you might also consider placing a car at the South Monte Sano Trailhead and one near the Bankhead Parkway Blockade to avoid a long walk back to your vehicle.

Distance: 3.4 mi.
Hiking Time: 1.5 hours
Elevation Gain/Loss: +239 ft., -276 ft.
Hiking Difficulty: Easy to moderate
Location: Land Trust of North Alabama Monte Sano Nature Preserve, 2442 Bankhead Pkwy. NE, Huntsville, AL 35801
Facilities: There are no facilities and no sources of potable water near the trailhead.
Driving Directions: See page 64 and use the directions for the South Monte Sano Trailhead.

Highlights

Creeks and Streams: When the rainstorms arrive in spring, rushing waters fill the creeks and streams along the High Trail. At 1.8 mi., a footbridge crosses Fagan Creek, which flows through a shadowy forest. On a warm, sunny day, this is a nice spot to enjoy cool shade.

Hotel Basin Trail: At 2.2 mi., a side trail leads to the ruins of the Hotel Monte Sano's Roman-style baths. Operating from 1887 to 1900, the five-story hotel stood on a bluff high above the bath ruins. For more information on the Hotel Monte Sano, See page 72.

Waypoint/Mile

Trailhead (Waypoint 23) (34.7468, -86.5394) You can reach the High Trail from two main parking areas. The first option is the South Monte Sano Trailhead parking area beside Monte Sano Boulevard on the southwest end of the mountain. The second option is roadside parking near the Bankhead Parkway Blockade Trailhead at the "hairpin curve" close to the top of Monte Sano. For the trail description in this book, the High Trail begins at the trail's southern terminus at the South Monte Sano Trailhead. At the north end of the gravel parking area, follow the wooden walkway marked "High Trail" and travel north.

23-1 (34.7229, -86.5375) (0.16 mi.) Cross Monte Sano Boulevard and bear right to pass to the right side of the large metal gate on the opposite side of the road. (**Warning: Use extreme caution and watch for oncoming traffic while crossing the road.**)

Follow the double-track gravel path through an opening in the forest for about 0.4 mi., and then enter shaded woods. At 0.75 mi., begin a gradual descent on a series of switchbacks.

23-2 (34.7298, -86.5411) (1.27 mi.) The Bluff Line Trail intersects on the left. Go straight, traveling north, to continue on the High Trail.

The narrow path climbs briefly and then rolls along, rising and falling easily.

24 (34.7416, -86.5375) (2.2 mi.) The Hotel Basin Trail intersects on the right and rises moderately to the east. This path stretches for about 0.1 mi. and ends at the ruins of the old Hotel Monte Sano baths. Continue straight and head south to stay on the High Trail.

23-3 (34.74676, -86.53933) (2.6 mi.) The High Trail crosses the wide and rocky Toll Gate Trail heading northeast.

The trail rises gradually, covering rocky ground and a shallow drainage. When you've hiked nearly 3 mi., you'll reach level ground, and the path transitions to packed earth.

A dusting of snow covers the forest along the High Trail.

23-4 (34.75000, -86.53357) (3.1 mi.) A connector trail intersects on the right and climbs steeply for 336 ft. to meet the Toll Gate Trail. To continue on the High Trail, go straight and descend while traveling southeast. The path soon drops more steeply and curls to the northwest.

23-5 (34.7468, -86.5394) (3.2 mi.) The High Trail ends at a three-way trail junction. On the left, the Dummy Line Trail heads northwest. On the right, a connector trail heads southeast and rises to end at the shoulder of Fearn Street, just above the hairpin curve.

Trail Facts

Fagan Creek and the "Foul Breath of Slander": Fagan Creek is named for Peter Fagan, who was a barber in Huntsville in the 1800s and owned property on Monte Sano, according to an online report from the Huntsville History Collection. Fagan was also a fiddler who performed at balls and parties, charging "75 cents for each man present." When Fagan died in 1829, a newspaper story concerning his death noted, "No more will Peter inspire the dance; no more will his music resound from the hall." Touting the man's honorable life, the report proclaimed, "The foul breath of slander never dared to impeach the honest and stern integrity of Peter Fagan."

24. Hotel Basin Trail

For an interesting side trip, follow this short path to the ruins of a bath facility operated by the Hotel Monte Sano in the late 1800s.

Distance: 0.12 mi.
Hiking Time: 5 minutes
Elevation Gain/Loss: +72 ft., -0 ft.
Hiking Difficulty: Easy
Location: Land Trust of North Alabama Monte Sano Nature Preserve, 2442 Bankhead Pkwy. NE, Huntsville, AL 35801
Facilities: The Monte Sano Preserve Bankhead Trailhead area has a portable toilet and a pavilion with picnic tables, but no source of potable water.
Driving Directions: See page 65 and use the directions for the Bankhead Trailhead.

Highlights

Hotel Monte Sano Bath Ruins: During the late 1800s, the Hotel Monte Sano served as a sanitorium where guests sought cures for a wide range of illnesses. Because many people believed in the healing power of mineral water at the time, the hotel constructed Roman-style baths that were fed by the nearby springs. At the end of the Hotel Basin Trail, you'll see a rectangular stone structure, which is the remnants of the baths. When they were operational, there were benches on each side for people to sit on. Also, there was a gate at one end of the bath structure that could be raised and lowered to adjust the water level.

Waypoint/Mile

Trailhead (Waypoint 24) (34.7416, -86.5375) To reach the Hotel Basin Trail, begin at the Monte Sano Preserve Bankhead parking lot. When you enter the parking area, there is a trailhead immediately on the left, near Bankhead Parkway. A sign indicates that this path leads to the Toll Gate, High, and Bluff Line trails. Ascend the Toll Gate Trail for 0.5 mi., turn right onto the High Trail and walk 0.4 mi. On the left (east) side of the High Trail, you will see a sign that reads "To Hotel Basin." The path makes a moderate ascent through the hardwood forest. Be aware that it can be difficult to follow the trail when leaves cover the forest floor.

At 0.1 mi., you'll reach a sign that says, "This marked trail and the basin at its end are available to the public for noncommercial hiking and sightseeing . . ." (This sign is present because this trail is on private land, but the owners allow the public to access it.)

24-1 (34.7421, -86.5356) (0.12 mi.) The path ends at the stone structure for the baths.

Trail Facts

A Quarter for a Bath: Hotel guests paid 25 cents to get a ticket to use the baths, plus a bar of soap and a towel. They would then descend wooden steps that stretched from the hotel to the baths.

Moss blankets stone walls that were once part of the Hotel Monte Sano baths.

SECTION 2:
Toll Gate Trail and Gaslight Trail

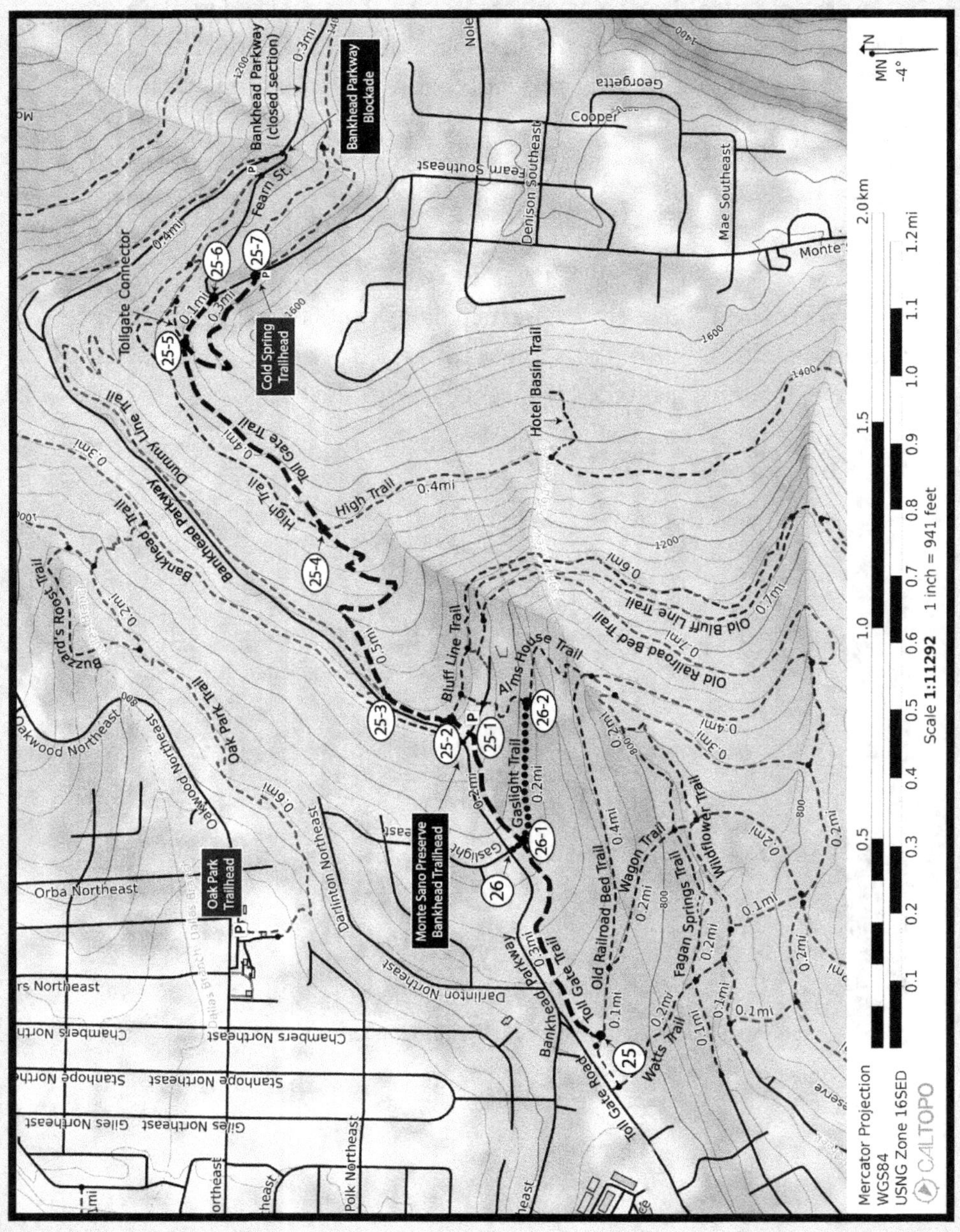

25. Toll Gate Trail

Following the route of an old road from the 1800s, the Toll Gate Trail climbs steadily up Monte Sano, gaining more than 600 ft. of elevation. For at least half a mile, the path is a rough and rocky ankle twister, so it's wise to hike in sturdy, supportive footwear. At its northern end, the trail ends at Fearn Street near the Cold Spring Trailhead, so you could leave a car at each end of the hike and shuttle back, rather than retracing your steps.

Distance: 1.5 to 1.7 mi.

Hiking Time: 1 to 1.5 hours

Elevation Gain/Loss: +668 ft., -29 ft.

Hiking Difficulty: Moderate

Location: Land Trust of North Alabama Monte Sano Nature Preserve, 2442 Bankhead Pkwy. NE, Huntsville, AL 35801

Facilities: The Monte Sano Preserve Bankhead Trailhead area has a portable toilet and a pavilion with picnic tables, but no source of potable water.

Driving Directions: See page 65 and use the directions for the Bankhead Trailhead.

Highlights

Hiking a Historic Road: The Toll Gate Trail follows the route of a wagon road built more than 160 years ago. In the 1800s, a man by the last name of Johnson lived in the Five Points area and operated a livery service delivering supplies to people living on Monte Sano. Because no roads ran up the mountain—only paths—Johnson could only transport small items that would fit on the backs of horses and mules. He knew his business would be more lucrative if he could deliver large items via wagon. So, in the spring of 1859, Johnson and members of his family constructed a road up Monte Sano. It began at the northwest corner of Maple Hill Cemetery and headed east up the mountain. Johnson built the road for his business but allowed others to use it for a fee. About a quarter-mile from the cemetery, he set up a toll gate near the current location of the Fagan Springs Apartments. Over time, the route became known as Toll Gate Road.

Waypoint/Mile

Trailhead (Waypoint 25) (34.7410, -86.5528) The Toll Gate Trail begins 265 ft. from the beginning of the Old Railroad Bed Trail. The Old Railroad Bed Trail starts beside Bankhead Parkway, across the street from Fagan Springs Apartments.

There are a couple of ways to access the actual beginning of the Toll Gate Trail. First, you can park on the shoulder of Toll Gate Road near a set of boulders, a few yards southwest of Waypoint 25. (Keep in mind that the space on the shoulder of the road is small and accommodates only a few vehicles.) From this parking spot, enter the Old Railroad Bed Trail and walk southeast for about 265 ft. to reach the beginning of the Toll Gate Trail.

The most popular place to access the Toll Gate Trail is the large Monte Sano Preserve Bankhead parking lot on Bankhead Parkway. When you enter this parking area, the Toll Gate Trail can be accessed on either the right or left side. The beginning of the Toll Gate Trail is 0.6 mi. to the southeast of the parking lot.

The following hike description begins at the southern terminus of the Toll Gate Trail at Waypoint 25.

Beginning at Waypoint 25, travel northeast. For the first 0.5 mi., the Toll Gate Trail is mostly packed earth and occasionally rocky. As you climb gradually toward the Monte Sano Preserve Bankhead parking lot, you'll probably hear traffic noise as you parallel the nearby Toll Gate Road.

26-1 (34.7426, -86.5475) (0.4 mi.) At a Y junction, the Gaslight Trail intersects on the right and heads southeast. Bear left and ascend the rocky path.

25-1 (34.7437, -86.5448) (0.6 mi.) The trail reaches the Monte Sano Preserve Bankhead parking lot. Head north and walk about 50 ft. across the parking lot to a trail sign that says the path leads to the Toll Gate, High, Panther Knob, Bluff Line and Old Railroad Bed trails. Ascend this trail and walk 160 ft. to a four-way trail junction.

25-2 (34.7441, -86.5444) (0.63 mi.) At the four-way junction, bear left and climb gradually to the northwest on the very rocky path. If you're not an experienced hiker or trail runner, proceed cautiously and step carefully for the next 0.5 mi. The trail is a jumble of loose rock, and you can easily twist an ankle.

25-3 (34.7455, -86.5437) (0.7 mi.) The Dummy Line Trail intersects on the left and briefly parallels the Toll Gate Trail.

25-4 (34.7467, -86.5394) (1.1 mi.) The Toll Gate Trail crosses the High Trail. Continue straight, climbing gradually to the northeast on the rocky path.

After you walk another 580 ft., the path becomes less rocky, and after 400 more ft. the trail becomes more level.

25-5 (34.7497, -86.5344) (1.5 mi.) At the end of a long, gradual climb, you'll reach a four-way junction. To the left, a connector trail descends 336 ft. to meet the High Trail. The Toll Gate Trail continues in two different directions. If you continue straight and travel east, you'll go another 408 ft. to the end of the trail on the shoulder of Fearn Street at Waypoint 25-6. From Waypoint 25-5, you can also turn right to begin a moderate to steep climb to the southeast. This stretch of trail continues for another 0.2 mi. and ends at Fearn Street (Waypoint 25-7), where a sign says, "Leaving Monte Sano State Park." The Cold Spring parking area is across Fearn St. and a few yards uphill.

25-6 (34.74921, -86.53336) (1.6 mi.) The Toll Gate Trail ends beside Fearn Street, on the western side of a tight curve.

25-7 (34.74816, -86.53272) (1.8 mi.) The Toll Gate Trail ends on the western side of Fearn Street, about 90 ft. north of the Cold Spring Trailhead.

Trail Facts

The Toll to Travel the Road: People on foot paid a penny to travel Toll Gate Road. If you were riding a horse or mule, you paid 2 cents, and people in wagons paid 5 cents.

Folks Who Traveled for Free: The state of Alabama authorized the toll road and stipulated that people didn't have to pay the toll if they were traveling between farms, going to a funeral, headed to a house of worship, reporting for militia duty or traveling to vote. Also, you didn't have to pay if you were walking to or from your job at a grist mill or blacksmith shop. (*Source: "Alabama Laws and Joint Resolutions of the Legislature of Alabama," Skinner Printing Company, 1860.*)

26. Gaslight Trail

The Gaslight Trail primarily serves as an access path that allows people in nearby neighborhoods to reach the Toll Gate Trail and other paths in the Monte Sano Nature Preserve. It mostly runs level as it connects the Toll Gate and Alms House trails.

Distance: 0.2 mi.
Hiking Time: 5 minutes
Elevation Gain/Loss: +10 ft., -9 ft.
Hiking Difficulty: Easy
Location: Land Trust of North Alabama Monte Sano Nature Preserve, 2442 Bankhead Pkwy. NE, Huntsville, AL 35801
Facilities: The Monte Sano Preserve Bankhead Trailhead area has a portable toilet and a pavilion with picnic tables, but no source of potable water.
Driving Directions: See page 65 and use the directions for the Bankhead Trailhead.

Highlights

A Taste of the Wild: At 0.2 mi., the junction of the Gaslight Trail and Alms House Trail is surprisingly impressive. The rocky Alms House Trail and surrounding cedars create a pocket of forest that feels like rugged wilderness.

Waypoint/Mile

Trailhead (Waypoint 26) (34.7427, -86.5478) There is no parking at the trailhead beside Bankhead Parkway. The nearest parking is the Monte Sano Preserve Bankhead parking lot, 0.2 mi. to the northeast. From the west end of the parking area (the end near Bankhead Pkwy.), walk southwest on the Toll Gate Trail. Go 0.2 mi. to the junction with the Gaslight Trail, which goes right (northwest) and left (southeast). If you turn right, you can walk 95 ft. to the actual beginning of the Gaslight Trail beside Bankhead Pkwy. at Waypoint 26. If you turn left, you can follow the Gaslight Trail for 0.2 mi. to its junction with the Alms House Trail at Waypoint 26-2.

26-1 (34.7426, -86.5475) (95 ft.) At the junction with the Toll Gate Trail, go straight and travel east. You'll hike through a hallway of dense honeysuckle and pass through a forest with tall cedar trees.

26-2 (34.7426, -86.5440) (0.2 mi.) The Gaslight Trail ends at a Y junction with the Alms House Trail. To the left, the Alms House Trail ascends to the northeast and reaches the parking lot in 0.1 mi. To the right, the Alms House Trail descends a stony path.

Trail Facts

The "Gaslight" Name: The path is named for its proximity to the road Gaslight Way, which is directly across Bankhead Parkway from the trailhead.

SECTION 3:
Old Railroad Bed Trail, Belue Trail, Watts Trail, Fagan Springs Trail, Wildflower Trail and Sink Hole Trail

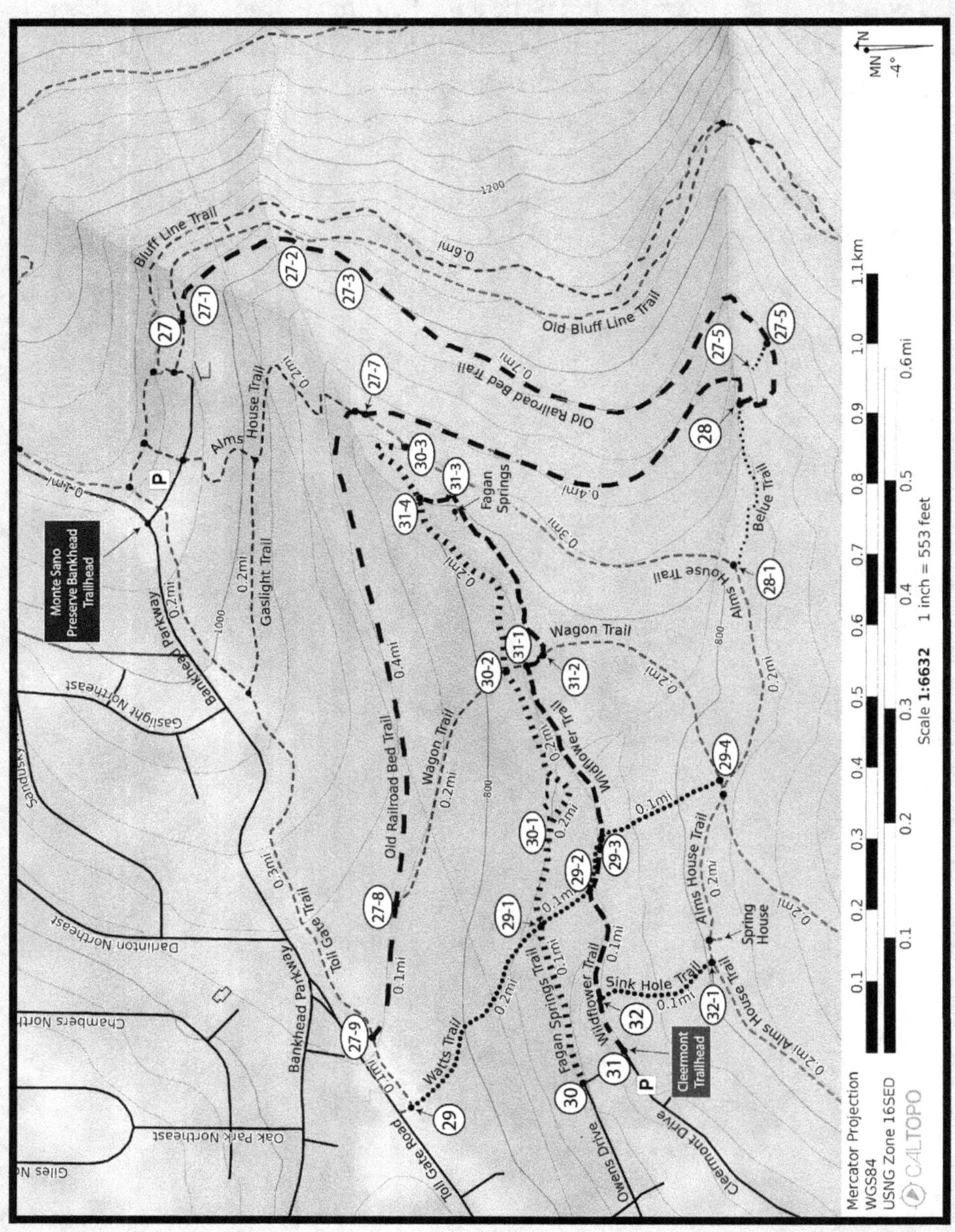

27. Old Railroad Bed Trail

Trace early Huntsville history by walking this entertaining trail that follows a railroad route from the 1800s. The railroad tracks are long gone, but support structures remain along the way, and interpretive signs provide details of the train's operation.

Distance: 1.7 mi.

Hiking Time: 30 to 45 minutes

Elevation Gain/Loss: +37 ft., -265 ft.

Hiking Difficulty: Moderate

Location: Land Trust of North Alabama Monte Sano Nature Preserve, 2442 Bankhead Pkwy. NE, Huntsville, AL 35801

Facilities: The Monte Sano Preserve Bankhead Trailhead area has a portable toilet and a pavilion with picnic tables, but no source of potable water.

Driving Directions: See page 65 and use the directions for the Bankhead Trailhead.

Highlights

Early Huntsville History: In the 1800s, cholera, yellow fever and other ailments swept through the United States. To avoid disease or find a cure, people flocked to mountaintop resorts such as the Hotel Monte Sano. (In Spanish and Italian, Monte Sano means "Mountain of Health.") These retreats offered fresh air and a variety of curative treatments. But getting to the Monte Sano summit involved a bumpy four-hour carriage ride. To ease the journey, the Monte Sano Railway Dummy Line was launched in 1888. (It was called a "dummy line" because it went point-to-point and made no connections.)

Passengers paid 25 cents each way for an 8.5-mi. ride that went from downtown Huntsville to the Hotel Monte Sano and took about 20 minutes. Unfortunately, the railway had a short life. In 1896, the Hotel Monte Sano failed to open, so the railroad couldn't operate and make payments on its equipment. Soon after, the Baldwin Locomotive Works in Philadelphia repossessed the train and the tracks. Over time, other evidence of the railway disappeared as roads and homes were developed on the mountain. However, the Old Railroad Bed Trail follows a 1.6-mi. stretch of the railway that is still recognizable.

Invasive Species Education: The Old Railroad Bed Trail not only provides a glimpse of Huntsville's past, but also the precarious future of its forests. Near the end of the trail, you pass through an "Invasive Species Treatment Demonstration Area." Here, the path moves through a hallway of invasive plants, including non-native honeysuckle and privet. On the left side of the trail, the land has been divided into plots where various eradication methods have been used on the invasive plants. At each plot, an interpretive sign explains the method and the thinking behind it.

Waypoint/Mile

Trailhead (Waypoint 27) (34.7473, -86.5421) To reach the beginning of the Old Railroad Bed Trail, begin at the trailhead near the far end of the Bankhead Trailhead parking area. You will see a wooden sign marked "Bluff Line" and "Old Railroad Bed," plus an interpretive sign that covers the history of the Monte Sano Railway. Enter the dirt path and walk about 200 feet to reach the junction with the Bluff Line Trail. Turn right onto the Bluff Line Trail, and then travel east 460 feet to the junction with the Old Railroad Bed, which intersects on the right. Turn right onto the Old Railroad Bed Trail and descend.

A wooden walkway crosses the wide creek bed on the Old Railroad Bed Trail.

27-1 (34.7434, -86.5417) (166 ft.) The Old Railroad Bed Trail intersects the old Bluff Line Trail route. Cross the old Bluff Line Trail and bear left on the path marked Old Railroad Bed Trail.

27-2 (34.7432, -86.5413) (144 ft.) Beside the path is the sign for "First Trestle/Wooden Foot Bridge." From here on, as you proceed down the path, you'll encounter several creek drainages and gullies. As you reach these, look to the side of the trail to see stacks of stones, which served as supports for the railroad trestles and bridges. Because the train couldn't manage steep grades, it had to make a series of switchbacks, gradually snaking its way up the mountain. This required the train to repeatedly cross creeks and other depressions.

27-3 (34.7421, -86.5405) (0.1 mi.) The trail crosses Fagan Creek and reaches the sign for "Slope Excavation," which explains that "mini canyons" were cut into the land to create a corridor for the train. Walk another 326 ft. to Waypoint 27-4.

27-4 (34.7413, -86.5408) (0.19 mi.) The trail passes between large berms and reaches the "First Bridge" sign, which explains how bridges and trestles were supported differently along the route.

27-5 (34.7361, -86.5422) (0.66 mi.) At the Y trail junction, the Old Railroad Bed Trail bears left and climbs gradually to the west. If you bear right at the Y junction, you'll take a side path that goes about 130 feet to a spot where a large train trestle once spanned the creek below.

27-6 (34.7364, -86.5425) The side path ends at the edge of a high bank along the creek. A "Mega Trestle" interpretive sign explains that it took workers almost two months to construct a trestle measuring 175 feet.

28 (34.7365, -86.5429) (0.74 mi.) The Belue Trail intersects on the left and descends gradually to the northwest. Turn right and travel east to continue on the Old Railroad Bed Trail.

Walk 615 feet and then turn left to follow a 70-foot-long wooden footbridge that crosses the creek.

27-7 (34.7411, -86.5433) (1.1 mi.) Near Fagan Creek, you reach a Y junction with the Alms House Trail. To continue on the Old Railroad Bed Trail, bear right and travel northeast, dropping down to cross the bed of Fagan Creek.

After you cross the creek bed, turn left to head northwest. (Look for a brown sign with Railroad Bed in red letters.)

At 1.4 mi., you cross the powerline corridor and enter the Invasive Species Treatment Demonstration Area.

27-8 (34.7408, -86.5510) (1.5 mi.) The Wagon Trail intersects on the left and descends gently to the southeast. Continue straight, traveling west.

27-9 (34.7410, -86.5528) (1.6 mi.) The Old Railroad Bed Trail ends at a junction with the Toll Gate Trail. If you turn right onto the Toll Gate Trail and head northeast, you'll walk about a half-mile to reach the Land Trust parking lot.

Trail Facts

A Train Wreck: Apparently, the Monte Sano Railway got off to a shaky start. "Early on in its operation, the train was wrecked when the brakes failed coming down the mountain," according to a document from the Land Trust of North Alabama. Fortunately, there weren't any serious injuries, but a new train had to be purchased for $15,000, which impacted profits for the railway and the Hotel Monte Sano. Plus, the accident no doubt spooked potential passengers. According to Montesano.org, the railway owners tried to ease riders' fears by declaring that the train was safe and that traveling by carriage wasn't necessarily a better option. They claimed that during carriage rides there had been "crowns broken" and "fair ladies bruised" due to "faulty harness, bad driving and balking horses."

28. Belue Trail

This easy path primarily serves a connector trail between the Old Railroad Bed Trail and the Alms House Trail. If you're walking on the Old Railroad Bed Trail, you can take the Belue Trail to quickly reach the Alms House Trail, then access other trails on the western side of the preserve. The pleasant Belue Trail offers views of the creek as it meanders through open hardwood forest.

Distance: 0.17 mi.
Hiking Time: 3 to 5 minutes
Elevation Gain/Loss: + 0 ft., -60 ft.
Hiking Difficulty: Easy
Location: Land Trust of North Alabama Monte Sano Nature Preserve, 2442 Bankhead Pkwy. NE, Huntsville, AL 35801
Facilities: The Monte Sano Preserve Bankhead Trailhead area has a portable toilet and a pavilion with picnic tables, but no source of potable water.
Driving Directions: See page 65 and use the directions for the Bankhead Trailhead.

Waypoint/Mile

Trailhead (Waypoint 28) To reach the Belue Trail, begin at the Monte Sano Preserve Bankhead parking lot. Follow the Bluff Line Trail to its junction with the Old Railroad Bed Trail. Follow the Railroad Bed Trail 0.74 mi. to its junction with the Belue Trail. Turn left onto the Belue Trail and gradually descend to the west on the single-track path.

The trail runs near the creek for the first 400 feet, then bends left to move slightly higher and traverse the base of a slope. But, after another 260 feet, it drops to meet the creek again. The packed-earth path descends gently and crosses a couple of rocky stream beds along the way.

28-1 (34.7366, -86.5455) (0.17 mi.) The Belue Trail ends at the junction with the Alms House Trail.

29. Watts Trail

The Watts Trail serves as an easy and convenient way to move between the Toll Gate Trail and several interior trails on this Land Trust property. It first reaches the Fagan Springs and Wildflower trails, where you can enjoy exploring the creek. Then it continues south, providing access to the Wagon Trail, Alms House Trail and other paths that wind throughout the recreation area.

Distance: 0.4 mi.
Hiking Time: 15 minutes
Elevation Gain/Loss: +92 ft., -101 ft.
Hiking Difficulty: Easy
Location: Land Trust of North Alabama Monte Sano Nature Preserve, 2442 Bankhead Pkwy. NE, Huntsville, AL 35801
Facilities: The Monte Sano Preserve Bankhead Trailhead area has a portable toilet and a pavilion with picnic tables, but no source of potable water.
Driving Directions: See page 65 and use the directions for the Bankhead Trailhead.

Waypoint/Mile

Trailhead (Waypoint 29) (34.7406, -86.5541) The Watts Trail begins near the shoulder of Toll Gate Road, across from Fagan Springs Apartments. There are a couple of ways to reach the beginning of the trail. One option is to park on the shoulder of Toll Gate Road near a set of boulders and the Old Railroad Bed Trail. Take the path that begins at the boulders and turn right onto the Toll Gate Trail, which is the first path on the right. Walk southwest on the Toll Gate Trail about 265 ft. to reach the junction with the Watts Trail. Turn left onto the Watts Trail and head southeast.

The trail drops gently while rocks and roots cover the ground. Dense underbrush dominates the hardwood forest, and downed limbs are scattered throughout the woods.

29-1 (34.7391, -86.5512) (0.2 mi.) The Watts Trail crosses the Fagan Springs Trail. Continue straight, descending gradually to the southeast toward Fagan Creek. Walk about 300 ft. to reach Waypoint 29-2.

29-2 (34.7384, -86.5506) (0.25 mi.) The Watts Trail crosses Fagan Creek. After you cross, turn left to follow the Watts Trail, which shares a path with the Wildflower Trail.

29-3 (34.7383, -86.5498) (0.3 mi.) At the junction, bear right to travel southeast on the Watts Trail, which begins to climb. To the left, the Wildflower Trail goes east and continues to parallel Fagan Creek.

29-4 (34.7368, -86.5489) (0.4 mi.) The Watts Trail ends at the junction with the Wagon Trail.

30. Fagan Springs Trail

The Fagan Springs Trail doesn't hug Fagan Creek for much of its length, so it's not as popular as its cousin, the Wildflower Trail. But the Fagan Springs Trail does have its own attractive qualities. Primarily, it provides easy access to Fagan Creek. Also, you can combine it with many other neighboring paths to create entertaining loop hikes.

Distance: 0.6 mi.
Hiking Time: 15 to 20 minutes
Elevation Gain/Loss: +134 ft., -23 ft.

Hiking Difficulty: Easy

Location: Land Trust of North Alabama Monte Sano Nature Preserve, 2442 Bankhead Pkwy. NE, Huntsville, AL 35801

Facilities: There is no restroom or source of potable water at the trailhead.

Driving Directions: From the junction of U.S. 231/431 (Memorial Parkway) and Governors Drive (U.S. 431), travel east on Governors Dr. for 1 mi., and then turn left onto California Street. Travel 0.7 mi. on California St., and then turn right onto McClung Avenue. Go 0.7 mi., and then turn left onto Owens Drive. Travel 0.8 mi. to the end of Owens Dr. Note that there is no dedicated parking area for this trailhead. For nearby dedicated parking, see page 64 and use the directions for the Cleermont Trailhead.

Highlights

Fagan Creek: On a warm day in spring or summer, when Fagan Creek is flowing, it's the perfect spot to take the kids. The trails leading to the creek aren't steep, so young ones can walk them easily. Plus, paths run right beside the water, offering easy access to shallow pools and small riffles. Best of all, the creek is shallow, so it's a safe place for kids to splash and play.

Fagan Family History: As you're hiking along Fagan Creek, imagine trying to raise sheep and cows on the rugged land. That's exactly what the Fagan family planned to do after emigrating from Ireland. In 1818, they became some of the first people to set up a homestead on Monte Sano. They began clearing the land around the creek so that animals could graze and produce milk, which the family would sell downtown. Unfortunately, the forest wasn't conducive to dairy farming, so instead the Fagans cut trees and sold firewood. They lived there until April of 1863, when the Union Army knocked on their door one morning and told them to leave immediately. With the family booted out, the soldiers transformed the area around the spring into a field hospital. By the time the next census was conducted, the Fagan family had disappeared from the rolls and never returned to the homestead.

Waypoint/Mile

Trailhead (Waypoint 30) (34.7385, -86.5536) You can access the trail at the end of Owens Drive or begin at the parking area for the Wildflower Trail on Cleermont Drive. From Cleermont Dr., follow the Wildflower Trail for 0.14 mi. and then turn left onto the Watts Trail. Cross the creek and walk 275 ft. to the junction of the Watts Trail and Fagan Springs Trail. To reach the beginning of the Fagan Springs Trail, turn left and travel southwest 0.14 mi. to where the trail meets Owens Dr.

The trail begins with an easy walk through a recovering forest with modest-sized trees and plenty of underbrush. At this point, Fagan Creek is mostly out of view and nearly 200 ft. away to the south. When you've walked almost 170 ft., you'll pass a large, lone magnolia. After about 0.1 mi., the trail begins to rise gradually.

29-1 (34.7389, -86.5512) (0.15 mi.) You'll reach a four-way junction with the Watts Trail. If you want to begin exploring Fagan Creek, turn right and you'll reach it after about 275 ft. To continue on the Fagan Creek Trail, continue straight, climbing to the northeast.

30-1 (34.7390, -86.5496) (0.2 mi.) At the Y junction, an old stretch of the trail continues straight to the east. To continue on the Fagan Springs Trail, bear right and descend to the southeast.

At 0.3 mi., you'll see to the left another junction with that old section of trail. Bear right and climb gradually to the northeast. Walk another 511 ft. to reach Waypoint 30-2.

30-2 (34.7394, -86.5472) (0.39 mi.) You reach a four-way junction with the Wagon Trail. To the left, the Wagon Trail climbs to the northwest. To the right, it drops and quickly meets Fagan Creek. Compared to other paths in the area, the Wagon Trail is much wider and rockier. It's easy to imagine that it was once part of a rough road that climbed the mountain. To continue on the Fagan Springs Trail, go straight, traveling east. Not far down the trail, at 0.4 mi., look to the right for a rocky, moss-covered path. It stretches about 30 ft. and leads to a patch of sloped rock where you can sit beside the stream.

31-4 (34.7405, -86.5446) (0.5 mi.) Cross Fagan Creek, stepping carefully, as the stone creek bed can be very slippery here. On the opposite side of the creek, the Fagan Creek Trail and Wildflower Trail intersect. To continue on the Fagan Springs Trail, turn left and travel northwest, gaining elevation gradually.

After walking another 0.1 mi. on the Fagan Springs Trail, look down and to the left to see a wide part of the creek that forms a rocky bowl. Skirt the creek for another 70 ft., and then look to the right for a sharp turn. The path seems to disappear as it hooks to the right and climbs through a rocky section.

30-3 (34.7407, -86.5438) (0.66 mi.) As you climb into a mature hardwood forest, the Fagan Springs Trail ends at the junction with the Alms House Trail.

Trail Facts

An Important Water Source: From the 1940s to the 1960s, Fagan Springs served as a major water source for Monte Sano residents and people living in the neighborhood now known as Blossomwood. Near the spring on Fagan Creek sits the cement foundation of an old building. It held two 65-horsepower diesel water pumps used to deliver the water.

31. Wildflower Trail

In spring and summer, this is one of the most popular trails in town. Many people visit to enjoy the wide array of wildflowers that bloom along the path. When the weather's warm and the creek is flowing, families bring their kids to splash in shallow pools, search for crayfish and try to spy lizards.

Distance: 0.58 mi.
Hiking Time: 15 to 20 minutes
Elevation Gain/Loss: +99 ft., -13 ft.
Hiking Difficulty: Easy
Location: Land Trust of North Alabama Monte Sano Nature Preserve, 2442 Bankhead Pkwy. NE, Huntsville, AL 35801
Facilities: There is no restroom or source of potable water at the trailhead.
Driving Directions: From the intersection of Governors Drive and California Street, drive north on California St. for 0.6 mi., and

then turn right onto Hermitage Avenue. Travel east on Hermitage Ave. for 0.9 mi., and then turn left onto Cleermont Drive. Travel 0.9 mi., and near the end of Cleermont Dr. you'll see a parking area on the left.

Highlights

Abundant Wildflowers: A wide variety of wildflowers thrive in the moist soil surrounding Fagan Creek. After you've parked and approach the trail, you get the hint that you're in for something special during your trek. Lining the road are brilliant red Indian pink flowers as well as lush ferns, hydrangeas and Solomon's seals. From sunny yellow trout lilies to brilliant white Alabama snow-wreath blossoms, the Wildflower Trail delivers a colorful array of fascinating plants.

Bursts of Color: In northeast Alabama, there are three major blooming periods for wildflowers. The timing depends on how cold the winter is and the soil temperature, but here's a rough estimate:

First Burst: By mid-March (before the tree canopy closes), the ephemerals bloom. This includes trilliums, Virginia bluebells, anemones, spring beauties, violets, Solomon's seal and many others.

Second Burst: In mid-May, there is an explosion of grasses, sedges, rushes and water plants. This is the rainy season, when plants rush to produce their offspring so that during summer all they have to do is mature their seeds. During this period, you'll see a colorful palette of plants, including Indian pink, fire pink, spiderwort, orchids and varieties of beardtongue.

Third Burst: From mid-June until the frost, you see the blooming of the aster plants and members of the bean family. In the woods around the Wildflower Trail, you might see butterweeds and ragworts from early spring through June. In summer and fall, goldenrods, black-eyed Susans and clover species thrive along the trail.

Waypoint/Mile

Trailhead (Waypoint 31) (34.7380, -86.5530) From the parking area on the side of Cleermont Drive, continue down the road 293 ft. and enter the trail at the kiosk. In early spring, you might see a large stand of trout lilies as the path immediately descends. Under a thick canopy of trees, the shadowy forest floor is home to lush green ferns, making this place feel ancient. The most common fern here is ebony spleenwort, which grows year-round. In late March, you might also see Virginia bluebells just off the trail.

32 (34.7383, -86.5522) (300 ft.) The Sink Hole Trail intersects on the right and crawls uphill. Continue straight, traveling east, to follow the Wildflower Trail.

About the same time that Virginia bluebells display their deep purple color, mayapple also blossoms. A single bloom or fruit dangles beneath an umbrella of deep-green leaves. Here and along other Huntsville trails, you'll find large stands of mayapples. The entire group is actually one plant, and a large population indicates a plant that has been around for a very long time.

This damp, shaded forest is also home to deep-red trillium and brilliant wild blue phlox. Also, scan the surrounding woods for a jack-in-the-pulpit, whose small flower is tucked into a conical stem with red and green stripes, as well as a hood that drapes over the flower.

As the trail continues, it runs beside a wide bank that is exposed when the water level is low. In late winter and early spring, look for bloodroot flowers, with their collection of eight to 12 small petals surrounding a yellow blossom. During most of the winter you won't see these plants, as they're buried underwater.

As you walk the Wildflower Trail, you can see on the opposite bank rows of bush honeysuckle and privet, two prominent invasive species in this part of Alabama. Both plants are in the top 10 of most harmful non-native plants in the area. As these plants take over the land, they prevent wildflowers from reaching the surface to be pollinated. Over time, the honeysuckle and privet wipe out the native wildflowers.

As the trail moves close to the creek, you might see stands of Alabama switch cane, which people have traditionally used to make fishing poles. Classified as a type of grass, it typically grows near streams, but it's also found near seeps or in depressions at higher elevations. As you near a short wood footbridge, look for native hydrangea, with large white blossoms hovering over broad green leaves.

29-2 (34.73838, -86.55057) (0.16 mi.) The Wildflower Trail and the Watts Trail intersect. Turn right and follow the path shared by the Watts Trail and Wildflower Trail.

29-3 (34.73825, -86.54980) (0.2 mi.) The Wildflower Trail continues east and runs parallel to the creek, while the Watts Trail goes right and heads south.

At several points along the trail, the forest is draped with thick vines. Most of these are muscadine vines. On the other end of the spectrum is the string-thin crossvine that crawls up trees lining the trail. On the crossvine, you'll see at regular intervals groupings of four narrow leaves, two on each side. Unlike some vines, these aren't harmful to trees, and they feature golden yellow flowers, making them a nice landscaping plant.

Indian pink blooms beside the Wildflower Trail.

At 0.26 mi., a side stream enters from the right and feeds into a wide section of Fagan Creek. Just before you cross the side stream, look at the left side of the trail where it meets the water and you might find Saint John's wort, which has been used for medicinal purposes going back to the ancient Greeks. Ominously, a sprig of bush honeysuckle has sprouted right next to it and may one day wipe it out.

31-1 (34.73911, -86.54708) (0.36 mi.) Wildflower Trail and the Wagon Trail intersect. This spot is home to a large population of Alabama snow-wreath plants, one of the state's most uncommon wildflowers. In April and May, these plants produce beautiful cream-colored blossoms. To continue on the Wildflower Trail, turn right to head south where the Wildflower Trail and Wagon Trail share a path for about 90 ft.

31-2 (34.73896, -86.54686) (0.38 mi.) The Wildflower Trail goes to the left and heads northeast, while the Wagon Trail bends to the right and heads southeast.

31-3 (34.74007, -86.54452) (0.54 mi.) Near Fagan Springs, the path goes right to make a horseshoe bend and cross a stream.

31-4 (34.74050, -86.54455) (0.58 mi.) The Wildflower Trail ends where the Fagan Springs Trail intersects on the left.

Trail Facts

Invasive Species: You might be wondering how invasive species made their way into Alabama forests. In most cases, the U.S. Forest Service brought them in to stabilize landscapes. Nurseries have also brought in non-native species, and people have used them to decorate their yards. Birds then feed on the invasive plants, fly into forests and leave their droppings, which include the seeds from the plants. It just so happens that bird poop has everything a seed needs when it's ready to germinate. So the fertilized seeds allow privet and bush honeysuckle, among other invasive plants, to spread easily.

The Pawpaw Patch: If you've ever heard the tune "Way Down Yonder in the Pawpaw Patch," you might be interested to know that pawpaw plants grow along the Wildflower Trail. In some spots, a tall pawpaw tree is surrounded by many smaller pawpaw plants—this is a pawpaw "patch." This plant produces the largest edible fruit of any plant native to North America (three to six inches long). There are stories that Native Americans and early settlers cultivated pawpaw plants. And, according to the Smithsonian Institution, pawpaws "kept members of the Lewis and Clark Expedition from starving during their travels west in 1804-1806." Also, they were a "favorite fruit of folk hero Daniel Boone and fed escaping African-American slaves during their dangerous journeys."

32. Sink Hole Trail

The short Sink Hole Trail serves as a connector between the Wildflower and Alms House trails, enabling hikers to piece together loops of varying lengths. Compared to other hikes on the mountain, this is also the shortest trail that will lead you to a sinkhole. While it is not especially dramatic, it does offer a close-up view of how water erodes rock and can eventually open large fractures in the stone.

Distance: 0.17 mi.
Hiking Time: 5 to 10 minutes
Elevation Gain/Loss: +81 ft., -0 ft.
Hiking Difficulty: Easy
Location: Land Trust of North Alabama Monte Sano Nature Preserve, 2442 Bankhead Pkwy. NE, Huntsville, AL 35801
Facilities: There are no facilities and no sources of potable water at the trailhead.
Driving Directions: See page 89 and use the directions for the Wildflower Trail.

Highlights

Sinkholes: These openings in the land are signature features of Monte Sano Mountain. This trail provides the easiest path to see one and get a better understanding of the natural forces affecting the land. Also, the Sink Hole Trail leads to several other interior trails, allowing you to create a loop hike that's the perfect distance for you.

Waypoint/Mile

Trailhead (Waypoint 32) (34.7383, -86.5522) To reach the Sink Hole Trail, enter the Wildflower Trail at the end of Cleermont Drive and walk 300 ft. The Sink Hole Trail intersects on the right and crawls uphill to the south.

After walking 0.1 mi., you'll see on the left side of the trail a small opening in a jumble of boulders. This is the first evidence of a sinkhole. Continue uphill for about 80 ft. to see another cavity in the rock.

32-1 (34.7384, -86.5506) (0.17 mi.) The Sink Hole Trail ends at the intersection with the Alms House Trail, which runs left (northeast) and right (west). If you turn left, you can combine the Alms House Trail with a variety of other trails in the area to form long or short loops, depending on how long you'd like to hike.

For a good short hike, follow the Alms House Trail northeast for 0.2 mi., and then turn left onto the Wagon Trail. Travel northeast on the Wagon Trail for 0.2 mi., and then turn left onto the Wildflower Trail. Head southwest on the Wildflower Trail and follow Fagan Creek for a little more than 0.4 mi. to return to the trailhead on Cleermont Drive. This makes a total trip of about 0.9 mi.

For a longer walk, follow the Alms House Trail for 0.7 mi. to the intersection with the Fagan Springs Trail. Turn left onto the Fagan Springs Trail, head southwest (going downstream) for 0.16 mi. and turn left onto the Wildflower Trail. Walk southwest on the Wildflower Trail for 0.58 mi. to return to the trailhead on Cleermont Drive. This makes a total trip of about 1.6 mi.

Trail Facts

High and Dry on Monte Sano: Early settlers on Monte Sano found that there was very little water on top of the mountain. This was due to the abundance of sinkholes. When rain reached the mountain, it flowed into the sinkholes and disappeared. As a result, settlers were forced to make their way to lower elevations to find springs where they could retrieve water.

SECTION 4:
Alms House Trail, Three Caves Loop Trail and Waterline Trail

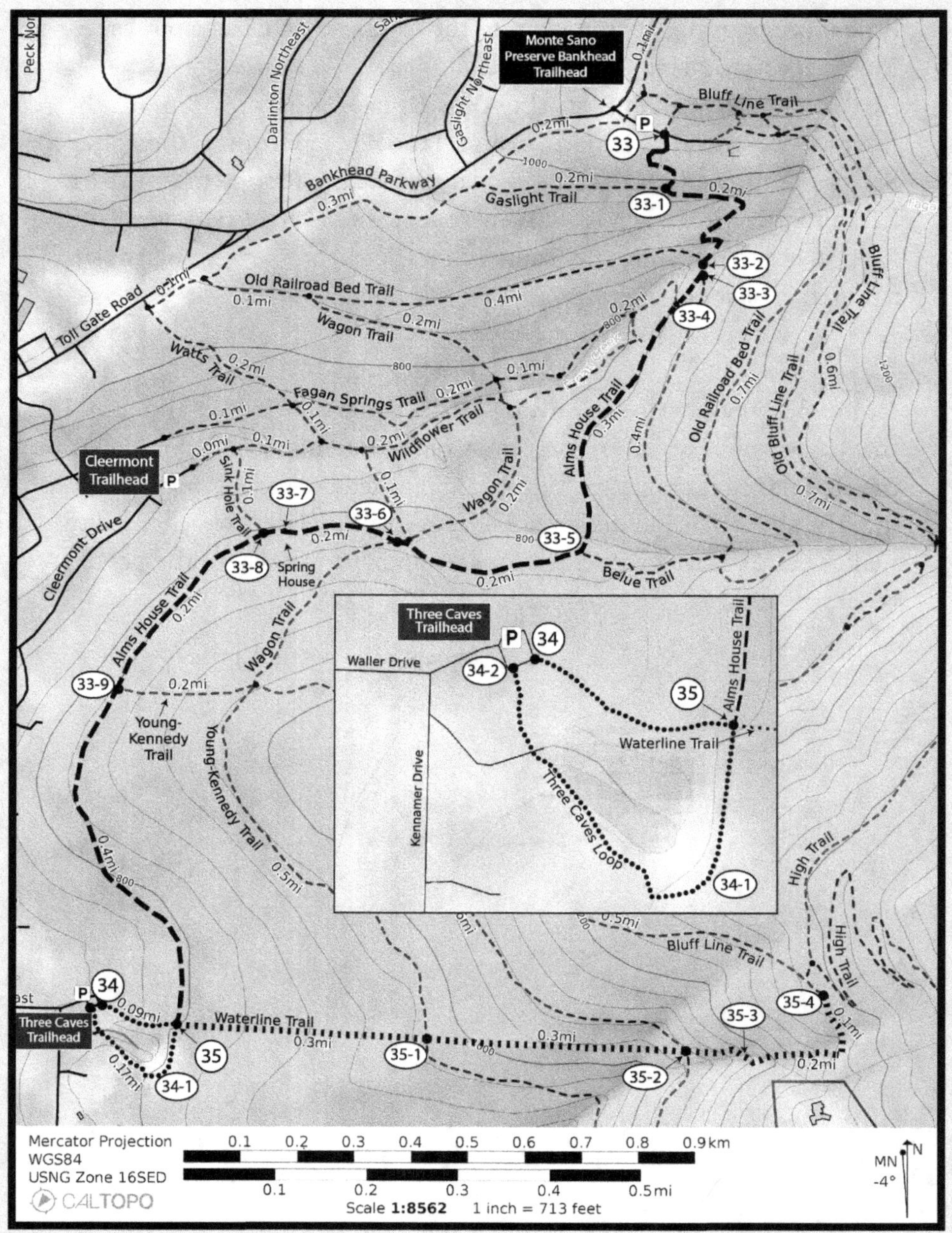

33. Alms House Trail

The Alms House Trail runs most of the length of this Land Trust property, offering hikers a long walk over moderate terrain. If you have a few hours to hike, you can combine this path with the Waterline Trail and other interior trails for a long loop back to the parking lot. The Alms House Trail also leads to the Three Caves Quarry, one of the mountain's more impressive and popular hiking destinations

Distance: 1.7 mi.

Hiking Time: 45 minutes to 1 hour

Elevation Gain/Loss: +118 ft., -380 ft.

Hiking Difficulty: Moderate to strenuous

Location: Land Trust of North Alabama Monte Sano Nature Preserve, 2442 Bankhead Pkwy. NE, Huntsville, AL 35801

Facilities: The Monte Sano Preserve Bankhead Trailhead area has a portable toilet and a pavilion with picnic tables, but no source of potable water.

Driving Directions: See page 65 and use the directions for the Bankhead Trailhead.

Highlights

Historic Springhouse: Just before the Alms House Trail meets the Sink Hole Trail, a short side path leads to the ruins of a historic springhouse. The moss-covered boulders you see at the site were once part of a small, two-room structure used to store food. A spring supplied water that kept the building at a constant cool temperature all year. Before electric refrigerators were invented, people in rural areas used springhouses to store meat, dairy products, fruit and other foods that could spoil.

Access to the Three Caves Quarry: The Alms House Trail ends near the Three Caves Quarry. A short walk takes you to the rim of the old limestone quarry, where you can peer into a massive pit with sheer rock walls 60 ft. high. It operated from 1945 to 1952, when it closed for a few reasons. As the quarry moved deeper into the mountain, it became more expensive to operate. Also, residents in the surrounding neighborhood complained about the noise, dust and debris from the blasting.

One dynamite charge blew a rock into the roof of the Alms House, and another charge hurled a brick into a woman's "brand new sporty 1949 Ford," according to the Historic Huntsville Quarterly.

Waypoint/Mile

Trailhead (Waypoint 33) (34.7434, -86.5440) On the southeast side of the Monte Sano Preserve Bankhead parking lot, enter the Alms House Trail at the edge of the pavement. The trail, which is marked with white diamond blazes, make a steep descent through boulders. This section is really the only part of the trail that might be strenuous. Going down it's not so bad, but if you return this way, you'll end your hike with a heart-pounding climb.

33-1 (34.7425, -86.5441) (0.1 mi.) The Gaslight Trail intersects on the right at a junction that's especially appealing. Overhead, a break in the tree canopy allows sunlight to flood the boulder-strewn Alms House Trail. Mature cedars, with their rough and twisted trunks, line the craggy path that swoops down through the forest. From this junction, bear left and descend to the west to stay on the Alms House Trail.

The path soon levels out and consists of rock and packed earth for easier walking. When you cross the powerline break, look to your right. If there are clear skies, you should be able to see in the far distance the Saturn V rocket at the U.S. Space & Rocket Center. You can get even better views of the rocket from the Old Railroad Bed Trail and Bluff Line Trail, which cross the powerline break higher on the mountain. After you cross the break, you'll descend another rocky section of the trail.

33-2 (34.7413, -86.5432) (0.3 mi.) The Alms House Trail crosses Fagan Creek and intersects with the Old Railroad Bed Trail. Walk 100 ft. to reach Waypoint 33-3.

33-3 (34.7411, -86.5432) (0.3 mi.) At another intersection with the Old Railroad Bed Trail, bear right and travel southwest through a nice section of the forest with mature hardwoods. To the right, deep-green moss blankets boulders strewn across the slope.

33-4 (34.7407, -86.5439) (0.4 mi.) At the T intersection, the Fagan Springs Trail intersects on the right and heads north. Turn left and travel southwest to stay on the Alms House Trail. For about the next half mile the trail gains and loses little elevation, making it a pleasant walk in remote woods.

33-5 (34.7366, -86.5455) (0.66 mi.) The Belue Trail intersects on the left. Go straight and travel southwest to continue on the Alms House Trail.

33-6 (34.7368, -86.5491) (0.8 mi.) The Alms House Trail intersects with the Wagon Trail. On the left, the Wagon Trail climbs to the west, and on the right, it descends to the east. To continue on the Alms House Trail, bear right and travel northwest.

The Historic Springhouse ruins lie just 60 feet from the Alms House Trail.

33-7 (34.7369, -86.5514) (1 mi.) To the left, a trail that stretches about 60 ft. leads to the Historic Springhouse. Continue on the Alms House Trail and in 126 ft. you'll reach Waypoint 33-7.

33-8 (34.7369, -86.5518) (1.1 mi.) The Sink Hole Trail intersects on the right. For a quick side trip, you can walk a few yards down the Sink Hole Trail to see where large fissures have formed in the rock slope.

33-9 (34.7341, -86.5546) (1.3 mi.) The Young-Kennedy Trail intersects on the left, climbs through a narrow, rocky corridor for 0.2 mi., and intersects with the Wagon Trail. Continue straight and travel southwest on the Alms House Trail. As you continue toward Three Caves, the path becomes significantly rockier, and cedar trees dominate the forest.

35 (34.7289, -86.5534) (1.7 mi.) The Alms House Trail ends at the intersection with the Waterline Trail. Continue straight to reach the rim of the quarry.

Trail Facts

A Place for the Poor: The trail is named for an Alms House, or "poorhouse," that operated from 1922 until the late 1950s and sat where the Mountain Springs Swim Club is now located on Kennamer Drive.

Measuring 80 ft. by 30 ft., it was a clay brick structure with a tin roof and was heated with coal oil. It cost about $557 a month to operate the facility. For the most part, the Alms House provided quarters for women and children, but in later years some employees of the Three Caves Quarry also lived there.

The Alms House Closes: In the late 1950s, the Alms House shut down, partly because it had few tenants as the city changed its policies and services for indigent people. Over time, it was no longer economical to keep the house open. Also, the blasting and debris from the Three Caves Quarry made life in the Alms House miserable. In 1958, the house was torn down.

34. Three Caves Loop Trail

Distance: 0.27 mi.

Hiking Time: 10 to 15 minutes

Elevation Gain/Loss: +148 ft., -12 ft.

Hiking Difficulty: Easy to moderate

Location: Land Trust of North Alabama Monte Sano Nature Preserve, 901 Kennamer Dr., Huntsville, AL 35801

Facilities: There is no restroom or water source at the trailhead.

Driving Directions: From the intersection of Governors Drive and California Street, drive north on California St. 0.5 mi. and then turn right onto Hermitage Avenue. Travel east on Hermitage Ave. 1.1 mi., and then turn left onto Kennamer Drive. Travel 0.2 mi., and then turn right at Waller Road to enter the trailhead parking area.

Highlights

Historic Limestone Quarry: Known today as "Three Caves," the Madison Limestone Company quarry operated from 1945 to 1952. In its heyday, the quarry employed 25 people, who extracted limestone to build local roads and bridges. Initially, the quarry used a "drill and shoot" method, placing dynamite into the ground vertically and igniting it to blast out chunks of rock. After about four years, the quarry changed to the "room and pillar" method, placing charges at the base of the rock to create a horizontal blast. This technique formed massive pillars that supported the roof of the quarry cavern and separated large "rooms" (*source: Historic Huntsville Quarterly*). The quarry closed in 1952 due to the increased cost of extracting limestone deeper into the mountain. Also, people in the surrounding neighborhood complained about the noise and debris from blasting. The floor of the quarry and the caverns are usually closed to the public, but the quarry floor is accessible during special events hosted by the Land Trust of North Alabama (www.landtrustnal.org).

Waypoint/Mile

Trailhead (Waypoint 34) (34.7293, -86.5548) There are trailheads for the Three Caves Loop Trail on the southwest and southeast corners of the parking area. This hike description begins at the southeast trailhead. At the trailhead kiosk, follow the path that enters the shaded forest and climbs gradually to the east.

35 (34.7289, -86.5534) (0.09 mi.) The Three Caves Loop Trail intersects with the Waterline Trail. To continue on the Three Caves Loop, turn right to walk south, skirting the rim of the quarry. If you continue straight, you'll enter the Waterline Trail, which climbs gradually to the east.

34-1 (34.7281, -86.5537) (0.1 mi.) On the right, a railing at the edge of the bluff provides a safe spot to get a good view of the quarry below.

The path then descends along the southwest side of the quarry. After walking another 500 ft., you'll cross a gravel road that leads down into the quarry. However, a fence blocks entry to the quarry. In another 100 ft., you'll reach the trailhead parking area.

34-2 (see inset map) (34.7292, -86.5550) The Three Caves Loop Trail ends at the parking area.

Trail Facts

A Nuclear Fallout Shelter: During the Cuban missile crisis in 1962, the Madison County Commission decided that Three Caves would be a good fallout shelter. In preparation, engineers with the Alabama

National Guard removed rubble from the entrance and interior of the caverns.

Hollywood History: In 1978, the movie *Ravagers* was filmed at Three Caves. Released in 1979, the film starred Richard Harris and Ernest Borgnine. Set in 1991, the film concerns a small group of people who survive a nuclear holocaust. The group lives in the cave to avoid the "ravagers," a mutated bunch of marauders. During filming, about 350 Huntsville residents served as extras. Also, parts of the movie were filmed at the U.S. Space & Rocket Center, which served as an abandoned missile base.

35. Waterline Trail

This is another Jekyll & Hyde path with two distinct personas. For the first half-mile, this trail shows its friendly side. From the trailhead, you can begin with a quick and easy side trip to get a lofty view of the impressive Three Caves Quarry. As you continue the Waterline Trail, you'll stroll easily along a narrow spine of land for about a half-mile, rising gradually through the forest. Then, suddenly, the path shows its more daunting personality, requiring hikers to scramble up a craggy slope and climb one of the steepest sections of trail on the mountain.

Distance: 0.8 mi.
Hiking Time: 30 to 45 minutes
Elevation Gain/Loss: +552 ft., -2 ft.
Hiking Difficulty: Strenuous
Location: Land Trust of North Alabama Monte Sano Nature Preserve, 901 Kennamer Dr., Huntsville, AL 35801
Facilities: There is no restroom or water source at the trailhead.
Driving Directions: See page 64 and use the directions for the Three Caves Trailhead.

Highlights

Three Caves Quarry: Before you proceed up the Waterline Trail, take a few minutes to visit the nearby Three Caves Loop Trail and view the quarry. From the high rim of the quarry, you can peer into the large pit and see three massive entryways that resemble cave openings.

Dry Falls: At 0.6 mi., the trail crosses what appears to be a waterfall area that's simply not flowing at the moment. The path first crosses a rock shelf at the base of a short, vertical drop in the creek bed. While there is often a trickle or small stream of water flowing onto the shelf, it's rarely a true waterfall. After crossing the shelf, you need both hands to grab rocks and small trees to pull yourself up the steep slope. Then the path skirts the main rock formation of Dry Falls, where a broad, high bluff forms a massive crescent. Looking at its size, you can imagine massive amounts of water pouring down. But, even after a good rain, there's usually just a narrow curtain of water slipping over the lip of the bluff.

Waypoint/Mile

Trailhead (Waypoint 35) (34.7289, -86.5534) To access the Waterline Trail, begin at the southeast corner of the Three Caves Trailhead parking area. Take the Three Caves Loop Trail to its junction with the Alms House Trail and Waterline Trail. Continue straight and walk east on the Waterline Trail.

35-1 (34.72870, -86.54852) (0.2 mi.) The Waterline Trail crosses the Young-Kennedy Trail. Continue straight, heading east.

35-2 (34.72856, -86.54345) (0.5 mi.) The Waterline Trail crosses the Wagon Trail. Continue straight, traveling east.

35-3 (34.72848, -86.54238) (0.6 mi.) Just below the Dry Falls, traverse a rocky shelf to cross the stream drainage. Once across, make the steep scramble up the right side of the drainage. The path then becomes extremely steep—one of the steepest sections of any trail in the Monte Sano Nature Preserve.

At 0.73 mi., the trail takes a sharp left turn and undulates as it traverses the slope.

35-4 (34.7291, -86.5408) (0.8 mi.) The Waterline Trail ends at the Y junction. Go left to follow the Bluff Line Trail or turn right to ascend gradually on a connector trail that stretches 356 feet to meet the High Trail.

Trail Facts

Waterline Trail History: Up until the mid-1950s, residents on the south part of Monte Sano received a portion of their water from Fagan Spring near the base of the mountain. The water was delivered through pipes constructed by the Civilian Conservation Corps. A pump house near the Three Caves Quarry housed a 20-horsepower pump that pushed the water 1,184 ft. up the mountain. In 1955, the city of Huntsville proposed the annexation of Monte Sano, and one condition was that the mountain would be added to the city water system.

SECTION 5:
Wagon Trail and Young-Kennedy Trail

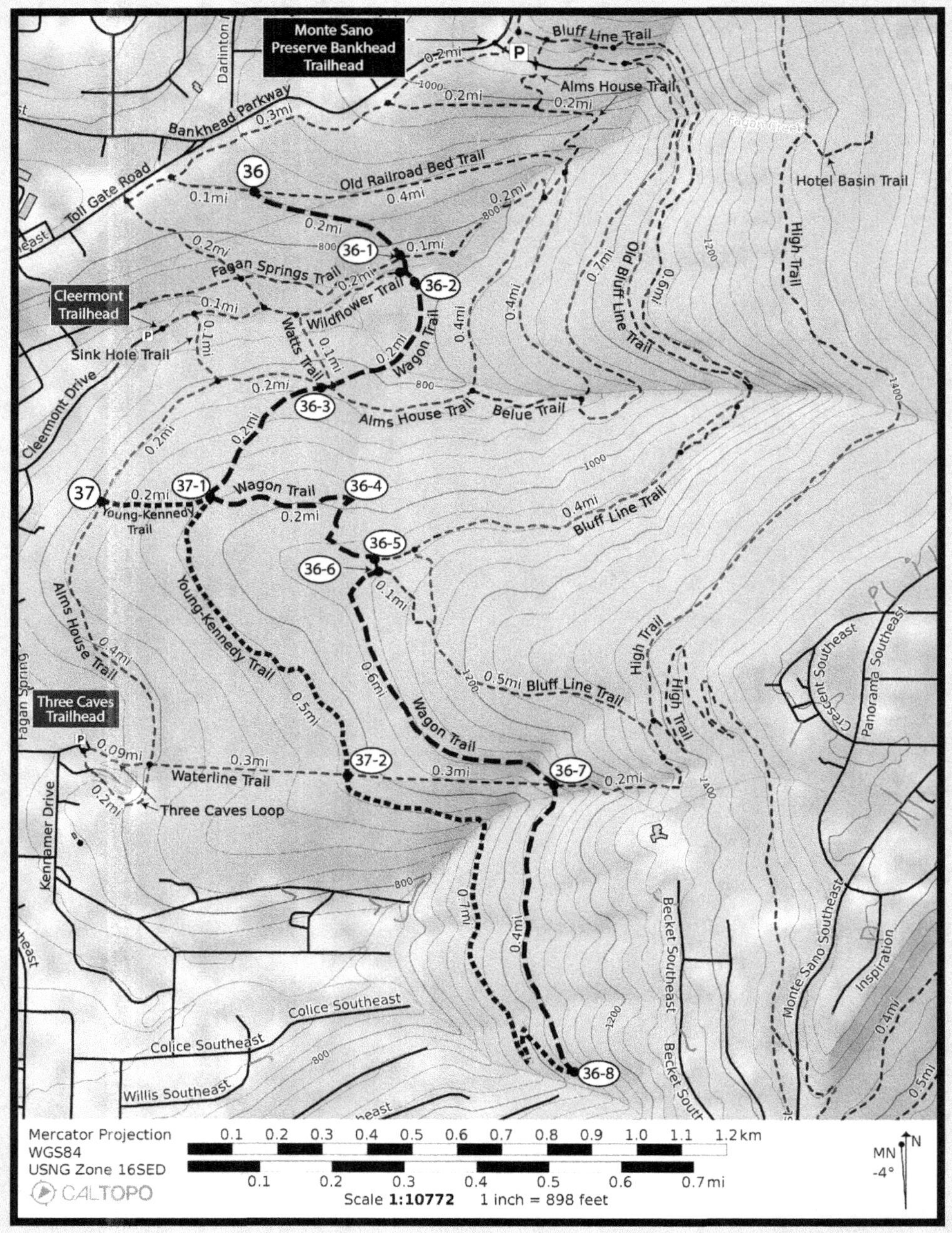

36. Wagon Trail

Following a wagon route from pioneer days, this trail takes ambitious hikers through the heart of the Monte Sano Preserve. The path mostly covers moderate ground, but it requires hikers to do a long out-and-back trip or a lengthy loop that includes the Young-Kennedy Trail or another nearby path. For another good option, combine portions of the Wagon Trail with the Young-Kennedy Trail or Waterline Trail to reach Three Caves, an old, abandoned quarry.

Distance: 2 mi.

Hiking Time: 1 to 1.5 hours

Elevation Gain/Loss: +330 ft., -152 ft.

Hiking Difficulty: Moderate

Location: Land Trust of North Alabama Monte Sano Nature Preserve, 2442 Bankhead Pkwy. NE, Huntsville, AL 35801

Facilities: The Monte Sano Preserve Bankhead parking lot has a portable toilet and a pavilion with picnic tables, but no source of potable water.

Driving Directions: See page 65 and use the directions for the Bankhead Trailhead.

Highlights

Pioneer Wagon Route: This path follows the route of a wagon road that dates to pioneer days. In 1859, a toll road was constructed so that people could more easily travel up and down Monte Sano Mountain. But some Monte Sano residents thought it was outrageous that they had to pay to move between their homes and town. So, in 1860, the mountain residents built their own road. Unfortunately, the new road was not maintained regularly. To travel it successfully, you needed enough muscle and supplies to remove downed trees and other debris that occasionally blocked the road. This meant traveling with at least two people in a wagon and carrying tools such as shovels, pickaxes and a crosscut saw.

Waypoint/Mile

Trailhead (Waypoint 36) (34.74101, -86.55083) From the Monte Sano Preserve Bankhead parking lot, travel southwest on the Toll Gate Trail. (As you enter the parking area, the trail is near the entrance on the right.) Walk 0.53 mi. to the junction where the Old Railroad Bed Trail intersects on the left. Turn left onto the Old Railroad Bed Trail and travel east for 0.1 mi. to the junction with the Wagon Trail, which intersects on the right. Turn right onto the Wagon Trail and travel southeast, following the white diamond blazes marked "Wagon Trail."

At 0.2 mi., you leave dense woods to cross a powerline break that's about 140 ft. wide. On the opposite side of the break, you enter more thick forest with stands of honeysuckle lining the path.

36-1 (34.73956, -86.54702) (0.38 mi.) The Wagon Trail crosses the Fagan Springs Trail. Continue straight, traveling south. Soon, the Wagon Trail and the Wildflower Trail share a path heading southeast.

36-2 (34.73887, -86.54658) (0.42 mi.) The Wildflower Trail intersects on the left and heads east. Go straight and travel southeast to continue on the Wagon Trail.

A moderate climb carries you through mature hardwoods. The surrounding thickets of bushes and brush thin out as you climb. At 0.5 mi., the Watts Trail intersects on the right and heads northwest.

36-3 (34.73695, -86.54937) (0.51 mi.) The Wagon Trail crosses the Alms House Trail. Continue straight and ascend to the west.

At 0.86 mi., the path becomes rockier and steeper, but the rough terrain only lasts for another 150 ft. Then the trail flattens and becomes a stone pathway of rounded rocks.

37-1 (34.73447, -86.55216) (0.8 mi.) At the four-way intersection, the first path

Water flows down a moss-covered rock face near the junction of the Wagon Trail and Young-Kennedy Trail.

to your right and the middle path are the Young-Kennedy Trail, which forms a V. To continue on the Wagon Trail, take the trail to your left and head southeast.

36-4 (34.73434, -86.54848) (0.9 mi.) Straight ahead is an old, closed section of the Wagon Trail. Turn right and climb to the south to continue on the Wagon Trail.

36-5 (34.73331, -86.54766) (1 mi.) The Bluff Line Trail intersects on the left and heads east. Continue straight to take the Wagon Trail southeast. Walk another 30 ft. to reach Waypoint 36-6.

36-6 (34.73288, -86.54754) (1.1 mi.) The Bluff Line Trail intersects on the left and climbs gradually to the southeast. Bear right to continue on the Wagon Trail, which bends back to the southwest.

36-7 (34.72856, -86.54341) (1.5 mi.) The Wagon Trail crosses the Waterline Trail. Continue straight and descend to the south.

36-8 (34.72258, -86.54287) (2 mi.) The Wagon Trail ends at the junction with the Young-Kennedy Trail, which intersects on the right and heads northwest. If you turn onto the Young-Kennedy Trail, you can walk north for 1.2 mi. to reach the northern section of the Wagon Trail at Waypoint 37-1. From that point you can follow the Wagon Trail another 0.7 mi. to return to the parking area.

37. Young-Kennedy Trail

This hike takes you through a wild and remote shoulder of Monte Sano covered in mature oaks and cedars. For at least a mile, you're surrounded by woods, with no signs of city life. If possible, hike this trail during winter or spring when there is frequent rain. Along the way, you'll encounter several large creek drainages, including Dry Branch Falls, which often boasts a steady gush of water. For the most part, the path covers easy terrain, but I've rated it "Moderate," because you'll walk a long distance if you hike the entire length and then return to your starting point.

Distance: 1.4 mi.
Hiking Time: 45 minutes to 1 hour
Elevation Gain/Loss: +263 ft., -95 ft.

Hiking Difficulty: Moderate
Location: Land Trust of North Alabama Monte Sano Nature Preserve, 2442 Bankhead Pkwy. NE, Huntsville, AL 35801
Facilities: At the Bankhead Trailhead, there is a portable toilet near the pavilion, but no water sources. There are no facilities and no potable water sources at the Cleermont Trailhead or the Three Caves Trailhead.
Driving Directions
Bankhead Trailhead: See page 65.
Cleermont Trailhead: See page 64.
Three Caves Trailhead: See page 64.

Highlights

A Wild Mile: Once hikers begin the Young-Kennedy Trail, they'll enjoy a mile-long walk with no signs of civilization. Tall oaks and cedars surround the trail and obscure views of the distant city. When you've walked a little more than a mile, look to the west for glimpses of Huntsville. Prominent city features include Huntsville Hospital, the 229-ft. steeple at First Baptist Church, and the 363-ft. replica of the Saturn V rocket.

Waypoint/Mile

Trailhead (Waypoint 37) (34.73415, -86.55457) The Young-Kennedy Trail begins at a junction with the Alms House Trail on the western side of the Monte Sano Preserve. There are three access points for the beginning of the Young-Kennedy Trail:

1. **Bankhead Trailhead:** Follow the Alms House Trail for 1.3 mi. to the beginning of the Young-Kennedy Trail.

2. **Cleermont Trailhead:** Take the Wildflower Trail and then the Sink Hole Trail to reach the Alms House Trail. Turn right onto the Alms House Trail and go 0.2 mi. to the junction with the Young-Kennedy Trail, which intersects on the left. This walk to the trailhead is a little more than 0.3 mi.

3. **Three Caves Trailhead:** From the Three Caves Trailhead parking area, take the Three Caves Loop path to the left and go nearly 0.1 mi. to the junction with the Alms House Trail. Turn left and travel

north on the Alms House Trail for 0.4 mi. to reach the Young-Kennedy Trail, which intersects on the right.

The hike begins with a gradual ascent on a narrow path that runs between low boulders. From this point until the end of the trail, the forest is mainly a mix of hardwoods and cedars, with occasional thickets of honeysuckle crowding the trail.

37-1 (34.73440, -86.55191) (0.15 mi.) At a four-way junction, turn right onto the path marked Young-Kennedy Trail and head southwest.

The path descends through woods where breaks in the forest and a thin tree canopy invite ample sunshine. During winter, the path is especially bright. The trail rises and falls gently, crossing narrow, thin streams that snake down the mountainside.

37-2 (34.72863, -86.54847) (0.6 mi.) The Young-Kennedy Trail crosses the Waterline Trail, which extends across the forest like a spine. Go straight, traveling south, to stay on the Young-Kennedy Trail.

You'll continue through a mountainous landscape, where wide, rocky streambeds cut across the trail and forested ridges ahead seem to rise higher and higher. Not far from the 1-mi. mark, the trail crosses a wide, rocky drainage. Walk another 180 ft. and look to the right for views of Huntsville to the west.

The path crosses another wide drainage and then begins a moderate climb, winding its way up the mountainside. At 1.3 mi., a large creek named Dry Branch Creek appears ahead. After periods of rain, a significant amount of water flows through this drainage, which eventually meets Fagan Creek in southeast Huntsville. After passing stacks of boulders, the trail bends to the east to parallel Dry Branch Creek.

36-8 (34.72258, -86.54287) (1.5 mi.) The Young-Kennedy Trail ends at the junction with the Wagon Trail. After it rains, this can be a peaceful spot, with the creek rushing below and nearby falls pouring down a jumble of moss-covered stone.

Trail Facts

The Young Family: The trail is named in recognition of the parents of David Young, who has supported the Land Trust of North Alabama for decades and served as a member of its board of directors.

SECTION 6:
Dummy Line Trail and Bankhead Trail

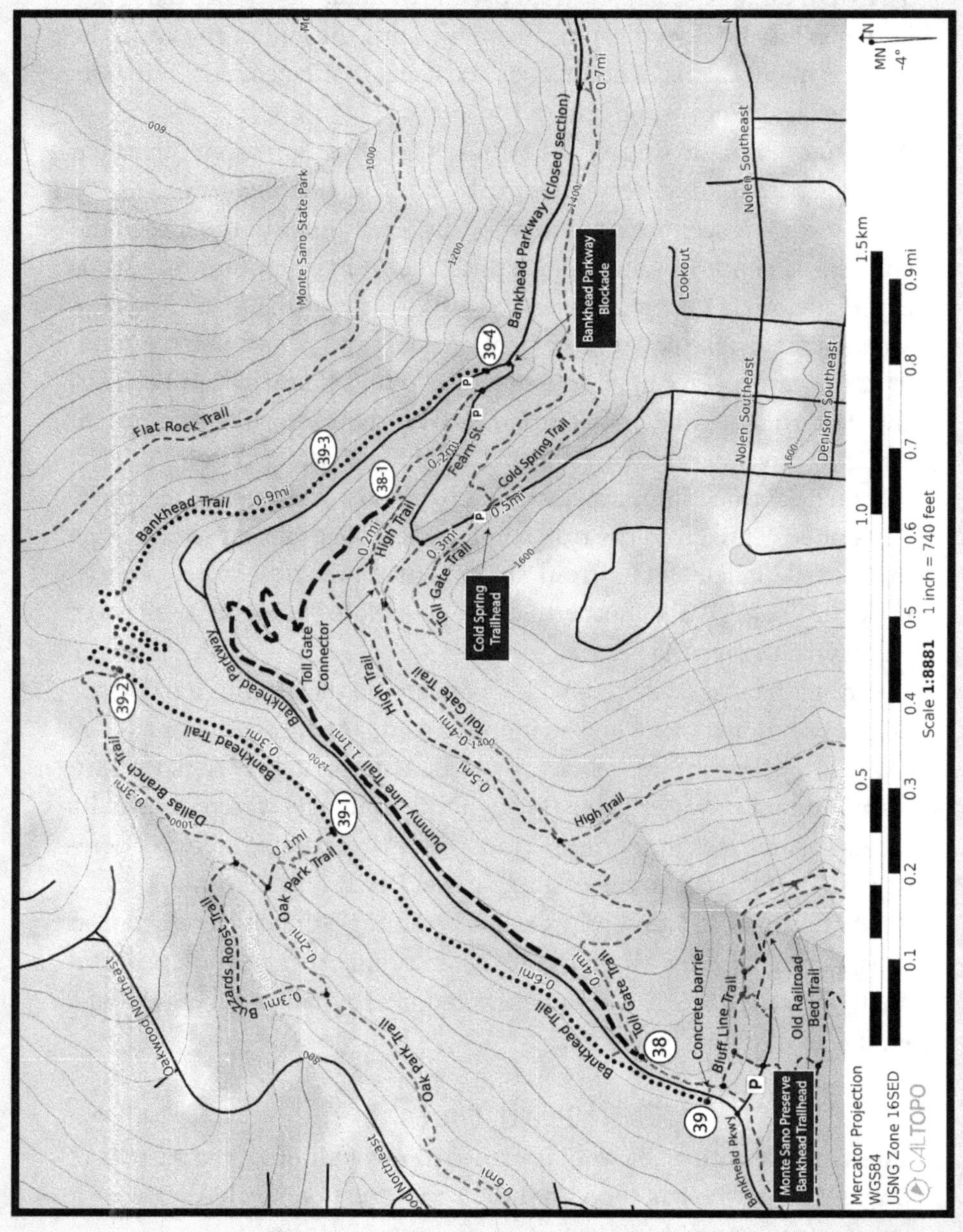

38. Dummy Line Trail

Around 2012, the Huntsville Area Mountain Bike Riders built the Dummy Line Trail to provide riders with a single-track path that's more rideable than the extremely rocky Toll Gate Trail. As an added benefit, the Dummy Line Trail gives mountain bikers and hikers another route to travel between the Bankhead Trailhead near the base of the mountain and the higher Bankhead Parkway Blockade, also known as the "hairpin curve." From the northern or southern ends of the Dummy Line Trail, you can link to the High Trail and Toll Gate Trail to do loops and lengthen your outing. As you're walking, keep an eye out for mountain bikers who might be moving swiftly as they descend the trail.

Distance: 1.17 mi.
Hiking Time: 35 to 45 minutes
Elevation Gain/Loss: +269 ft., -2 ft.
Hiking Difficulty: Moderate
Location: Land Trust of North Alabama Monte Sano Nature Preserve, 2442 Bankhead Pkwy. NE, Huntsville, AL 35801
Facilities: The Monte Sano Preserve Bankhead parking lot has a portable toilet and a pavilion with picnic tables, but no source of potable water.
Driving Directions: See page 65 and use the directions for the Bankhead Trailhead.

Highlights

Scenic Woods: Hikers beginning at the Bankhead Trailhead will climb steadily through a mature hardwood forest scattered with rock gardens. In winter, you'll enjoy views of the Chase Valley, which lies far below to the north.

Waypoint/Mile

Trailhead (Waypoint 38) (34.7455, -86.5436) To reach the trail, begin at the Monte Sano Preserve Bankhead parking lot and go to the Trailhead sign on the northwest end of the parking area. (As you enter the parking area, this trailhead is on the left near the entrance.) Walk northeast on the Toll Gate Trail for about 750 ft., to where the Dummy Line Trail intersects on the left. Follow the white diamond blazes marked Dummy Line Trail.

The Dummy Line Trail is a popular route for hikers and mountain bikers.

The single-track path starts off level but soon alternates between flat sections and places where the trail rollercoasters, rising and falling gently. Occasional rock gardens and rugged stream crossings entertain mountain bikers on this part of the trail. Along the way, you'll also cross several wood footbridges.

At the half-mile mark, the trail begins to rise more steeply. At times, the path is composed of packed earth, while at other times it's a rocky, bumpy route. Moving up Monte Sano, the path veers away from Bankhead, and winter hikers can look to the north for views of the distant Chase Valley on the northeast edge of Huntsville.

38-1 (34.7496, -86.5323) (1.1 mi.) The Dummy Line Trail ends at the junction with the High Trail. From here you can turn right to ascend the High Trail or continue straight on a path that ends beside Fearn Street, just above the hairpin curve and blockaded section of Bankhead Parkway.

Trail Facts

What's a "Dummy Line"? The Dummy Line Trail is named for the Monte Sano Railway train that ran between downtown Huntsville and the Hotel Monte Sano in the late 1800s. It was called a "dummy line" because it went point-to-point and made no connections. While the old railroad inspired the name of the trail, the path does not actually follow the train route. If you'd like to trace a portion of the real route and see remains of trestles and bridges, hike the Old Railroad Bed Trail (see page 80), which begins beyond the eastern end of the Monte Sano Preserve Bankhead parking lot.

39. Bankhead Trail

Especially popular with mountain bikers and trail runners, the Bankhead Trail rises steadily through a forest of mature hardwoods and winds among boulders and rocky bluffs. Like the Dummy Line Trail, this single-track path enables people traveling by foot or bike to link the lower Bankhead Trailhead and the upper trailhead at the Bankhead Parkway Blockade.

Distance: 1.8 mi.

Hiking Time: 1 hour

Elevation Gain/Loss: +432 ft., -137 ft.

Hiking Difficulty: Moderate

Location: Land Trust of North Alabama Monte Sano Nature Preserve, 2442 Bankhead Pkwy. NE, Huntsville, AL 35801

Facilities: The Monte Sano Preserve Bankhead parking lot has a portable toilet and a pavilion with picnic tables, but no source of potable water.

Driving Directions: See page 65 and use the directions for the Bankhead Trailhead.

Highlights

Beautiful Open Forest: Not far beyond 0.6 mi., you'll encounter one of the more beautiful and inviting sections of trail on this side of the mountain. To the left is a broad swath of open forest floor covered in leaves. The land falls away gradually, and mature trees dot the sunny slope. The path rises and drops comfortably as it moves among rock gardens and runs along the base of a craggy bluff.

Waypoint/Mile

Trailhead (Waypoint 39) (34.7443, -86.5447) To reach the trail, begin at the Monte Sano Preserve Bankhead parking lot and go to the Trailhead sign on the northwest end of the parking area. (As you enter the parking area, this trailhead is on the left near the entrance.) Walk up the Toll Gate Trail, traveling northeast, for about 250 ft. At the concrete barrier on the left side of the trail, walk to the right of the barrier and cross Bankhead Parkway, carefully watching for traffic. After crossing, enter the path on the right that heads northeast.

The trail begins by running parallel to Bankhead Parkway and stays fairly level. You might notice that there are no trail markers in this area, but the single-track path is clear and easy to follow. A little farther ahead, the trail zigzags through the open hardwood forest, and there are few obstacles to negotiate, save for a few boulders and trees hugging the path.

39-1 (34.7506, -86.5393) (0.6 mi.) The Oak Park Trail intersects on the left and descends to the northwest. Continue straight, traveling northeast.

39-2 (34.7541, -86.5359) (0.9 mi.) The Dallas Branch Trail intersects on the left and immediately bends back to the north to parallel the Bankhead Trail. Continue straight and climb into dense forest with stands of cedars.

The trail turns south and tours an intriguing area where an impressive field of boulders covers the slope. As you continue to climb, be on the lookout for mountain bikers, who pick up momentum along this stretch of trail. At 1.2 mi., you'll get glimpses of distant ridges to the northwest. The path seems especially wild and remote as it winds among boulders in dense woods. At 1.4 mi., a sign on the right side of the trail says "State Lands" on the downslope (east) side and "Leaving Monte Sano State Park" on the upslope (west) side. The path starts to climb gradually and runs parallel to nearby Bankhead Parkway.

39-3 (34.7505, -86.5315) (1.6 mi.) The trail crosses a footbridge constructed in 2016 by SORBA Huntsville, the Huntsville Track Club and Polaris Industries.

39-4 (34.7479, -86.5295) (1.8 mi.) The Bankhead Trail ends at the information kiosk near the Bankhead Parkway Blockade and the hairpin curve.

Trail Facts

The Bankhead Family: The trail is named for its proximity to the Bankhead Parkway, which in turn is named for William Brockman Bankhead, who came to Huntsville in 1895 to practice law. In 1916, Bankhead was elected to the U.S. House of Representatives, and he eventually served as Speaker of the House. He was also the father of famed actress Tallulah Bankhead, who was born in Huntsville in 1903 (*Source: Why Is It Named That? Stories Behind the Names of 250 Places in Madison County and Huntsville, Alabama.*)

SECTION 7:
Oak Park Trail, Buzzards Roost Trail and Dallas Branch Trail

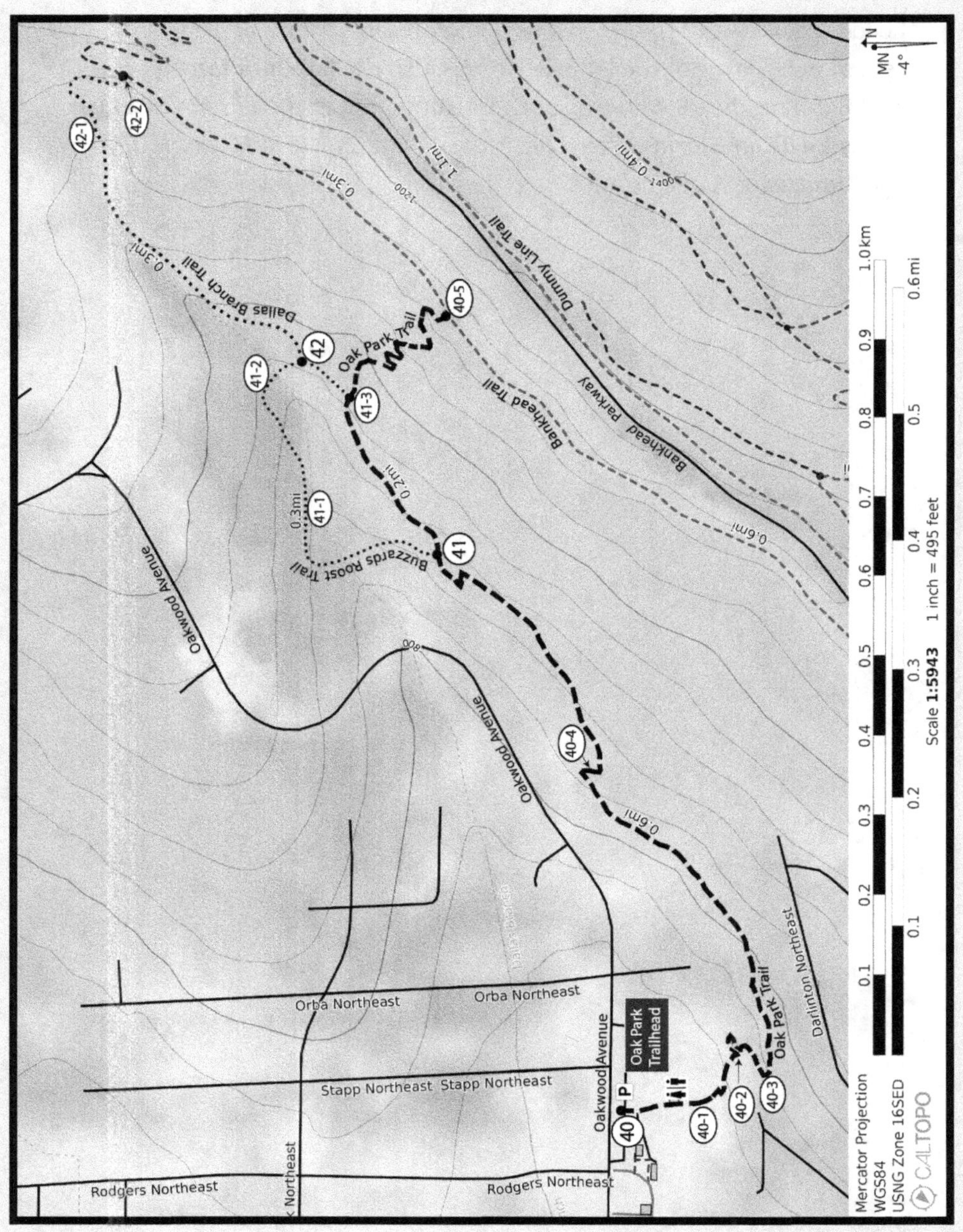

40. Oak Park Trail

The Oak Park Trail explores the beautiful northwestern slope of Monte Sano. In this mature forest, you'll wind among stout hardwood trees and traverse fields of moss-covered boulders. For the most part, the woods feel spacious and free of dense brush. On clear fall days, sunshine illuminates a forest floor covered in thick blankets of leaves. If you're seeking a short hike, the Oak Park Trail makes a great out-and-back trip. But you can also link to other trails for long hikes that end at the Bankhead Parkway Blockade (aka the "hairpin curve") or the Bankhead Trailhead near the base of the mountain.

Distance: 1 mi.

Hiking Time: 30 to 45 minutes

Elevation Gain/Loss: +422 ft., -35 ft.

Hiking Difficulty: Moderate

Location: Land Trust of North Alabama Monte Sano Nature Preserve, 2250 Oakwood Ave. NE, Huntsville, AL 35801

Fees: There are no fees to use the trail.

Facilities: There is a restroom near the trailhead, but it might be closed when teams are not playing or practicing at the ballpark.

Driving Directions: From the intersection of Memorial Parkway (U.S. 431) and Oakwood Avenue, travel east on Oakwood Ave. for 1.5 mi. and then turn right into the Oak Park parking area.

Highlights

Handcrafted Footbridge: At the 0.5-mi. mark, you'll cross a wooden footbridge and likely notice that the planks are much rougher than what you typically see on Huntsville trails. That's because in April of 2017, local volunteers constructed the bridge using only hand tools. They began the 3.5-day project by felling black locust trees with a two-person saw and wooden wedges. Then they employed a drawknife and other blades to shape the wood. Without any power tools, they also created wood pegs, which were used to connect the bridge pieces.

Waypoint/Mile

Trailhead (Waypoint 40) (34.7486, -86.5501) Near the midpoint of the parking area, you'll see a wooden sign with red letters reading "Oak Park Trail." Follow the paved path that heads south toward the forest and walk between two baseball fields. After walking 365 ft., you'll reach the trailhead kiosk at the edge of the woods.

40-1 (34.7475, -86.5499) (365 ft.) At the kiosk, enter the trail, which climbs gradually in a mature hardwood forest and heads southeast.

40-2 (34.7473, -86.5494) (492 ft.) At the Y junction, the main Oak Park Trail goes left and climbs to the northeast. To the right is the Oak Park Alternate Trail, which measures about 244 ft., climbs to the southwest, and then turns east to meet with the main Oak Park Trail again.

40-3 (34.7470, -86.5496) (0.1 mi.) At the second junction with the Oak Park Alternate Trail, turn left and climb to the east on the single-track path. The trail skirts a residential area, so houses are visible off to the left.

As the trail rollercoasters across the slope, you can see the rooftops of houses in the adjoining neighborhood. At 0.4 mi., the trail passes very close to a home and then begins to move away from the residential area.

40-4 (34.7490, -86.5454) (0.5 mi.) Cross the handmade wooden footbridge. After another 0.1 mi., you'll pass through a field of boulders in a younger section of forest filled with dense brush.

41 (34.7507, -86.5427) (0.7 mi.) At the Y junction, the Buzzard's Roost Trail goes left and runs mostly level to the northeast. To continue on the Oak Park Trail, bear right and ascend to the east. Be on the lookout for two trees with large burls. These

Volunteers used only hand tools to construct the rugged foot bridge on the Oak Park Trail.

odd-looking round masses on tree trunks are calluses that form after the tree suffers an injury. A burl could be the result of storm damage, pruning, insect damage or disease.

Up ahead, the woods feel more primitive, as you walk among moss-covered boulders and thick vines that curl around tree trunks like fat snakes. Following switchbacks, you'll climb moderately through attractive woods where sunshine floods the forest floor.

41-3 (34.7516, -86.5404) (0.9 mi.) The Buzzards Roost Trail intersects on the left. To continue on the Oak Park Trail, bear right and then hook back left to the southwest.

40-5 (34.7505, -86.5393) (1 mi.) The Oak Park Trail ends at the intersection with the Bankhead Trail.

41. Buzzards Roost Trail

If you hike the Oak Park Trail after a hard rain, take this short detour to see a waterfall on Dallas Branch Creek. Just be aware that these falls don't typically run unless there's a real downpour in the area.

Distance: 0.3 mi.

Hiking Time: 10 to 15 minutes

Elevation Gain/Loss: +111 ft., -38 ft.

Hiking Difficulty: Easy to moderate

Location: Land Trust of North Alabama Monte Sano Nature Preserve, 2250 Oakwood Ave. NE, Huntsville, AL 35801

Facilities: There is a restroom near the trailhead, but it might be closed when teams are not playing or practicing at the ballpark.

Driving Directions: See page 65 and use the directions for the Oak Park Trailhead.

Highlights

Buzzards Roost Falls: After walking 0.2 mi., you'll reach a large rock outcrop that transforms into a waterfall after significant rain. Most of the time, the falls are dry, and even when the water's running it's typically just a trickle. That's led some local hikers to refer to it jokingly as the "beautiful and spectacular Buzzards Roost Falls." Even if no water is running, this is still an interesting feature, as the path traverses the top of the outcrop to provide a lofty view of the rocks below and the surrounding forest.

Waypoint/Mile

Trailhead (Waypoint 41) (34.7507, -86.5427) To reach the Buzzards Roost Trail, begin at the Oak Park Trailhead parking area and follow the Oak Park Trail for 0.6 mi. At the Y junction, go left to take the Buzzards Roost Trail, which runs mostly level to the northeast.

A drainage tunnel passes through a berm along the Buzzards Roost Trail.

You'll cross a slope where thick moss blankets boulders and then move into dense woods. The path runs level on the spine of an earth berm and climbs gradually. **41-1** (34.75206, -86.54197) (0.1 mi.) The trail passes a man-made stone tunnel that allows water from the Dallas Branch Creek to pass through a berm. The path moves along the floor of the creek drainage and then rises steeply along the side of the waterfall rock outcrop. If it has been raining, be very careful as you climb up the rocks, as they can be very slippery.

41-2 (34.7525, -86.5401) (0.26 mi.) Cross the top of the Buzzards Roost Falls and walk in the shade of tall cedars. You'll walk another 158 ft. to reach Waypoint 42.

42 (34.7521, -86.5399) (0.29 mi.) The Dallas Branch Trail intersects on the left and goes northeast. To continue on the Buzzards Roost Trail, bear right and go southwest. Walk another 211 ft. to reach Waypoint 41-3.

41-3 (34.7516, -86.5404) (0.33 mi.) The Buzzards Roost Trail ends at the intersection with the Oak Park Trail, which goes right (northwest) and left (southeast).

42. Dallas Branch Trail

From the junction with the Buzzards Roost Trail, the Dallas Branch Trail climbs steadily to meet the Bankhead Trail. For much of the way, you pass through dense forest, so this route isn't as scenic as other nearby trails. But the Dallas Branch Trail is a good option if you want to explore a path that feels much more secluded.

Distance: 0.3 mi.
Hiking Time: 15 minutes
Elevation Gain/Loss: +154 ft., -4 ft.
Hiking Difficulty: Easy
Location: Land Trust of North Alabama Monte Sano Nature Preserve, 2250 Oakwood Ave. NE, Huntsville, AL 35801
Facilities: There is a restroom near the trailhead, but it might be closed when teams are not playing or practicing at the ballpark.
Driving Directions: See page 65 and use the directions for the Oak Park Trailhead.

Highlights

Isolated Woods: The Dallas Branch Trail runs along the extreme north end of the Land Trust property, and hundreds of feet of thick forest lie between it and the Bankhead Trail. As a result, it offers hikers the chance to walk through a quiet and remote corridor. Just stay alert, as you'll likely encounter mountain bikers moving through the area.

Waypoint/Mile

Trailhead (Waypoint 42) (34.7521, -86.5399) To reach the Dallas Branch Trail, begin at the Oak Park Trailhead parking area. Near the midpoint of the parking area, you'll see a wooden sign with red letters reading "Oak Park Trail." Follow the paved path that heads south toward the forest and walk between two baseball fields. After walking 365 ft., you'll reach the trailhead kiosk at the edge of the woods. Follow the Oak Park Trail for 0.8 mi. to its northernmost junction with the Buzzards Roost Trail. Then take the Buzzards Roost Trail and walk 211 ft. to the junction with the Dallas Branch Trail. To take the Dallas

Branch Trail, bear right at the junction and travel northeast.

The Dallas Branch Trail immediately begins its ascent and parallels the rocky bed of Dallas Branch Creek. The path climbs through an attractive, open forest and weaves through a field of boulders.

42-1 (34.7544, -86.5368) (0.2 mi.) An old, unnamed path intersects with the Dallas Branch Trail. Continue east on a gradual ascent.

The forest becomes choked with heavy brush and saplings. In this area, mountain bikers must negotiate tight turns with trees hugging the path. At 0.32 mi., take a sharp turn south to parallel the Bankhead Trail. The trail continues for another 260 ft. and becomes steeper.

42-2 (34.7541, -86.5359) (0.37 mi.) The Dallas Branch Trail ends at the junction with the Bankhead Trail.

Trail Facts

Dallas Mill: The Dallas Branch Trail and Dallas Branch Creek derive their names from Dallas Mill, which was the largest cotton mill in Alabama and operated in Huntsville from 1892 to 1949. The mill was named for Trevanion B. Dallas, who was the principal stockholder in the operation and served as the mill's treasurer and general manager. Trevanion's uncle was George Dallas. According to some people, Dallas, Texas, is named for George. However, others believe the city is named for Trevanion himself. And some people say the city is named for Alexander Dallas, a hero of the War of 1812. (*Sources: Texas Monthly, Why Is It Named That? Stories Behind the Names of 250 Places in Madison County and Huntsville, Alabama.*)

CHAPTER 3

Monte Sano Preserve and Monte Sano State Park

The trails in this chapter traverse portions of both the Monte Sano Nature Preserve (managed by the Land Trust of North Alabama) and Monte Sano State Park. Be aware that Land Trust trails and Monte Sano State Park trails have different fees and rules for visitors. Land Trust trails generally do not have required fees, though hikers are encouraged to make donations at trailheads that have donation boxes. Monte Sano State Park requires visitors to pay entrance fees. (See page 2 for fee details.) Also, Land Trust trails are generally open dawn to dusk, while Monte Sano State Park trails officially open at 8 a.m. and close 30 minutes before sunset. Both the Land Trust and State Park allow leashed dogs on trails.

SECTION 1:
Cold Spring Trail

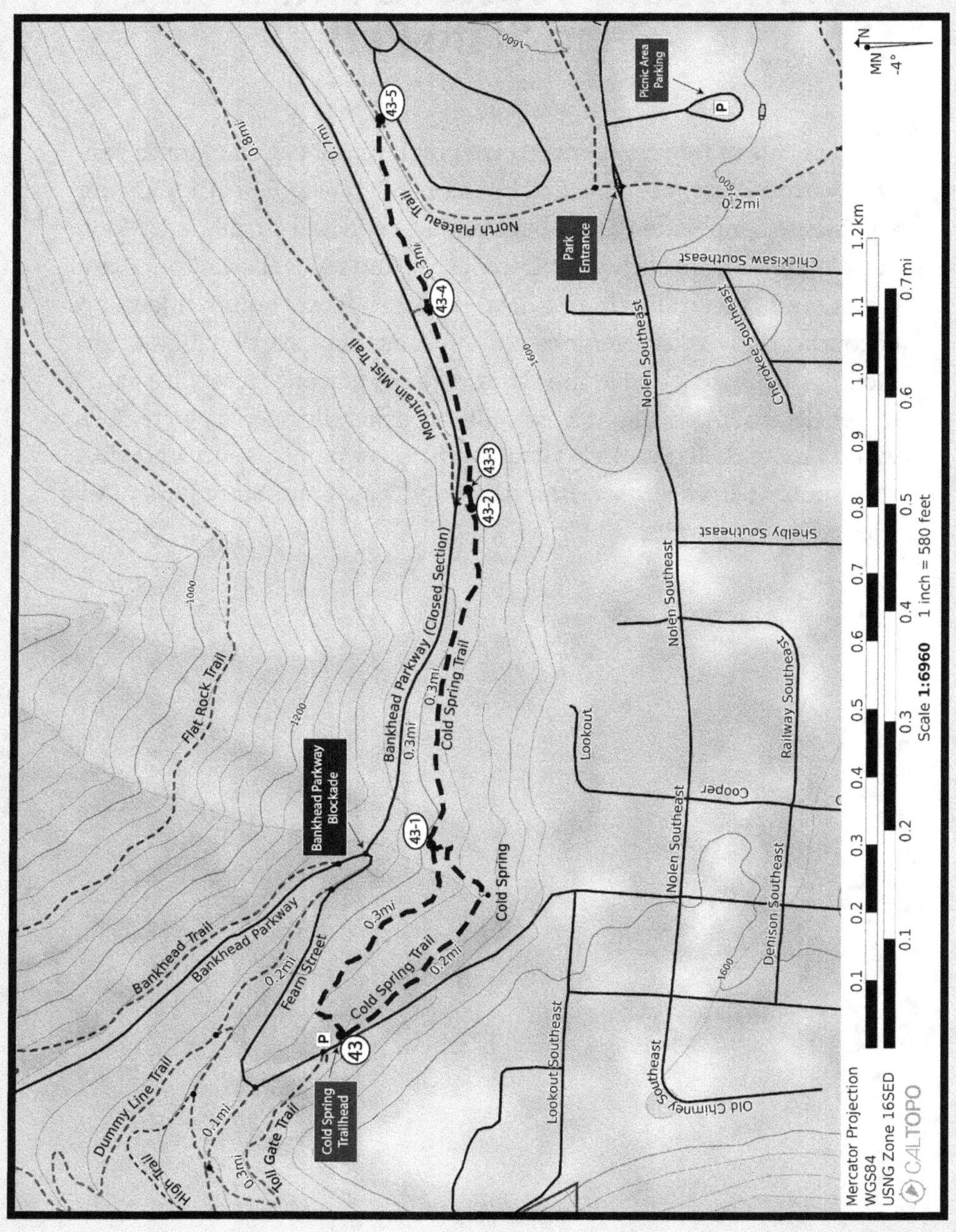

43. Cold Spring Trail

The Cold Spring Trail combines two different types of hikes. A short loop near the trailhead includes several labeled trees and plants, providing a good opportunity to educate kids on local wildlife. East of the loop, the path rises gradually and parallels the closed section of Bankhead Parkway. The hike ends with a steep ascent to the top of the mountain plateau, where you'll enjoy nice views of the Chase Valley.

Distance: Loop, 0.5 mi.; entire trail, 1.2 mi.
Hiking Time: Loop, 20 minutes; entire trail, 45 minutes to 1 hour
Elevation Gain/Loss: Loop, +128 ft., -128 ft.; entire trail, +270 ft., -80 ft.
Hiking Difficulty: Loop, easy; entire trail, moderate to strenuous
Location: Land Trust of North Alabama Monte Nature Sano Preserve, Bankhead Parkway, Huntsville, AL
Fees: There are no fees collected at the Cold Spring Trailhead.
Facilities: There are no facilities or sources of potable water at the Cold Spring Trailhead.
Driving Directions: See page 65 and use the directions for the Cold Spring Trailhead.

Highlights

Kid-Friendly Interpretive Loop Trail: Measuring 0.5 mi., the loop portion of the Cold Spring Trail is a good option for kids. It's long enough to work off some energy, but not so long that you'll be carrying them toward the end. Along the loop, signs identify certain trees and plants, giving you the chance to educate kids about the mountain ecosystem.
Bluff Views: At its eastern end, the Cold Spring Trail makes a steep climb to the top of the plateau. The high bluff offers good views of the distant valley to the north and the Chase community.

Waypoint/Mile

Trailhead (Waypoint 43) (34.7478, -86.5324) From the small parking area on the northeast side of Bankhead Parkway, walk uphill for 130 ft. to an orange gate and the trailhead kiosk. Facing the kiosk, turn right and travel southeast on the level path that parallels Bankhead Pkwy. The Cold Spring Trail is marked with red blazes.

Walk down the trail about 295 ft. to see a marked basswood tree. These trees can grow to be 60 to 80 ft. tall. At about 375 ft., you'll encounter a marked sassafras tree. Native Americans and early European settlers used the leaves, bark and roots of sassafras trees to treat a variety of ailments and to create spices for food and drinks. At 0.17 mi., the path crosses the burbling stream fed by Cold Spring on the right.

43-1 (34.7469, -86.5293) (0.2 mi.) At the T junction, continue the loop by turning left and traveling west. To leave the loop and explore the rest of the Cold Spring Trail, go right and travel east.

Cold Spring Loop (Waypoint 43 to Waypoint 43-1 and back)

When you continue on the loop, you'll pass a yellow buckeye tree and red oak tree before reaching a Christmas fern plant at 0.3 mi. The plant gets its name from the fact that it stays green through the holiday season and has traditionally been used as a decoration. Next on the loop tour is the tulip poplar, which can live for more than 200 years.

At 0.4 mi., mayapple plants line the trail, along with a chestnut oak. At 0.48 mi., keep an eye out for a spicebush. When you crush the leaves and stems of this plant, it creates a citrusy aroma. Not far ahead you'll pass a shagbark hickory, with its rough, peeling bark. Then the route becomes steep and passes a white oak at about 0.5 mi. Continue uphill for another 138 ft. to return to the trailhead at Waypoint 43.

Cold Spring Trail East of Loop (Waypoint 43-1 to 43-5)

From Waypoint 43-1, turn right and head east. The path soon leaves the Land Trust property and enters Monte Sano State Park. (A sign says "Leaving Monte Sano State Park" on the opposite, uphill side.)

The trail parallels the closed section of Bankhead Parkway, which is visible below and to the left. The Cold Spring Trail rises gradually and occasionally runs level.

43-2 (34.7463, -86.5240) (0.5 mi. from trailhead) At the Y junction, there's a sign with an arrow pointing left for the Mountain Mist Trail, which descends to Bankhead Parkway and continues to the northeast.

The sign indicates this is the shortest route back to park roads and facilities. To continue on the Cold Spring Trail, take the right side of the Y and head east. Walk another 100 ft. to reach Waypoint 43-3.

43-3 (34.7463, -86.5235) (0.6 mi. from trailhead) To the left is a trail that connects to Bankhead Parkway. Continue straight to follow the Cold Spring Trail.

43-4 (34.74689, -86.52055) (0.76 mi. from trailhead) A path on the left drops gradually for 65 ft. to meet Bankhead Parkway. Go straight to continue on the Cold Spring Trail.

At 0.8 mi. from the trailhead, the path becomes much steeper. The climbing gets even more difficult for the next 300 ft., but you can catch your breath at a more level spot at 0.9 mi. When you

Mature hardwoods tower over the Cold Spring Trail.

can breathe again, continue climbing another 315 ft. to reach the end of the trail at Waypoint 43-5.

43-5 (34.7475, -86.5176) (0.96 mi. from the trailhead) Just below the top of the bluff, the Cold Spring Trail ends at the junction with the North Plateau Loop Trail, which is marked with blue blazes. From this vantage point, there are nice views of the valley below stretching from the northwest to the north. Retrace your steps to return to the trailhead.

Trail Facts

Water Source for Early Settlers: Cold Spring was an important water source for early settlers in the 1880s like the Martin family, whose home was on the mountain plateau where water is scarce. Any time they needed water, they had to walk down to the spring.

Historic Toll Road: The eastern section of the Cold Spring Trail, where it rises to meet the North Plateau Loop, was originally part of a toll road built in 1859. Two brothers built the road to ferry supplies to people living on top of Monte Sano. They allowed other people to use their road for a fee, ranging from a penny to 5 cents, depending on whether you were walking, riding a horse, or pulling a wagon.

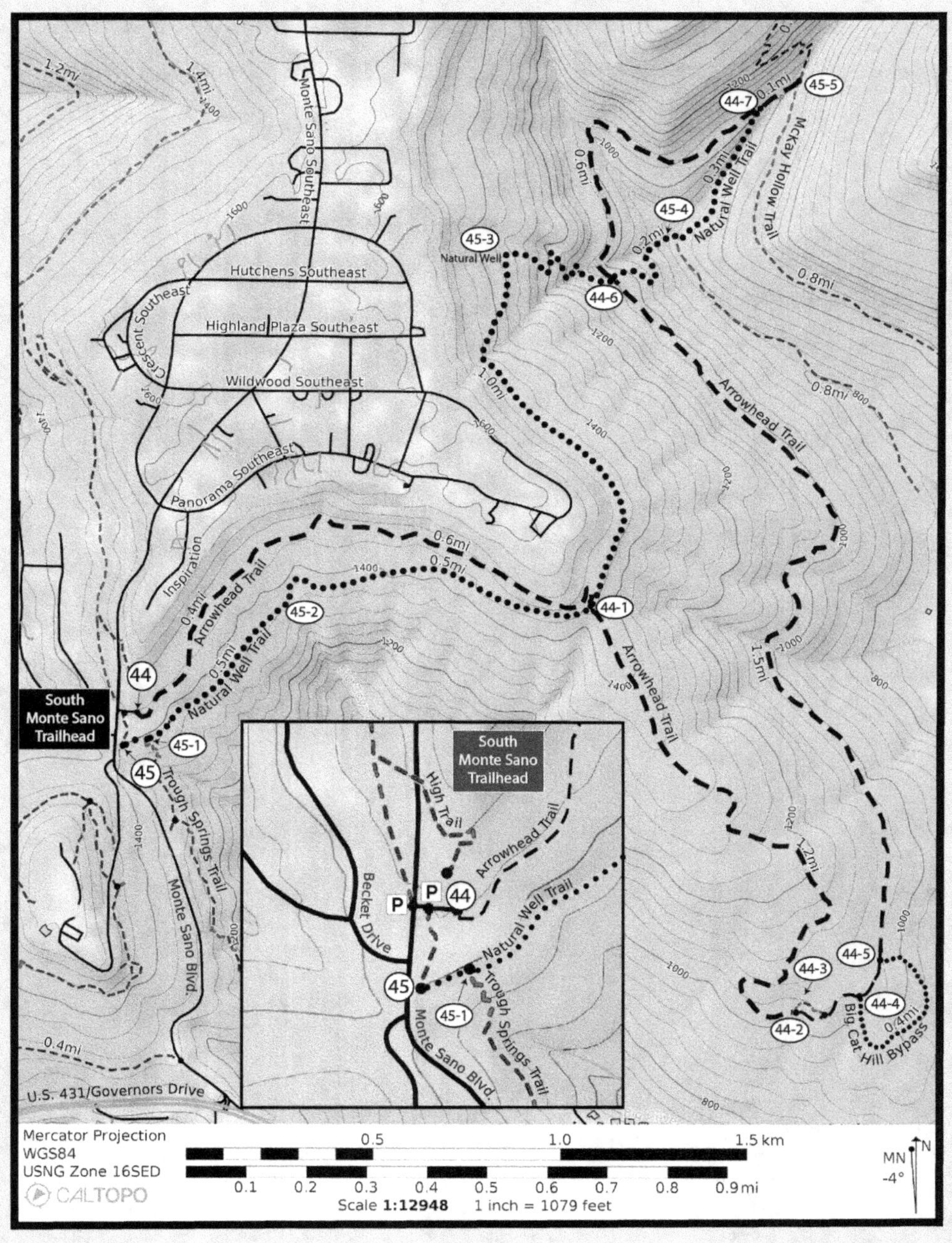

SECTION 2:
Arrowhead Trail, Big Cat Hill Bypass
and Natural Well Trail
1.2mi
1.4mi
Monte Sano Southeast
44-7
45-5
0.1mi
McKay Hollow Trail
0.6mi
45-4
Natural Well Trail
0.3mi
45-3
Natural Well
0.2mi
Hutchens Southeast
44-6
0.8mi
Crescent Southeast
Highland Plaza Southeast
1200
0.8mi
800
Wildwood Southeast
Arrowhead Trail
1.0mi
Panorama Southeast
0.6mi
0.5mi
Inspiration
Arrowhead Trail
45-2
44-1
Arrowhead Trail
0.4mi
0.5mi
Natural Well Trail
1.5mi
44
South
Monte Sano
Trailhead
45-1
45
Trough Springs Trail
Monte Sano Blvd.
High Trail
South
Monte Sano
Trailhead
Becket Drive
Arrowhead Trail
P P 44
Natural Well Trail
45
Trough Springs Trail
45-1
1.2mi
44-5
44-3
Monte Sano Blvd.
44-4
44-2
0.4mi
0.4mi
Big Cat Hill Bypass
800
U.S. 431/Governors Drive
Mercator Projection
WGS84
USNG Zone 16SED
CALTOPO
0.5   1.0   1.5 km
MN   N
-4°
0.1 0.2 0.3 0.4 0.5 0.6 0.7 0.8 0.9mi
Scale 1:12948   1 inch = 1079 feet

44. Arrowhead Trail and Big Cat Hill Bypass

Jonesing for an all-day trek? The Arrowhead Trail measures 5.5 mi. one way, making it one of the longest trails on Monte Sano Mountain. The trail lies within the boundaries of Monte Sano State Park, but it begins at the Land Trust South Monte Sano Trailhead. From the trailhead parking lot, the path heads east to McKay Hollow, exploring one of the mountain's most remote areas. For the most part, the terrain isn't especially challenging. Just make sure you're properly prepared if you set out to hike the whole thing. Allow ample time and carry plenty of water, because the hike takes 2 to 3 hours (one way). When you've hiked a little more than 0.2 mi., you'll reach the Big Cat Hill Bypass, a brief, 0.3-mi. detour that traverses a beautiful stretch of open forest with mature hardwoods. If you take this path, you'll face a short, steep climb to reconnect with the Arrrowhead Trail, but it's worth the effort. **Returning to the Trailhead:** Keep in mind that the Arrowhead Trail ends near the McKay Hollow Trail in the state park. Consider leaving a car at the South Monte Sano Trailhead and another one in the state park so you can shuttle back, rather than retracing your steps. If you do this, be aware that you'll travel 0.1 mi. on the Natural Well Trail and 0.6 mi. on the McKay Hollow Trail to reach the park picnic area, and this includes a steep climb. But negotiating this 0.7-mi. stretch is much quicker than retracing your steps for 5.5 mi.

Distance: 4.6 mi.
Hiking Time: 3 to 4 hours
Elevation Gain/Loss: +626 ft., -1,058 ft.
Hiking Difficulty: Moderate to strenuous
Location: Land Trust of North Alabama Monte Sano Nature Preserve, South Monte Sano Trailhead, 1970 Monte Sano Blvd. SE, Huntsville, AL 35801
Fees: At the South Monte Sano Trailhead, there is a box for donations that benefit the Land Trust of North Alabama.
Facilities: There are no facilities and no sources of potable water

at the trailhead.

Driving Directions: From the intersection of California Street and Governors Drive, head southeast on Governors Dr. for 2.6 mi. Turn left onto Monte Sano Boulevard and head up the mountain. Travel 0.8 mi. and turn right into the gravel parking area for the South Monte Sano Trailhead. If parking isn't available, you can park on the opposite (west) side of Monte Sano Blvd.

Highlights

Remote Woods: As the Arrowhead Trail heads east, it moves farther into remote woods and drops deeper into McKay Hollow. When you've walked 4 mi., you're in one of the most secluded pockets of Monte Sano. If it's rained recently, take a side trip and follow the Natural Well Trail to the floor of the hollow. If you're searching for a wilderness experience in Huntsville, you'll find it where two large creeks converge and the sound of rushing water floods the ravine.

The Real Trough Springs? Beginning at the South Monte Sano Trailhead, the Trough Springs Trail heads south and reaches a spring after a little more than a mile. But some veteran Monte Sano hikers say that this seep is not the real Trough Springs. The spring with an actual cement trough is near the 2-mi. mark on the Arrowhead Trail. There, you'll see a side trail marked, "To Historical Cistern." This path climbs to a spring that flows into a shallow, rectangular trough made of cement. It's believed that this trough was built to hold water for horses and other livestock. In the 1800s, this section of the Arrowhead Trail was part of an old road that came from Guntersville. Travelers would stop at the trough so their animals could drink.

The historical cistern near the Arrowhead Trail likely held water for horses and other livestock.

Civil War History: In May of 1865, the Rev. Milus E. "Bushwhacker" Johnston surrendered to Union troops on Monte Sano Mountain. According to some historians, it took place at the site of the cement trough near the Arrowhead Trail. Before the Civil War, Johnston worked as a Methodist minister, traveling a circuit through the South. Johnston initially intended to stay out of the war. But in 1863, Union troops burned the farm of Johnston's in-laws, some of whom were members of the Confederate Army. Suspecting that Johnston was a Confederate sympathizer, they tried to arrest the reverend, but he escaped. Fed up with the actions of the Union troops, Johnston joined the Confederate Army. In 1863, Union officials sought to arrest Johnston on the suspicion that he was a spy for the Confederacy and part of a group that waged guerrilla war against the Union Army. Johnston was labeled a "bushwhacker," a term for unofficial fighters who used unconventional tactics. The federal troops put a $5,000 bounty on Johnston, and many Union soldiers wanted him hanged. While he eventually surrendered and was put in jail, he survived the war. For more on Bushwhacker Johnston, see page 145.

Waypoint/Mile

Trailhead (Waypoint 44) (34.7213, -86.5372) At the east side of the parking area, enter the gravel path a few yards to the left of the information kiosk. A few feet down the trail, look to the right near the ground to see a diamond-shaped Arrowhead Trail marker. As you continue, follow the teal blazes. The path is generally level, though you'll encounter sections that are really rocky, so be prepared for this if you plan to run this trail.

44-1 (34.7240, -86.5238) (1 mi.) The Arrowhead Trail meets the Natural Well Trail, which is very wide and level. Turn right, travel 58 ft., and then turn left onto the Arrowhead Trail, which descends the ridge heading southeast. You'll soon pass through a cedar grove and continue winding downward through a boulder-strewn forest.

44-2 (34.7139, -86.5179) (2.1 mi.) A sign beside the trail says, "Bike Route." The Arrowhead Trail continues straight, heading northeast, and crosses a stream. At this junction, a trail intersects on the left and a sign says, "To Historical Cistern." This path goes to the cement trough that is believed to be the real Trough Springs and the spot where Bushwhacker Johnston surrendered. Travel north on this path 180 ft. to reach the trough.

44-3 (34.7142, -86.5176) (180 ft.) You reach the trough, or cistern. From here, continue east for 256 ft. to rejoin the Arrowhead Trail.

44-4 (34.7143, -86.5159) (2.2 mi.) At the Y junction, the Arrowhead Trail bears left, while the Big Cat Hill Bypass goes to the right and heads south.

The Big Cat Hill Bypass (0.3 mi.)

The Big Cat Hill Bypass drops gradually through open hardwood forest for about 0.2 mi. It turns to the northeast and cuts across a finger of land where the woods are fantastic. Large, mature hardwoods tower over a broad, clear forest floor, and a distant ridge dominates the horizon ahead. Behind you, high terrain blocks any noise from civilization, making this a quiet and peaceful pocket of woods. The trail swings to the north and begins climbing for another 0.1 mi., ending with a brief steep climb.

44-5 (34.7153, -86.5153) (2.58 mi.) The Big Cat Bypass Trail intersects the Arrowhead Trail. To continue on the Arrowhead Trail, travel north on a fairly level path. The trail then begins a long run north, rising and falling gently in a forest that transitions between open hardwood and dense stretches with sweet gum trees and woods draped in thick vines.

44-6 (34.7321, -86.5232) (4.04 mi.) The Arrowhead Trail crosses the Natural Well Trail, which goes left (southwest) and right (north). The Arrowhead Trail goes straight, heading northwest, marked with teal blazes.

44-7 (34.7363, -86.5188) (4.6 mi.) The Arrowhead Trail drops down to end at the junction with the Natural Well Trail, which runs level to the left (north) and descends to the right (southwest). To continue to the state park picnic area, go straight to take the Natural Well Trail for 0.1 mi. Then turn left onto the McKay Hollow Trail and begin a 0.6-mi. climb to the park picnic area.

Trail Facts

Historical Cistern: As mentioned above, the cistern sat along an old road from Guntersville, and it was a popular place for travelers to stop. Some people say it's likely that a store was also located near the spring. One indicator of this is the collection of daffodils that grow on the slope above the trough. Back in the 1800s, people would plant these flowers around homes or businesses. Because daffodils are not a native species, their presence indicates that a structure of some kind once occupied the land.

45. Natural Well Trail

This hike begins with an easy walk to one of Monte Sano's most notable curiosities, the Natural Well. As is the case with the Arrowhead Trail, the Natural Well Trail lies within the Monte Sano State Park boundaries, but it begins at the Land Trust South Monte Sano Trailhead. From there, the trail is at times rocky and challenging as it drops to the base of the deep ravine known as McKay Hollow. Because this path can be muddy in spots and traverses rugged terrain, wear supportive and protective footwear with good traction.

The Natural Well Trail intersects the McKay Hollow Trail in the state park. Consider placing one car at the South Monte Sano Trailhead and another at the picnic area parking lot in the state park, so you can shuttle back rather than retracing your steps. Just be aware that you'll travel 0.6 mi. on the McKay Hollow Trail and face a steep climb to reach the park picnic area. However, it's easier to hike this 0.6-mi. stretch than retrace your steps on the Natural Well Trail for more than 3 mi.

Distance: 3.3 mi.
Hiking Time: 1.5 to 2 hours
Elevation Gain/Loss: +343 ft., -761 ft.
Hiking Difficulty: Strenuous
Location: Land Trust of North Alabama Monte Sano Nature Preserve, South Monte Sano Trailhead, 1970 Monte Sano Blvd. SE, Huntsville, AL 35801
Facilities: There are no facilities and no sources of potable water at the trailhead.

Driving Directions: See page 64 and use the directions for the South Monte Sano Trailhead.

Highlights

Natural Well: At 1.7 mi., the trail passes the gaping mouth of a natural pit with a 180-ft. vertical shaft. This deep shaft drops to a slanted rubble slope that continues to the pit floor, which is 245 ft. below the surface. **Warning: When you visit, don't plan on exploring the Natural Well, as it is extremely dangerous and requires expert caving skills and equipment.**

The Natural Well is 245 feet deep and connects to cavern rooms with ceilings 100 feet high.

McKay Hollow: From the highest spot on the Natural Well Trail (about 1,467 ft. of elevation), the trail drops 590 ft. to reach the floor of McKay Hollow. At the base of the ravine, you're greeted with a wild scene as two tumbling streams converge. After a good rain in winter or spring, there's no finer place to be, as the rushing water provides the perfect soundtrack for lunch or an afternoon nap.

Waypoint/Mile

Trailhead (Waypoint 45) (34.7213, -86.5373) When you enter the South Monte Sano Trailhead parking area, the Natural Well Trail begins at the kiosk located to the right, on the south side of the parking area. Facing the kiosk, go to the right and enter the path marked by the sign reading "Trough Springs Trl" and "To Natural Well Trl." As you hike, follow the light purple blazes.

45-1 (34.7206, -86.5369) (620 ft.) At the junction with the wide path, turn left and travel northeast to continue on the Natural Well Trail.

45-2 (34.7239, -86.5327) (0.4 mi.) The Natural Well Trail turns right to leave the wide treadway and descend into a wide drainage. (A purple blaze marks the turn.)

44-1 (34.7239, -86.5238) (1 mi.) The Natural Well Trail meets the Arrowhead Trail, which goes right and descends to the east. The Arrowhead Trail also continues straight and briefly shares a treadway with the Natural Well Trail. Continue straight and travel north. After walking 55 ft., you'll reach a junction where the Arrowhead Trail goes left and ascends gently to the north. At this junction, continue straight to take the Natural Well Trail, which runs level.

45-3 (34.7327, -86.5264) (1.7 mi.) The Natural Well is on the left, with a fence blocking part of the opening. From here, the path goes to the right and descends to the east, quickly becoming steeper and rockier.

44-6 (34.7322, -86.5232) (2.0 mi.) On a plateau, the Natural Well Trail and the Arrowhead Trail intersect. Continue straight and travel north on the Natural Well Trail.

At 2.2 mi., the trail crosses a creek bed. Because the rocks in this drainage are slippery, there's a rope you can use to keep your balance as you cross.

45-4 (34.7332, -86.5214) (2.3 mi.) The trail reaches the base of McKay Hollow and the confluence of streams. From here, travel northeast to continue on the Natural Well Trail and move into a narrow corridor surrounded by steep hillsides.

44-7 (34.7364, -86.5189) (2.6 mi.) The Arrowhead Trail intersects on the left and heads west. Continue straight, traveling northeast on the Natural Well Trail. After another 90 ft., you'll reach Waypoint 45-5.

45-5 (34.7371, -86.5177) (2.6 mi.) The Natural Well Trail ends at the junction with the McKay Hollow Trail. The McKay Hollow Trail offers the most direct route out of the hollow and back to the state park picnic area.

Trail Facts

The Space Walk Trail: The Natural Well Trail is part of a now-defunct path that was known as the Space Walk Trail. Measuring 11 mi., the route stretched from Green Mountain to Monte Sano State Park. In the 1960s, four Boy Scout troops developed the trail by combining several existing paths and blazed it with markers resembling the silhouette of the Gemini spacecraft. Over time, new versions of the Space Walk Trail were developed and blazed with markers shaped like the space shuttle. In later years, portions of the Space Walk Trail disappeared as new homes and roads were developed on Huntsville's mountains. While the Space Walk is no longer a functioning trail, you can still see the shuttle markers along several Monte Sano trails.

The Natural Well: While the pit has a floor 245 ft. down, there are cavernous rooms even beyond this point. According to a brochure on the Space Walk Trail produced by the Tennessee Valley Council of the BSA, "The cave opens into spectacular Cathedral Hall with a 100-foot ceiling. From there the cave narrows, branches and winds through a total length of 1,150 ft. Tapp Dome is another awesome hall with a 100-foot ceiling. Two other domes have ceilings of 70 ft. In one corridor is a 20-ft. waterfall." **Warning: Exploring the Natural Well is extremely dangerous and requires expert caving skills and equipment.**

SECTION 3:
Trough Springs Trail and Bushwhacker Johnston Trail

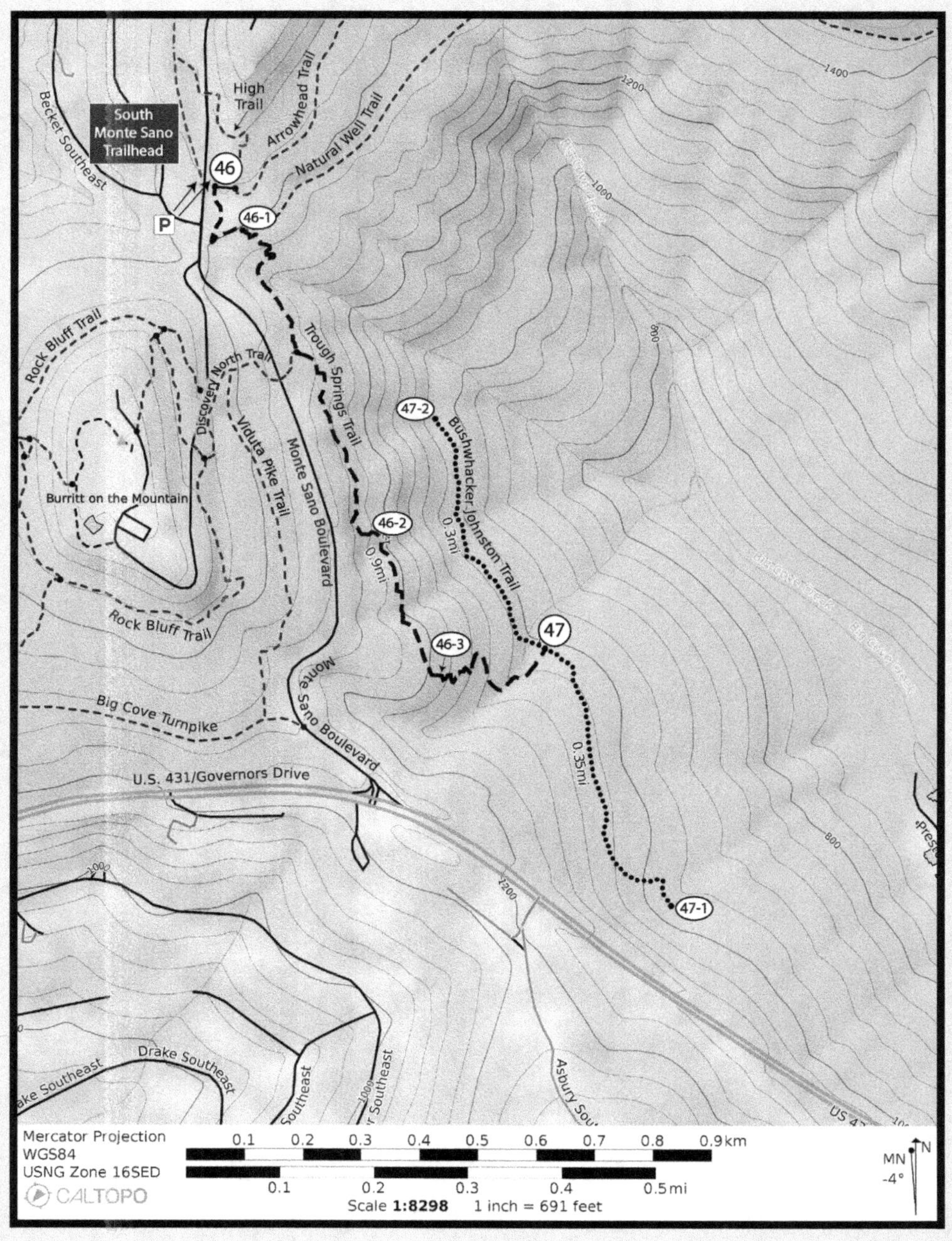

46. Trough Springs Trail

The Trough Springs Trail rollercoasters along a rugged slope and then makes a steep drop into secluded woods. The path intersects with the Bushwhacker Johnston Trail, which leads to a small water source known as Trough Springs.

Distance: 0.9 mi.

Hiking Time: 25 to 30 minutes

Elevation Gain/Loss: +45 ft., -476 ft.

Hiking Difficulty: Moderate to strenuous

Location: Land Trust of North Alabama Monte Sano Nature Preserve, South Monte Sano Trailhead, 1970 Monte Sano Blvd. SE, Huntsville, AL 35801

Facilities: There are no facilities and no sources of potable water at the trailhead.

Driving Directions: See page 64 and use the directions for the South Monte Sano Trailhead.

Highlights

Isolated Forest: The Trough Springs Trail parallels Monte Sano Boulevard for about half a mile, but it then veers east and descends 200 ft. into remote woods. The path meets the Bushwhacker Johnston Trail in an open and airy forest that feels far removed from the city.

Waypoint/Mile

Trailhead (Waypoint 46) (34.7213, -86.5373) The Trough Springs Trail begins at the kiosk on the south side of the South Monte Sano Trailhead parking area. (This kiosk is on the right when you drive into the parking lot.) Walk to the right of the kiosk, and enter the path marked "Trough Springs Trl" and "To Natural Well Trl." The path immediately turns left to run south. Follow the white diamond blazes marked "Trough Springs Trail."

46-1 (34.7206, -86.5370) (612 ft.) At the four-way junction, the Trough Springs Trail intersects the Natural Well Trail. Turn left to walk east, go about 30 ft., and then turn right onto the Trough Springs Trail. You'll begin a moderate to steep descent to the southeast.

At 0.2 mi., you'll probably hear traffic noise as the narrow path crosses a drainage and begins to rollercoaster along the upper part of the slope. At 0.29 mi., the Discovery Trail intersects on the right and climbs toward the road. If you hike this trail in winter, you might want to pause at the 0.34-mi. mark where a bench sits to the left of the trail. From this spot, you get a good view of the high ridge on the opposite side of the deep cove.

46-2 (34.7158, -86.5344) (0.5 mi.) The trail makes a hairpin turn to the north and descends. Keep your eyes peeled here because this turn is hard to see when leaves cover the path.

46-3 (34.7136, -86.5332) (0.7 mi.) You'll reach a bench and see a tree with a Trough Springs Trail diamond blaze. Walk past the tree and then go right to descend to the southeast. The trail is hard to make out here. Ahead, tight switchbacks take you winding down among mature hardwoods on the boulder-strewn slope.

47 (34.7140, -86.5312) (0.9 mi.) The Trough Springs Trail ends at the T junction with the Bushwhacker Johnston Trail.

Trail Facts

Site of Surrender: According to a historical marker at the South Monte Sano Trailhead, the Trough Springs Trail leads to the spring where Lt. Col. "Bushwhacker" Johnston surrendered to Union troops in 1865. The marker indicates that in the 1800s, this spring was a popular watering hole for livestock as people traveled the Big Cove Turnpike.

47. Bushwhacker Johnston Trail

This easy path in remote woods leads to the water source known as Trough Springs. The trail is named for Lt. Col. Milus E. "Bushwhacker" Johnston, who led the 25th Alabama Cavalry Battalion during the Civil War and reportedly surrendered to Union troops at Trough Springs.

Distance: 0.6 mi.

Hiking Time: Trailhead to southern terminus is 10 minutes; trailhead to northern terminus is 10 minutes

Elevation Gain/Loss: Trailhead to southern terminus +55 ft., -86 ft.; trailhead to northern terminus +51 ft., -35 ft.

Hiking Difficulty: Easy

Location: Land Trust of North Alabama Monte Sano Nature Preserve, South Monte Sano Trailhead, 1970 Monte Sano Blvd. SE, Huntsville, AL 35801

Facilities: There are no facilities and no sources of potable water at the trailhead.

Driving Directions: See page 64 and use the directions for the South Monte Sano Trailhead.

Highlights

Rev. Milus E. "Bushwhacker" Johnston, courtesy of David Frost

A Confederate Guerrilla Warrior: The most interesting aspect of this trail is its namesake. On May 11, 1865, Lt. Col. Milus E. "Bushwhacker" Johnston and about 150 Confederate soldiers surrendered to Union Army Col. William Given at Trough Springs. Johnston helped fight a guerrilla war against the Union, serving in Company E of Lemuel Mead's Cavalry Battalion and later leading the 25th Alabama Cavalry. Going behind enemy lines, he helped attack wagon trains and railroads in North Alabama and Tennessee. Before the Civil War, Johnston served as a Methodist minister and traveled a circuit in the Southeast. During the early years of the war, Union troops suspected that Johnston was a spy for the confederacy. In 1863, Union soldiers burned the home of Johnston's father-in-law and tried to capture Johnston, but he escaped. Johnston supposedly swam across the Tennessee River to join the Confederate Army and was sworn into service in 1864.

Waypoint/Mile

Trailhead (Waypoint 47) (34.7140, -86.5312) To reach the Bushwhacker Johnston Trail, begin at the South Monte Sano Trailhead. Follow the Trough Springs Trail for 0.9 mi. to where it intersects with the Bushwhacker Johnston Trail.

Southern Section (Waypoint 47 to Waypoint 47-1)

From the trailhead at Waypoint 47, turn right and travel southeast, following the blazes marked "Bushwhacker Johnston Trail." The leaf-covered path descends gradually and widens. As you approach the spring, the path runs along the base of a steep slope.

47-1 (34.7099, -86.5289) (0.35 mi. from Waypoint 47) The trail reaches a bench at Trough Springs, where you will likely find a trickle of water feeding a shallow, rocky stream. Honestly, it's not much to look at. But in the winter, when the forest is clear and the sun brightens the woods, you can appreciate being far away from most of the trail traffic on this side of the mountain. This marks the end of the trail, and from here you can retrace your steps to return to the trailhead. Note that you might see pathways that continue to the southeast. Just be aware that these paths gradually fade and become unrecognizable after another mile or so.

Northern Section (Waypoint 47 to Waypoint 47-2)

From the trailhead at Waypoint 47, turn left and begin climbing as you head northwest. While the path is pretty wide, it can be difficult to follow if it's covered in leaves, so keep an eye out for the diamond-shaped blazes marked "Bushwhacker Johnston Trail." After the trail crosses a small drainage, it traverses terrain that's more level. The trail rises and falls easily in a forest of widely spaced hardwoods and little underbrush. As you parallel a high, rocky bluff, you leave behind the traffic noise from Monte Sano Boulevard and enter a very quiet and peaceful pocket of woods.

47-2 (34.7176, -86.5333) (0.3 mi. from Waypoint 47) The trail ends and suddenly disappears. From this point, retrace your steps to return to the trailhead.

Trail Facts

The "Bushwhacker" Nickname: Union soldiers didn't consider guerrilla fighters like Johnston to be legitimate troops. Because they used unconventional tactics, Union troops referred to them derisively as "bushwhackers" (meaning "ambushers").

SECTION 4:
Bankhead Parkway

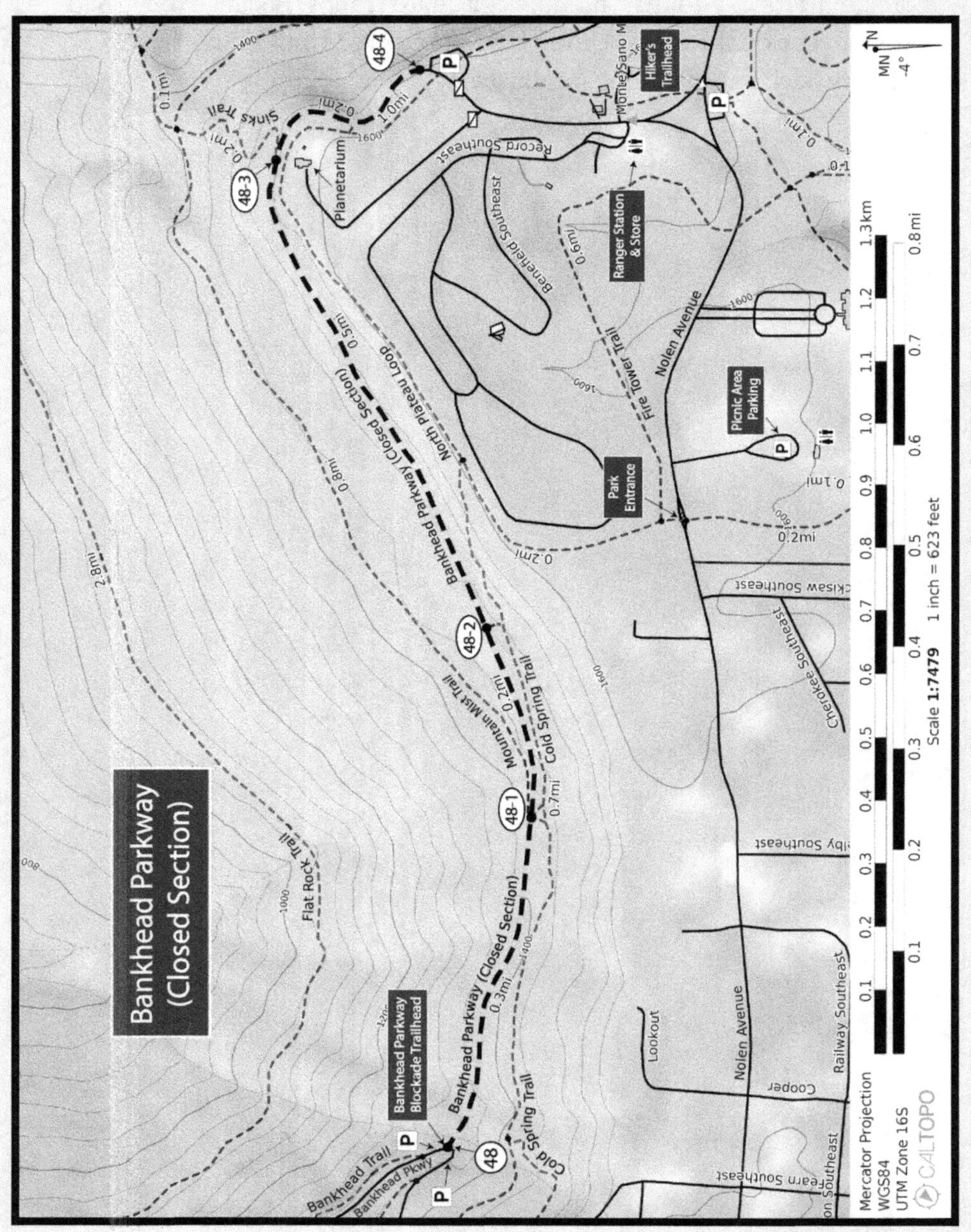

48. Bankhead Parkway
(Closed Section Beginning at the Blockade)

Walk, run, take the dogs for a stroll, or ride bikes on this closed section of Bankhead Parkway. Beginning at a hairpin curve, the asphalt road climbs gradually to an overlook in Monte Sano State Park. In the late 1980s, the city tried several times to repair this stretch of road when erosion caused sections to crumble and collapse. In the early 1990s, the road was closed permanently. Now, it serves as a spacious, safe and easily accessible path through a mature hardwood forest. Plus, the road provides access to several surrounding trails and serves as an alternate way to enter Monte Sano State Park.

Distance: 1.2 mi.

Hiking Time: 30 to 40 minutes

Elevation Gain/Loss: +258 ft., -13 ft.

Hiking Difficulty: Easy

Location: Monte Sano Mountain, Bankhead Parkway, Huntsville, AL 35801

Fees: There is an honor system pay box at the trailhead. Kids 12 years old and adults, $5; seniors, $2; kids 4 to 11 years old, $2; kids 3 years old and under, free.

Facilities: There are no facilities and no sources of potable water at the trailhead.

Driving Directions: See page 65 in Chapter 2 and use directions for the Bankhead Parkway Blockade Trailhead.

Highlights

An Excellent Exercise Path: A wide range of people like to exercise on this road because it's closed to traffic, the surface is mostly clear of debris, and the grade is consistent, with no steep sections. Plus, the surrounding trees provide plenty of shade.

Monte Sano State Park Overlook: Once you reach the top of the road, you're rewarded with beautiful views at an overlook in the state park. From the long, low stone wall at the overlook, a vast forested landscape unfolds before you. In the foreground, the steep slope drops into a long, narrow cut known as the Sinks. Looking left across the forested cut, you see Logan Point rising dramatically like a swollen knot. To its right, a long saddle sweeps up to meet a prominent ridge. Beyond the shoulder of the ridge, distant hills and mountains stack up like waves, shifting from gray to pale blue as your gaze drifts toward the horizon.

Waypoint/Mile

Trailhead (Waypoint 48) (34.74763, -86.52947) From your parking space along Bankhead Parkway, walk toward the cement barrier at the sharp curve. Go beyond the barrier and follow the asphalt road, climbing gradually to the southeast.

The road is immediately shaded by thick tree canopy. To the left is a clear view of the open forest, and in winter the distant Chase Valley is visible. On the right, the road is bordered by moss-covered stones and a steep, forested slope.

48-1 (34.74640, -86.52373) (0.3 mi.) At the trail junction, look left to see the Mountain Mist Trail, which runs parallel to the road. On the right, the Cold Spring Trail intersects and heads southwest and southeast. Just before this junction, a metal sign on the right indicates whether the trails are open to bikes. (Bikers are discouraged from using muddy trails after periods of rain to prevent trail damage.)

The scenery grows more impressive as a towering oak tree leans over the trail. The mature hardwood forest is also home to high-rise hickories and stout tulip poplars. Dangling from the boughs of tall trees are dark vines so thick they look like battleship rigging.

48-2 (34.74707, -86.52050) (0.5 mi.) On the right, a narrow path climbs slightly for 65 ft. to meet the Cold Spring Trail.

At 0.75 mi., you'll see on the left a 60-ft. section of road that has slumped—clear evidence of the erosion that forced this part of Bankhead to close. After walking another 0.1 mi., you'll notice you've really gained elevation. On the left, the tops of trees are now just above eye level. Not far ahead, small breaks in the trees offer lofty views of the valley to the north.

48-3 (34.75000, -86.51225) (1 mi.) On the left, the Sinks Trail dives down the slope.

Not far beyond 1 mi., Logan Point comes into view on the left. As you continue around a curve and bend to the south, you're rewarded with even better views of the point as well as its neighboring saddle and ridge. At 1.1 mi., more evidence of road damage appears. On the left shoulder, a chunk of road is missing, forming a crescent-shaped gap.

48-4 (34.74809, -86.51069) (1.2 mi.) The closed section of road ends at an overlook in Monte Sano State Park.

Trail Facts

The "Bankhead" Name: Bankhead Parkway is named for William Brockman Bankhead, who came to Huntsville in 1895 to practice law. In 1916, he was elected to the U.S. House of Representatives, and he eventually served as Speaker of the House. He was also the father of famed actress Tallulah Bankhead, who was born in Huntsville in 1903 (*Source: Why Is It Named That? Stories Behind the Names of 250 Places in Madison County and Huntsville, Alabama.*)

The closed section of Bankhead Parkway on Monte Sano Mountain

SECTION 5:
Warpath Ridge Trail and Red Lizard Trail

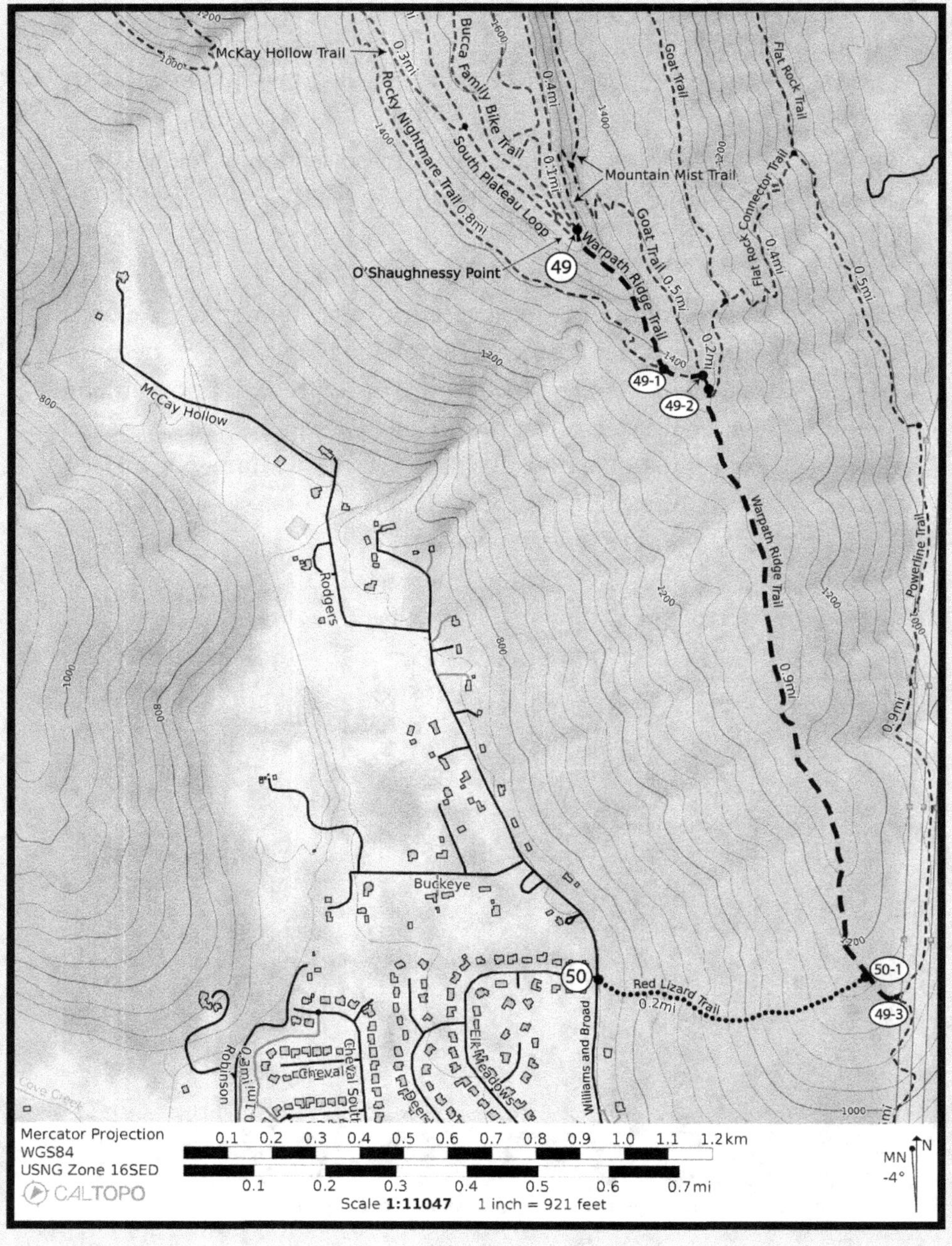

49. Warpath Ridge Trail

The Warpath Ridge Trail starts at O'Shaughnessy Point, one of the most popular spots on Monte Sano, and then dives down to explore the mountain's remote southern slope. Allow plenty of time for this hike. If you start at the state park Hiker's Trailhead on Bankhead Parkway, you'll walk more than a mile to reach the beginning of the Warpath Ridge Trail. Also, there is no road access at the southern end of the trail (and no parking for the adjoining Red Lizard Trail), so this is an out-and-back hike that will take at least a couple of hours.

Distance: 1.3 mi.

Hiking Time: 30 to 40 minutes

Elevation Gain/Loss: +33 ft., -473 ft.

Hiking Difficulty: Moderate

Location: Monte Sano State Park, 5105 Nolen Ave., Huntsville, AL 35801. (256) 534-3757

Fees: Kids 12 years old and adults, $5; seniors, $2; kids 4 to 11 years old, $2; kids 3 years old and under, free.

Facilities: At the Monte Sano State Park Hiker's Trailhead there are no facilities and no sources of potable water.

Driving Directions: See pages 2-3 and use the directions for the Monte Sano State Park entrance and the Hiker's Trailhead.

Highlights

O'Shaughnessy Point: Offering one of the best views on Monte Sano, this rock outcrop lies along the South Plateau Loop Trail, immediately west of the Warpath Ridge Trail. The bluff offers a sweeping view of McKay Hollow as well as Monte Sano's western ridge and the rural countryside to the south.

Ridge Walk: The Warpath Ridge Trail immediately wows hikers by taking them across the rugged spine of a ridge. As the terrain falls away steeply on each side of the path, you can look to the right for a bird's-eye view of McKay Hollow. While the path quickly dives away from the top of the ridge, this first section makes quite an impression and hints that you're setting off into the wilder parts of the mountain.

Waypoint/Mile

Trailhead (Waypoint 49) (34.7254, -86.5021) From the Hiker's Trailhead in the state park, there are several ways to reach the Warpath Ridge Trail. For one of the most direct routes, take the South Plateau Loop Trail to the Fire Tower Trail. Go left onto the Fire Tower Trail, travel south 0.8 mi., and then bear right to take the South Plateau Loop Trail once again. Finally, go 0.6 mi. to the junction with the Warpath Ridge Trail. Enter the Warpath Ridge Trail and travel southeast, crossing the crest of the ridge on the narrow path marked with orange blazes.

The trail runs level across the narrow ridge, affording views of McKay Hollow. In the distance, you'll see Highway 431 and Hampton Cove. After 150 ft., a sign cautions that a steep drop is ahead. After about another 60 ft., you begin a steep descent off the ridge, but it only lasts for about 150 ft. Soon, you're descending gradually with good views of distant peaks to the southwest. When you've gone about 0.2 mi., you dip low enough that the nice views disappear.

49-1 (34.7228, -86.4999) (0.2 mi.) The Rocky Nightmare Trail intersects on the right and descends gradually to the west. Continue straight and take the level Warpath Ridge Trail, heading southeast.

49-2 (34.7226, -86.4992) (0.3 mi.) At the Y junction, the level path to the left stretches 75 ft. to meet the Goat Trail. To continue on the Warpath

Descending the Warpath Ridge Trail on Monte Sano Mountain

Ridge Trail, take the right side of the Y and head south, descending gradually in a corridor of cedars.

The Warpath Ridge Trail continues to move down a finger of land and enters a short stretch of forest that feels very old. Downed trees are bone white and stripped of their bark, while bright-green moss hugs the trees and blankets pale gray boulders scattered about the area. Farther on, the woods are draped in thick twisted vines.

At 1.2 mi., the path winds through flat-topped boulders, and a powerline corridor comes into view on your left.

50-1 (34.7100, -86.4948) (1.2 mi.) The Red Lizard Trail intersects on the right and goes west through a field of moss-covered boulders. The Warpath Ridge Trail continues south for about 260 ft.

49-3 (34.7095, -86.4942) (1.3 mi.) The Warpath Ridge Trail ends at the powerline corridor. Some maps will show the Flat Rock Trail following the powerline break. But be aware that the path can be difficult to follow, and in places you'll wade through high brambles. I recommend that you turn around at 49-3 and retrace your steps.

Trail Facts

Indians on the Warpath? So, why is it named the Warpath Trail? Did Native Americans once follow this route to launch an attack on their enemies? No, not at all. Several Native American tribes hunted on the land around Huntsville, and they shared the area peacefully. The land wasn't owned by any one tribe, and there were no clashes, or any reason to be on the warpath. But the Boy Scouts developed the trail, and they often used terms related to Native Americans when naming them.

50. Red Lizard Trail

This steep path begins alongside a residential road and climbs a rocky slope to meet the Warpath Ridge Trail. While the trail technically begins beside Williams and Broad Drive, many people access it by traveling from Monte Sano State Park on the Warpath Ridge Trail. When you explore this path, be aware that there is no designated parking in the neighborhood near the trailhead.

Distance: 0.45 mi.
Hiking Time: 20 to 30 minutes
Elevation Gain/Loss: +453 ft., -3 ft.
Hiking Difficulty: Strenuous
Location: Williams and Broad Drive in the neighborhood near Dug Hill Road, off U.S. 431. **Note that this is a private trail that is not entirely within the property of Monte Sano State Park or the Land Trust of North Alabama. But I've included it in this section because of its proximity to the Warpath Ridge Trail.
Fees: There is no fee to use this trail.
Facilities: There are no facilities or water sources at the trailhead.
Driving Directions: From the junction of U.S. 431 and Dug Hill Road, travel northeast on Dug Hill Rd., going toward Legacy Preserve Drive. Travel 1.2 mi. on Dug Hill Rd., and then turn left onto Williams and Broad Drive. Go 0.4 mi. and look for the trailhead on the right, just before Elk Meadows Drive.

Highlights

A Heart-Pumping Hike: The Red Lizard Trail gains nearly 500 ft. in less than half a mile, making it one of the steepest trails on the mountain. If you're tired of your workout routine and need an alternate way to get your heart pumping, do a lap up and down this trail. Or, if you're hiking the Warpath Ridge Trail and want an added challenge, descend the Red Lizard Trail and climb back up, adding nearly a mile to your trek.

Waypoint/Mile

Trailhead (Waypoint 50) (34.7099, -86.5014) The Red Lizard Trail begins 37 ft. east of Williams and Broad Drive. From the road, you'll head east, crossing a ditch to reach the beginning of the path. Ascend the drainage to the right of a tree near the trailhead.

Immediately, you begin to climb a slope covered in hardwood trees and cedars. As the path winds among boulders, it ranges from moderately steep to very steep. After walking about 0.2 mi., you can take a breather on a narrow plateau. Enjoy the forgiving terrain here, because in 60 ft.

you'll begin another steep ascent through more jumbles of large rocks.

A little beyond 0.4 mi., the path reaches the top of the ridge and runs level among mossy boulders.

50-1 (34.7100, -86.4948) (0.3 mi.) The Red Lizard Trail ends at the junction with the Warpath Ridge Trail.

Trail Facts

Tree Lizards: You won't see a unique, red-colored species of lizard darting along this path. You might, however, spy the red, lizard-shaped tree markings for which the trail is named.

Burritt on the Mountain

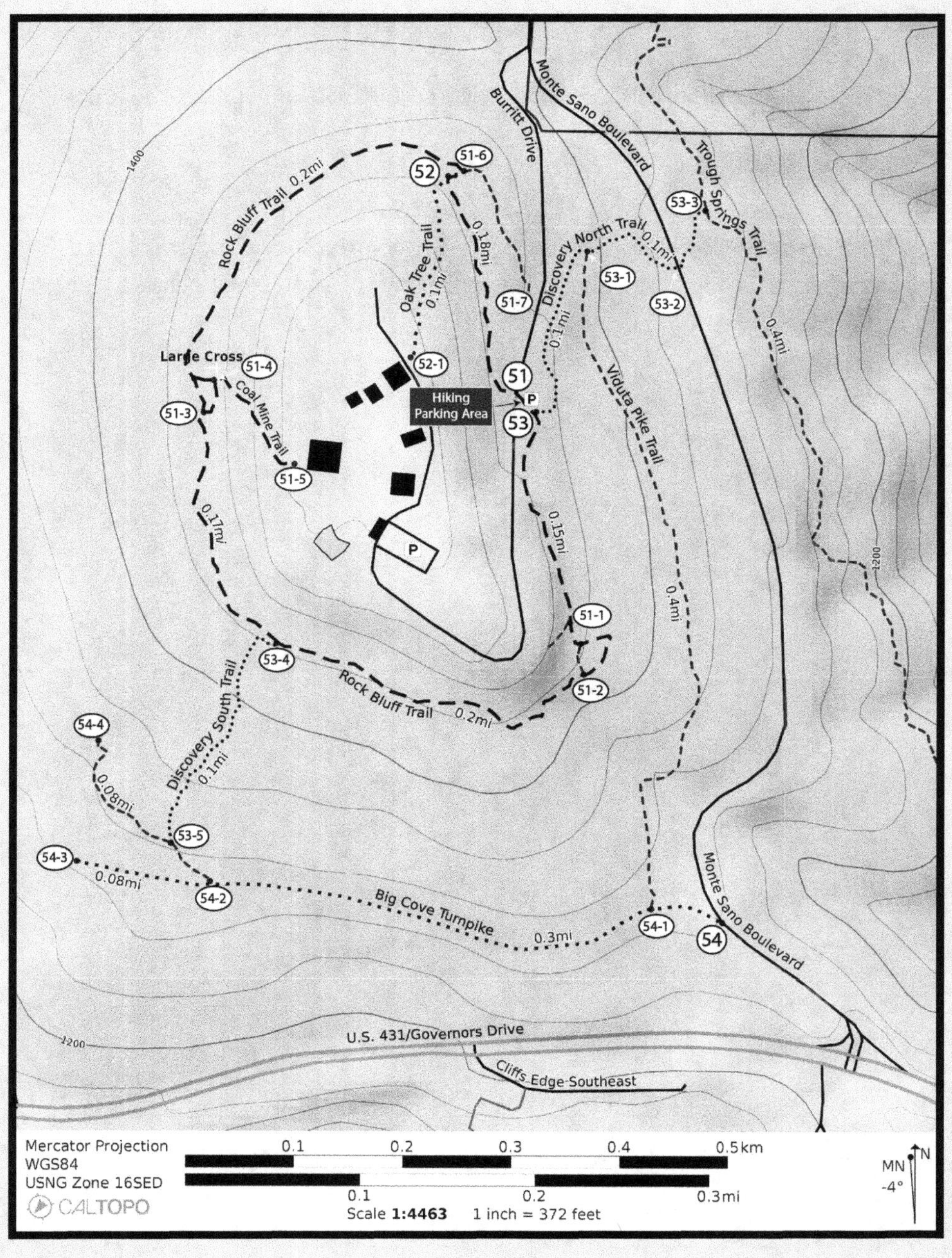

CHAPTER 4

Burritt on the Mountain

In 1934, physician William Henry Burritt built an eccentric mansion on Round Top Mountain, a plateau that connects to Monte Sano Mountain in Huntsville. He had become wealthy after years of working in farming, logging, mining and rubber production. Burritt constructed his mansion on 167 acres of land, where he spent his retirement years farming and raising goats. In 1955, when Burritt died, the house and property were donated to the city to be transformed into a museum. Today, Burritt on the Mountain is a unique destination with an outdoor museum, education programs for kids and adults, and hiking trails.

Burritt on the Mountain's trails measure a little more than two miles and include easy strolls, moderate treks, and short but steep hikes near the summit. On the low flanks of Round Top, the Big Cove Turnpike Trail takes you down a wide, level treadway that follows an old wagon road. Higher up, the rugged Discovery Trail scrambles up and down the forested mountainside. Probably the most popular path is the Rock Bluff Trail, which circles the mountain and includes interpretive signs to teach kids about Round Top's animals, plants, geology and geography.

Another popular spot is the mountain summit, where an overlook provides a panoramic view of Huntsville that you shouldn't miss. Also, a path links the summit to a massive, 74-foot-tall cross that sits high on a western slope.

As you plan your outing to hike Burritt's trails, consider participating in the many educational and recreational programs offered throughout the year. In October, Burritt offers Nature Rangers Camps for kids in kindergarten through fifth grade. In the heart of the Burritt complex, kids can visit the McCurdy Barnyard to see authentic farm animals and learn about their purpose on a farm. As part of the Alabama Birding Trails, Burritt is also a great place to join Audubon-led hikes. Plus, you can visit the Burritt mansion and explore several historic structures where living history interpreters provide insights on 19th-century farming.

General Information

Location: 3101 Burritt Dr., Huntsville, AL 35801

Hours: Trails are open during the same hours as the park. Winter (Nov.-March) hours: Tues.-Sat., 10 a.m.-4 p.m.; Sun., 12 p.m.-4 p.m. Summer (April-Oct.) hours: Tues.-Sun., 9 a.m.-5 p.m. Open Memorial Day, Fourth of July and Labor Day; closed Mondays, Thanksgiving Day, Christmas Day and New Year's Day.

Primary trail activities allowed: Hiking

Pets: Leashed pets allowed on trails.

Fees: There are no parking fees and no fees to use the trails.

Facilities: There are no facilities or water sources at the hiking parking lot on Burritt Drive. Restrooms, water fountains, snacks and beverages are available in the Welcome Center.

Information: (256) 536-2882; burrittonthemountain.com

Driving Directions: From the intersection of U.S. 231/431 (Memorial Parkway) and Governors Drive, travel east on Governors Dr. for 3.6 mi. Then turn left onto Monte Sano Boulevard. Travel 0.7 mi., and then turn left onto Burritt Drive. Follow Burritt Dr. for 0.2 mi. to reach the Burritt hiking parking area, on the left. Or travel 0.5 mi. on Burritt Dr. to reach the main parking area for Burritt on the Mountain.

Rock Bluff Trail, Oak Tree Trail, Discovery Trail and Big Cove Turnpike Trail

51. Rock Bluff Trail

A hike on the Rock Bluff Trail is the perfect way to teach children about the local environment in a fun and engaging way. Kids will have no problem navigating this flat, paved path. Along the way, they'll encounter interpretive signs that explain interesting natural features near the path. Also, you can travel the Rock Bluff Trail to reach the massive Burritt cross as well as the summit of the mountain, which offers impressive views.

Distance: Main trail, 0.9 mi.; Waypoint 55-5 to Waypoint 55-7 (the Burritt summit), 0.1 mi.

Hiking Time: 25 to 30 minutes with no stops, but allow an hour or so to give kids time to explore.

Elevation Gain/Loss: Main trail +134 ft., -134 ft.; Waypoint 55-5 to Waypoint 55-7 (the Burritt summit) +106 ft., -1 ft.

Hiking Difficulty: Main trail, easy; Waypoint 55-5 to Waypoint 55-7 (the Burritt summit), moderate to strenuous

Location: Burritt on the Mountain, 3101 Burritt Dr. SE, Huntsville, AL 35801

Fees, Facilities & Driving Directions: See page 160.

Highlights

A Fun Learning Experience for Kids: There's no better way to learn about the natural world than to experience it firsthand. While interpretive signs along the path provide valuable information, kids also interact with the environment (and get some exercise!) as they learn about nature. They can peer into a cave, touch the bark of a tree that resembles animal skin, and identify the tracks of animals that inhabit the forest.

Burritt Summit: The 3,000-sq.-ft. overlook atop Burritt provides a fantastic panoramic view of Huntsville. From the overlook and the lawn of the Burritt property, you can see for miles to the southwest. If you have a chance, attend one of the many concerts held on the Burritt summit, and enjoy great music with the valley serving as a sublime backdrop. Also, Burritt hosts Cocktails at The View every Wednesday from 5-8 p.m. April through October.

Burritt Cross: The massive cross on the high flank of Monte Sano is literally one of the biggest curiosities in Huntsville. Built in 1963, the concrete cross is 74 ft. tall with a cross beam measuring 31 ft. According to a report in the *Huntsville Times*, several groups of Christians across the city worked together to construct the cross and mark Huntsville as a city devoted to the "Prince of Peace."

Waypoint/Mile

Trailhead (Waypoint 51) (34.7171, -86.5378) The Rock Bluff Trail begins at the small Burritt hiking parking lot on Burritt Drive. From Monte Sano Boulevard, turn onto Burritt Dr. and travel 0.2 mi. to reach this parking area, which has room for just a few cars. From the southeast end of the parking area, take the asphalt Rock Bluff Trail, traveling southeast.

53 (34.7171, -86.5375) (27 ft.) The Discovery Trail intersects on the left and descends to the east. (The Discovery Trail sign sits about 50 ft. from the asphalt path.) To continue on the Rock Bluff Trail, go straight and head south.

51-1 (34.71528, -86.53737) (0.15 mi.) On the right, a short asphalt side trail leads to boulders. This path stretches 56 ft. and ends at a sign marked, "Caution Floating Rocks!"

If you take this side path, you'll reach a rock formation where layers of limestone resemble stacks of pancakes. An interpretive sign explains how the rock erodes and "floats" down the mountain about half an inch each year. From Waypoint 51-1, you'll walk 88 ft. and reach a trail junction (0.16 mi.). Turn left and head east. Walk about 190 ft. to see a persimmon tree whose bark resembles the skin of an alligator.

51-2 (34.71483, -86.53714) (0.2 mi.) On the right, a connector trail runs for about 100 ft. to meet with the main Rock Bluff Trail.

From Waypoint 51-2, go another 150 ft. to a sign on the right that says, "Falling Leaves Form Flowing Water." Here you'll learn about the formation of springs, which you'll encounter on many Monte Sano trails. Go another 500 ft. to see the "Underground Worlds" sign, which explains how caves form. A few yards beyond the sign, you'll see a small cave opening. Of course, kids are fascinated with caves, and they might want to go in and explore, but be aware that visitors are not allowed to enter.

53-4 (34.71509, -86.54017) (0.4 mi.) The Discovery Trail intersects on the left. Continue straight, traveling northwest on the Rock Bluff Trail.

51-3 (34.71708, -86.54097) (0.57 mi.) At the Y junction, you have a couple of options. If you bear left and travel north, you'll continue on the main Rock Bluff Trail, which traverses a clearing and passes the large cross. At Waypoint 51-3, you can also bear right to head toward the Burritt summit, which is just 0.1 mi. away. If you choose this option, you'll ascend gradually for 100 ft. to reach a junction at Waypoint 51-4.

51-4 (34.71732, -86.54087) (0.59 mi.) Turn right and ascend the stepped Coal Mine Trail for about 440 ft. to reach the summit.

51-5 (34.71662, -86.54009) (0.67 mi.) The Coal Mine Trail ends at the Baron Bluff Building. You'll notice a sign that says, "Trail to the Cross," as many Burritt visitors begin at the summit to take the shortest route to visit the cross.

If you don't climb to the summit from Waypoint 51-3, cross the clearing. After another 86 ft., you'll reach a junction where another path leads to Waypoint 51-5 at the summit. Continue past this junction to continue exploring the Rock Bluff Trail.

51-6 (34.71926, -86.53839) (0.8 mi.) At the Y junction, go right to continue on the main Rock Bluff Trail. (This path also leads to the Oak Tree Trail.) If you go left, you'll follow a wide path that continues about 500 ft. and ends at Burritt Drive at **Waypoint 51-7** (34.71815, -86.53771).

After going right at Waypoint 51-6 and walking 20 ft., you'll encounter another Y junction, where the Oak Trail begins.

52 (34.71910, -86.53867) (0.83 mi.) The Rock Bluff Trail intersects with the Oak Tree Trail. At the junction, turn left to continue on the Rock Bluff Trail and begin a steady, gradual climb.

After walking a little more than 0.1 mi., you'll reach Burritt Drive. Cross the road to reach the trailhead parking area.

The Big Cross beneath the Burritt summit measures 74 feet tall.

Trail Facts

Round Top Mountain: The 167-acre Burritt on the Mountain property sits atop Round Top Mountain, though you hardly ever hear that name. Most folks just call it Burritt.

Fire on the Mountain: When William Burritt built his mansion on the summit, he used straw insulation. Apparently, he had seen it used on a Missouri farm and was impressed by its ability to keep structures cool on hot days. Unfortunately, when Burritt moved into his mansion on June 6, 1936, it burned to the ground. An electrical fire sparked the blaze, and the straw insulation and protective metal panels added fuel to the fire. Undaunted, he rebuilt, and it is this second version you can visit today.

52. Oak Tree Trail

The Oak Tree Trail links the Rock Bluff Trail and the summit of the mountain. The brief, steep climb offers a bit of a challenge for hikers, but otherwise, it's not very noteworthy. However, people hiking the Rock Bluff Trail can use the Oak Tree Trail as a quick way to return to the mountain summit.

Distance: 0.1 mi.
Hiking Time: 5 to 10 minutes
Elevation Gain/Loss: +114 ft., -0 ft.
Hiking Difficulty: Moderate to strenuous
Location: Burritt on the Mountain, 3101 Burritt Dr. SE, Huntsville, AL 35801
Fees, Facilities & Driving Directions: See page 160.

Highlights

The Burritt Summit: The Burritt property on Round Top Mountain not only features the elaborate Burritt mansion, but also a collection of 19th-century buildings. In the 1960s and 1970s, the structures were moved from their original locations to the Burritt property to create an outdoor museum. On the grounds, you'll find a church that dates to 1884 and originally sat in downtown Madison. Another interesting building is the Smith-Williams House, which is a combination of two structures that were built in the 1840s and stood in McKay Hollow at the bottom of Monte Sano Mountain.

Waypoint/Mile

Trailhead (Waypoint 52) (34.71910, -86.53867) The Oak Tree Trail begins at the northeast portion of the Rock Bluff Trail. At the Y junction (Waypoint 56 on the map), go right and begin the steep ascent to the top of the mountain. Water and erosion have rutted out the path, which climbs through a corridor of oaks.

52-1 (34.71750, -86.53894) (0.1 mi.) The path ends at a gravel road atop the mountain.

53. Discovery Trail
(North and South Sections)

The Discovery Trail is split into two separate sections, one on the northeastern side of Round Top Mountain, and one on the southwestern side of the mountain. The northern path runs between the Burritt hiking parking area on Burritt Drive and the Trough Springs Trail. The southern trail links the Rock Bluff Trail and the Big Cove Turnpike Trail.

Discovery North Trail

This portion of the Discovery Trail primarily provides hikers a means to travel from Round Top Mountain to the Trough Springs Trail. For years, this path was difficult to follow because it was not well-marked. But it was recently rerouted, and hikers can now easily follow this dirt path, which makes an easy to moderate descent through an open hardwood forest.

Distance: 2 mi.
Hiking Time: 5 to 10 minutes
Elevation Gain/Loss: +0 ft., -99 ft.
Hiking Difficulty: Easy to moderate
Location: Burritt on the Mountain, 3101 Burritt Dr. SE, Huntsville, AL 35801
Fees, Facilities & Driving Directions: See page 160.

Highlights

Remnants of the Space Walk Trail: When you reach the base of Round Top Mountain and cross Monte Sano Boulevard, you'll see a telephone pole with a marker shaped like a space shuttle. This is a remnant of the now-defunct Space Walk Trail. In the 1960s, four Boy Scout troops created the route by combining several existing paths. Measuring 11 mi., the Space Walk Trail stretched from Green Mountain to Monte Sano State Park. Many Scouts used the path to train for long hikes on the Appalachian Trail. They originally blazed the Space Walk Trail with markers resembling the silhouette of the Gemini spacecraft. Over time, new versions of the Space Walk Trail were developed and blazed with markers shaped like the space shuttle. In later years, portions of the Space Walk Trail disappeared as homes and roads were constructed.

Waypoint/Mile

Trailhead (Waypoint 53) (34.71707, -86.53752) From the Burritt hiking parking area, enter the Rock Bluff Trail (an asphalt path) near the "Parking Hours" sign and walk 27 ft. Look to the left to see a Discovery Trail sign in the woods about 50 ft. from the Rock Bluff Trail. Head to this sign and take the narrow path that soon bends left and heads north.

The hike begins with an easy walk across the upper flank of the mountain, with Monte Sano Boulevard visible below.

53-1 (34.71844, -86.53711) (0.1 mi.) The Viduta Pike Trail intersects on the right. This path stretches 0.4 mi. and provides a pleasant route to reach the Big Cove Turnpike Trail. At Waypoint 53-1, go straight and descend to continue on the Discovery North Trail.

53-2 (34.71830, -86.53623) (0.16 mi.) The Discovery North Trail reaches Monte Sano Boulevard. Go straight and cross the street, walking toward a telephone pole with a newer trail marker and an older trail marker shaped like a space shuttle. When you see the space shuttle marker on the telephone pole, you'll notice that the nose is pointing east, toward the forest. This is a signal that you should enter the woods at this spot and follow the narrow trail that heads east. From the telephone pole, you'll walk 180 ft. to reach Waypoint 53-3.

53-3 (34.71876, -86.53603) (0.2 mi.) The Discovery Trail ends at the junction with the Trough Springs Trail.

Discovery South Trail

This portion of the Discovery Trail links the Rock Bluff Trail and the Big Cove Turnpike Trail. If you're hiking the Rock Bluff Trail, you can take this quick side hike to visit the Big Cove Turnpike Trail, which traces a segment of an old wagon road.

Distance: 0.13 mi.
Hiking Time: 5 minutes
Elevation Gain/Loss: +0 ft., -112 ft.
Hiking Difficulty: Easy

Highlights

Access to an Old Wagon Road: From the Rock Bluff Trail, you only have to walk downhill for a few minutes to explore a wagon road used in the 1800s. The corridor for the Big Cove Turnpike Trail is unusually wide, making it obvious that it was once an old road. While the path is pretty level, the ground is still rough, providing a sense of what early travelers would have endured while bumping along the road in horse-drawn wagons.

Waypoint/Mile

53-4 (34.71509, -86.54017) To reach the Discovery South Trail on the southwest side of the mountain, begin at the Burritt hiking parking area on Burritt Drive and enter the Rock Bluff Trail (an asphalt path) near the "Parking Hours" sign. Follow the Rock Bluff Trail for 0.4 mi. to where the Discovery South Trail intersects on the left. Turn left and head northwest on the Discovery South Trail.

Walk 97 ft. to where the path takes a left turn at a sign for the Geologic Loop and Rock Bluff Trail. After you walk another 37 ft., you'll see a sign that says, "To Discovery Trail & Big Cove Turnpike." A thick bed of leaves covers the narrow path, which winds down a moderate slope covered in hardwood trees.

53-5 (34.71339, -86.54132) (0.13 mi.) The Discovery South Trail ends at a junction with an old path that leads to the Big Cove Turnpike Trail. At this junction, turn left and head downhill for 177 ft. to reach the Big Cove Turnpike Trail.

54. Big Cove Turnpike Trail

Imagine yourself in a horse-drawn wagon, bumping along an old wagon trail in a mountain wilderness. When you walk the Big Cove Turnpike Trail, you'll get a glimpse of what passed as a "road" in pioneer days. Running mostly level on the flank of Round Top Mountain, the Big Cove Turnpike Trail follows a short section of a road that was developed in the 1800s. Hikers can also use the Big Cove Turnpike Trail to access higher-up trails surrounding the Burritt on the Mountain property.

Distance: 0.3 to 0.4 mi.

Hiking Time: 10 to 15 minutes

Elevation Gain/Loss: +42 ft., -38 ft.

Hiking Difficulty: Easy

Location: Burritt on the Mountain, 3101 Burritt Dr. SE, Huntsville, AL 3580. **Note that the trailhead for Big Cove Turnpike is on Monte Sano Boulevard, but there is no parking at this spot. You can park in the Burritt hiking parking area on Burritt Drive, or in the main Burritt on the Mountain parking lot, and then follow the Rock Bluff Trail and Discovery Trail to the Big Cove Turnpike Trail. I don't recommend parking at the Land Trust South Monte Sano parking area and walking along Monte Sano Blvd. to reach the trail. The shoulder of the road is very narrow in spots, and you risk getting hit by a car.

Fees: There are no fees to hike this trail.

Facilities: There are no facilities and no sources of potable water along the trail. The nearest restrooms and food and water are located at Burritt on the Mountain.

Driving Directions: See page 160.

Highlights

Remnants of the Old Turnpike: In the late 1800s, more people began settling on Monte Sano Mountain and farther northeast of Huntsville. This sparked construction of the Big Cove Turnpike, which allowed travelers from Big Cove and other points east to make their way over Monte Sano and into the valley that Huntsville inhabits. Portions of the turnpike roughly followed what is now Governors Drive and U.S. 431.

Waypoint/Mile

Trailhead (Waypoint 54) (34.71272, -86.53576) To reach the beginning of the Big Cove Turnpike Trail, begin at the Burritt hiking parking area. Then follow the Discovery North and Viduta Pike trails for a 0.52-mi. walk to the Big Cove Turnpike Trail at Waypoint 54-1. From this junction, the actual beginning of the Big Cove Turnpike Trail is just 200 ft. to the southeast, beside Monte Sano Boulevard at Waypoint 54.

The path is wide and rises and falls gradually in woods dominated by cedars. To the immediate left, bluff-side homes are visible, but soon a thick line of trees shrouds nearby homes and views of the valley. At around 400 ft., the path is level and grassy, and this section can become flooded after substantial rain.

54-1 (34.71286, -86.53645) (200 ft.) The Viduta Pike Trail intersects on the right. Go straight to continue on the Big Cove Turnpike Trail.

54-2 (34.71308, -86.54089) (0.3 mi.) At a clearing, you reach a Y junction where the official Big Cove Turnpike Trail bears left and descends to the west. When you reach this junction, look left to see an "Old Wagon Road" sign, indicating that this section of the trail was part of the old turnpike. From the sign, you can walk another 465 ft. to a point where the path ends.

54-3 (34.71333, -86.54228) (0.38 mi.) The Big Cove Turnpike Trail ends near a small stream and the backyards of two houses. Retrace your steps from here to continue.

Old Spur of the Big Cove Turnpike Trail

When you reach Waypoint 54-2, instead of bearing left at the Old Wagon Road sign, you can bear right to follow an old 0.1-mi. spur of the Big Cove Turnpike Trail. After you bear right at Waypoint 54-2 and walk 40 ft., you'll see on the right a sign for the Space Walk Trail. Now defunct, the Space Walk Trail was developed in the 1960s by the Boy Scouts. Measuring 11 mi., the route combined several existing trails and ran from Green Mountain to Monte Sano State Park.

After walking 177 ft., you'll reach a small drainage on the right that leads to the Discovery South Trail at Waypoint 53-5 (34.71339, -86.54132). From the drainage, you can look to the right and see uphill a wooden sign for the Discovery Trail. The Discovery South Trail leads to the Rock Bluff Trail and the Burritt on the Mountain property. If you don't wish to take the Discovery South Trail, continue straight at Waypoint 53-5, heading west. The trail goes for another 430 ft. to end at Waypoint 54-4. **54-4** (34.71422, -86.54204) (0.38 mi.) The path ends at a stream that is near a backyard and flows to the southwest between two houses.

Trail Facts

The Original Route into the Valley: The Big Cove Turnpike wasn't always a main route into Huntsville. Before the turnpike was created, early settlers and traders coming from the east took the Blevins Gap Road and crossed Green Mountain to enter the valley. By the late 1800s, a new road was needed to serve the growing number of people settling in northern sections of Huntsville. By 1875, a court had ordered that the Blevins Gap route no longer be considered a public road, and development of the Big Cove Turnpike became a priority.

Blevins Gap Preserve

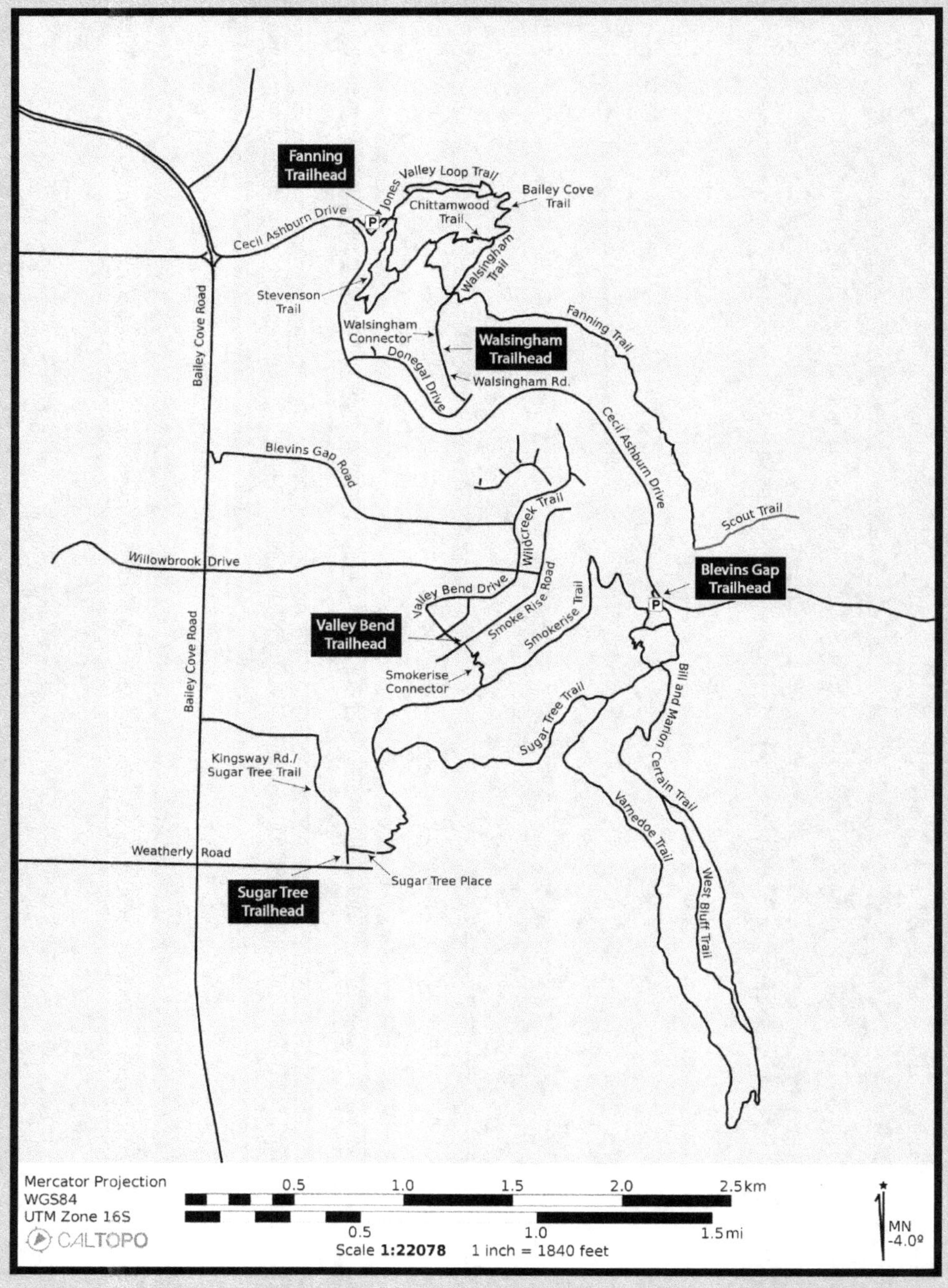

CHAPTER 5

Blevins Gap Nature Preserve

In 1988, Ed Stevenson donated 16.9 acres of land on Huntsville Mountain to the Land Trust of North Alabama, establishing what is now the Blevins Gap Nature Preserve. Now covering 1,086 acres, this preserve is unique because it's divided in two and includes separate trail systems on Huntsville Mountain and Green Mountain. The preserve is also special because it's close to major South Huntsville neighborhoods and shopping areas. From this part of the city, you'll drive just a few minutes to reach trails that explore beautiful creeks, remote woods, and high bluffs with inspiring views.

The main Blevins Gap Trailhead is located on Green Mountain, south of Cecil Ashburn Drive, which runs between Green Mountain and Huntsville Mountain. From this trailhead, hikers can reach eight miles of trails that explore 727 acres of the nature preserve. The 1.7-mile Varnedoe Trail and the 1.9-mile Bill and Marion Certain Trail are perfect for those seeking longer treks in remote woods. These trails, plus the West Bluff Trail, also offer excellent views of Huntsville and the lowlands east of town. It's also possible to reach the Green Mountain trails from the Sugar Tree Trailhead on the western edge of the preserve. The Sugar Tree Trail and Smokerise Trail pass through the secluded and quiet heart of the forest and link to the main Blevins Gap Trailhead.

Another main access point for the preserve is the Fanning Trailhead, located north of Cecil Ashburn Drive, behind Southeast Church of the Nazarene. This trailhead gives hikers access to 4.5 miles of trail on 267 acres. The most popular trail in this area is the Jones Valley Loop Trail, which circles around a stream known as Bailey Cove Branch. Its small, tumbling falls and shallow pools make a great playground for kids on warm spring and summer days.

General Information

Hours: Open dawn to dusk. **Due to church services, there is no parking at the Fanning Trailhead Wednesday evenings after 6 p.m., Sundays before noon, and during special church events.

Primary trail activities allowed: Hiking, biking

Pets: Leashed pets allowed.

Fees: There are no fees to use the trails, though donations are encouraged at trailheads with donation boxes.

Facilities: At the Blevins Gap Trailhead, there is a portable toilet but no source of potable water. At the Fanning Trailhead, there are no facilities and no sources of potable water.

Information: (256) 534-5263; www.landtrustnal.org/properties/blevins-gap-preserve/

Driving Directions

Fanning Trailhead

From the junction of U.S. 231 (Memorial Parkway) and Airport Road, travel east on Airport Rd. Travel 1.2 mi. to where Airport Rd. turns slightly right and becomes Carl T Jones Drive. Continue on Carl T Jones Dr. 1.9 mi., and then turn left onto Cecil Ashburn Drive. Travel 0.4 mi., and then turn left into the driveway for Southeast Church of the Nazarene. **Be aware that this turn sneaks up on you, so watch for it closely as you're traveling on Cecil Ashburn. Also, as you prepare to turn into the church, watch carefully for opposing traffic coming downhill, as people drive very fast here.* After you turn into the driveway for the church, go around the right side of the church to the parking lot in back. Continue to the far northeast end of the parking lot, where you'll see the trailhead. **Due to church services, there is no parking at the Fanning Trailhead Wednesday evenings after 6 p.m., Sundays before noon, and during special church events. Go to www.hsvsenaz.org for current church schedules.

Blevins Gap Trailhead

From the junction of U.S. 231 (Memorial Parkway) and Airport Road, travel east on Airport Rd. Go 1.2 mi. to where Airport Rd. becomes Carl

T Jones Drive. Continue 1.9 mi. on Carl T Jones Dr., and then turn left onto Cecil Ashburn Drive. Travel 2.3 mi. and then turn right into the parking area for the Blevins Gap Nature Preserve.

Sugar Tree Trailhead

From the junction of U.S. 231 (Memorial Parkway) and Weatherly Road, travel east on Weatherly Rd. for 1.9 mi. Then turn left onto Sugar Tree Trail, go 240 ft., and then turn right onto Sugar Tree Place. The trailhead is at the end of the road. While there are no designated parking spots, you can park on the side of Sugar Tree Pl.

SECTION 1:
Jones Valley Loop Trail, Bailey Cove Trail, Walsingham Connector and Walsingham Trail, and Chittamwood Trail

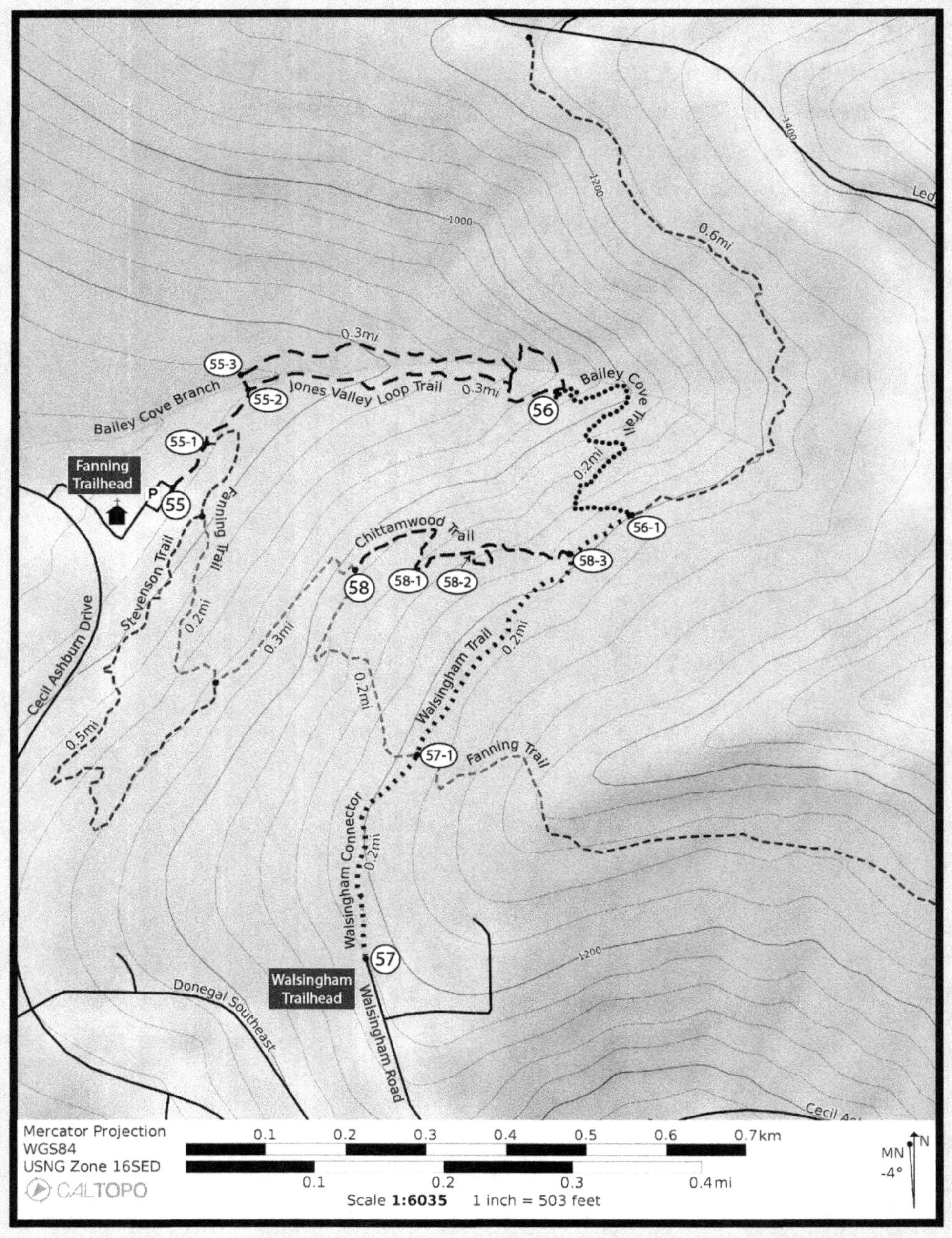

55. Jones Valley Loop Trail

Want to take the family for a quick and entertaining escape? This short loop explores a shallow stream teeming with miniature waterfalls and small pools. On a warm, sunny day, it's the perfect watery playground for young ones. Plus, people of all ages can handle this fairly easy trail that includes only modest amounts of climbing.

Distance: 0.7 mi.

Hiking Time: 30 minutes

Elevation Gain/Loss: +200 ft., -191 ft.

Hiking Difficulty: Easy to moderate

Location: Blevins Gap Nature Preserve, 2275 Cecil Ashburn Dr. SE, Huntsville, AL 35802

Facilities: There are no restrooms and no sources of potable water at the trailhead.

Driving Directions: See page 174 and use the directions for the Fanning Trailhead.

Highlights

Family-Friendly Hiking: The Jones Valley Loop Trail rises gradually as it moves east, but there are no steep sections, so most kids and adults can walk the path with no trouble. Also, the trail forms a loop that measures less than a mile, so it's a great destination for a short outing.

Bailey Cove Branch Stream: This beautiful stream is the centerpiece of the trail. The path parallels Bailey Cove Branch, which slips, slides and tumbles through a shaded forest of hardwoods and cedars. When you first reach the creek, a long wood footbridge provides a sublime spot to view a small waterfall that plunges right beside the bridge. As Bailey Cove Branch moves through the forest, it drops gradually, so it's possible to walk and play in portions of the stream. Along the way, you'll encounter many small falls and pools where you can cool off in the summer heat.

Waypoint/Mile

Trailhead (Waypoint 55) (34.67351, -86.53074) The Jones Valley Loop Trail begins at the northeast end of the Fanning Trailhead parking area. Follow the gravel path and short wooden footbridge. After 83 ft., you'll follow a longer wood walkway.

55-1 (34.67397, -86.53013) (136 ft.) The Fanning Trail intersects on the right. Continue straight to take the Jones Valley Loop Trail, traveling north.

55-2 (34.67455, -86.52946) (431 ft.) The trail reaches the southeast end of the 30-ft.-long wooden bridge that spans Bailey Cove Branch. This hike description follows the loop counterclockwise, so bear right and stay to the right side of the creek, traveling northeast. For a little more than 0.1 mi., the path hugs the stream, and you have easy access to small, shallow pools.

The path then rises more noticeably as it bends away from the stream. The trail runs parallel to the stream for about 0.2 mi.; then it turns right and climbs higher onto the slope. After another 350 ft., the trail moves toward the water again and runs parallel to the lively stream filled with small waterfalls. At 0.3 mi., the path once again rises moderately and turns away from the creek. When I've hiked here in spring, I've seen abundant blue phlox wildflowers, which add a splash of lavender to the drab leaves covering the slope.

56 (34.67458, -86.52537) (0.37 mi.) The Bailey Cove Trail intersects on the right and climbs the hill. To continue on the Jones Valley Loop Trail, bear left and travel north toward the creek.

Go another 100 ft. to cross the creek and ascend the opposite slope. The trail takes a sharp turn left and gradually descends the rocky slope that

The Jones Valley Loop Trail skirts a rushing creek with small falls.

parallels the stream. The wide path flirts with Bailey Cove Branch, approaching the stream briefly, only to soon turn away. But you can still see and hear the rushing water throughout the descent. Near the half-mile mark, the trail passes a large pool in Bailey Cove Branch and then bears right to turn away from the stream and cover fairly level ground.

55-3 (34.67479, -86.52963) (0.69 mi.) The trail reaches the northwest end of the bridge. To complete the loop, turn left and cross the bridge, and then retrace your steps to the trailhead.

Trail Facts

Jones Valley Farm: The loop trail is named for Jones Valley Farm, which Carl Jones established in 1939 when he purchased 2,500 acres of land southwest of Monte Sano Mountain. While the lush green valley has seen significant development, the farm still covers 1,700 acres where Hereford cattle graze on the fescue grass. It's considered one of the largest working urban farms in the United States.

56. Bailey Cove Trail

The short but steep Bailey Cove Trail is essentially a connector trail that provides a direct route between the Bailey Cove Branch stream basin and the top of the nearest ridge to the southeast. People seeking a longer, more challenging hike can ascend the Bailey Cove Trail and connect to several other paths in the area, choosing from several loop hikes that return hikers to the Fanning Trailhead.

Distance: 0.2 mi.
Hiking Time: 15 minutes
Elevation Gain/Loss: +250 ft., -0 ft.
Hiking Difficulty: Strenuous
Location: Blevins Gap Nature Preserve, 2275 Cecil Ashburn Dr. SE, Huntsville, AL 35802
Facilities: There are no restrooms and no sources of potable water at the trailhead.
Driving Directions: See page 174 and use directions for the Fanning Trailhead.

Waypoint/Mile

Trailhead (Waypoint 56) (34.67458, -86.52537) To reach the Bailey Cove Trail, begin at the Fanning Trailhead parking area. Follow the Jones Valley Loop Trail on the right side of the creek for 0.37 mi. to where the Bailey Cove Trail intersects on the right. The Bailey Cove Trail begins a steep climb, heading south.

56-1 (34.67311, -86.52424) (0.28 mi.) The Bailey Cove Trail ends at the intersection with the Walsingham Trail.

Trail Facts

Historic Bailey Cove: The area known as Bailey Cove is the pocket of low land where the Valley Bend shopping center sits just south of the Jones Farm. The cove is named for Lewis Winston Bailey. In 1879, Lewis and his wife, Mary M. McCay, purchased 287 acres of land in the area known as Bailey Cove (*Source: Why Is It Named That? Stories Behind the Names of 250 Places in Madison County and Huntsville, Alabama.*)

57. Walsingham Connector and Walsingham Trail

The Walsingham Connector and main trail traverse a high ridge in the heart of this portion of the Blevins Gap Preserve. To reach these paths you have to do some climbing, but there's a nice payoff. Once you're atop the ridge, the Walsingham trails offer an easy walk through a sunny forest with mature trees. These trails also allow hikers to do a variety of loop hikes that lead back to the Fanning Trailhead.

Distance: Walsingham Connector, 0.18 mi.; Walsingham Trail, 0.27 mi.

Hiking Time: Walsingham Connector, 5 to 10 minutes; Walsingham Trail, 7 to 10 minutes

Elevation Gain/Loss: Walsingham Connector, +56 ft., -4 ft.; Walsingham Trail, +31 ft., -54 ft.

Hiking Difficulty: Easy

Location: Blevins Gap Nature Preserve, 2275 Cecil Ashburn Dr. SE, Huntsville, AL 35802
Facilities: There are no restrooms and no sources of potable water at the trailhead.
Driving Directions: See page 174 and use the directions for the Fanning Trailhead.

Highlights

Easy Ridgetop Hiking: The Walsingham Connector and Walsingham Trail traverse the top of a ridge, allowing you to enjoy a comfortable stroll with very little change in elevation. Hikers who begin at the Fanning Trailhead and ascend from the stream valley can take the Walsingham trails to lengthen their hike without wearing out their legs.

Walsingham Connector
Waypoint/Mile

Trailhead (Waypoint 57) (34.66806, -86.52791) Officially, the Walsingham Connector begins at the Walsingham Trailhead on Walsingham Road. However, there is no designated parking at this trailhead, which is in a residential area.

To reach the Walsingham Connector, you could also begin at the Fanning Trailhead, where there is ample parking. From this point, follow the Jones Valley Loop Trail for 136 ft., and then turn right onto the Fanning Trail. Take the Fanning Trail 0.7 mi. to its junction with the Walsingham Connector Trail and Walsingham Trail at Waypoint 57-1 (34.67031, -86.52736). From Waypoint 57-1, it's 0.2 mi. to the Walsingham Connector Trailhead at Waypoint 57.

Whichever way you access the Walsingham Connector, you'll find that it makes an easy run along the upper portion of the ridge. In this area, keep an eye out for hawks, as I once saw three take flight at the same time. Along this stretch, the forest is fairly open, but there aren't really any views of the stream valley to the northwest. Still, you'll stroll through a nice stretch of trail where moss-covered boulders hug the narrow path.

Walsingham Trail
Waypoint/Mile

Trailhead (Waypoint 57-1) (34.67031, -86.52736) There are two ways to access the beginning of the Walsingham Trail. You can begin at the Walsingham Trailhead (Waypoint 57) at the end of Walsingham Road, or you can begin at the Fanning Trailhead. This hike description begins at the Fanning Trailhead because it offers parking.

At the northeast end of the Fanning Trailhead parking area, enter the gravel path and cross the wooden footbridge, traveling northeast. At 136 ft., you'll reach the junction with the Jones Valley Loop Trail and the Fanning Trail. Turn right to take the Fanning Trail and ascend for 0.7 mi. to the junction with the Walsingham Connector and Walsingham Trail at Waypoint 57-1. Turn left onto the Walsingham Trail and travel northeast.

The path begins in dense forest where storms have raked the ridge and blown down many trees. After 0.1 mi., the trail drops gradually through a boulder-strewn forest. If you look left, you can barely see the stream valley through the trees. At 0.15 mi., the path rises gently and cuts across the leaf-covered slope where widely spaced mature hardwoods allow ample sun to wash over the ridge top.

58-3 (34.67269, -86.52511) (0.2 mi.) The Chittamwood Trail intersects on the left. Go straight, traveling northeast, to follow the Walsingham Trail, which rolls along easily through the open forest.

56-1 (34.67311, -86.52424) (0.27 mi.) The official Walsingham Trail ends where the Bailey Cove Trail intersects on the left and makes its steep descent to Bailey Cove Branch and the Jones Valley Loop Trail. While this is where the Walsingham Trail officially ends, you'll see a clear path that continues to the northeast. This path continues another 0.59 mi. and dead-ends at Ledges Drive.

58. Chittamwood Trail

Home to an unusual number of rare chittamwood trees, the Chittamwood Trail begins along the Fanning Trail and makes a moderate to steep ascent to meet the Walsingham Trail. This path not only offers the opportunity to see a rare tree species, but also serves as one leg of a nice, 1.4-mi. loop hike combining the Fanning, Chittamwood, Walsingham, Bailey Cove and Jones Valley Loop trails.

Distance: 0.25 mi.

Hiking Time: 10 minutes

Elevation Gain/Loss: +170 ft., -7 ft.

Hiking Difficulty: Easy to moderate

Location: Blevins Gap Nature Preserve, 2275 Cecil Ashburn Dr. SE, Huntsville, AL 35802

Facilities: There are no restrooms and no sources of potable water at the trailhead.

Driving Directions: See page 174 and use directions for the Fanning Trailhead.

Highlights

The Rare, Exotic Chittamwood Tree: Also known as the American smoketree, chittamwood is a native tree that grows on limestone outcrops and is extremely tolerant of drought conditions. Its bright golden wood is very hard and heavy, and it's considered one of the rarest exotic woods in North America (especially a chittamwood burl). (*Source: Land Trust of North Alabama.*)

Waypoint/Mile

Trailhead (Waypoint 58) (34.67251, -86.52795) To reach the Chittamwood Trail, begin at the Fanning Trailhead and follow the Fanning Trail for half a mile. At a bend in the trail, the Chittamwood Trail intersects on the left and heads north.

The path begins to climb gradually as it cuts across the slope. You will likely find that the path is not well-marked, and there were no trail markers when I mapped it.

58-1 (34.67243, -86.52730) (0.1 mi.) Make a sharp turn to the right and climb the hill, heading northeast. Be aware that this turn is difficult to see.

58-2 (34.67271, -86.52648) (0.15 mi.) Turn right and head uphill to bypass the large fallen tree. When you're past the tree, turn left and go downhill to rejoin the original course of the Chittamwood Trail.

58-3 (34.67269, -86.52511) (0.25 mi.) The Chittamwood Trail intersects with the Walsingham Trail. If you turn left and travel northeast, you'll walk 244 ft. to reach the Bailey Cove Trail, which will carry you back to the Jones Valley Loop Trail and the Bailey Cove Branch creek. From Waypoint 58-3, if you go right and follow the Walsingham Trail to the southwest, you'll travel 0.2 mi. to intersect with the Fanning Trail. You can then descend the Fanning Trail for 0.7 mi. to return to the Fanning Trailhead parking area.

Trail Facts

Brilliant Chittamwood Flowers: During summer, chittamwood trees produce pink-gray flowers, but in fall their foliage is brilliant scarlet. Many people consider it the most intense fall color produced by any tree.

SECTION 2:
Fanning Trail, Stevenson Trail and Scout Trail

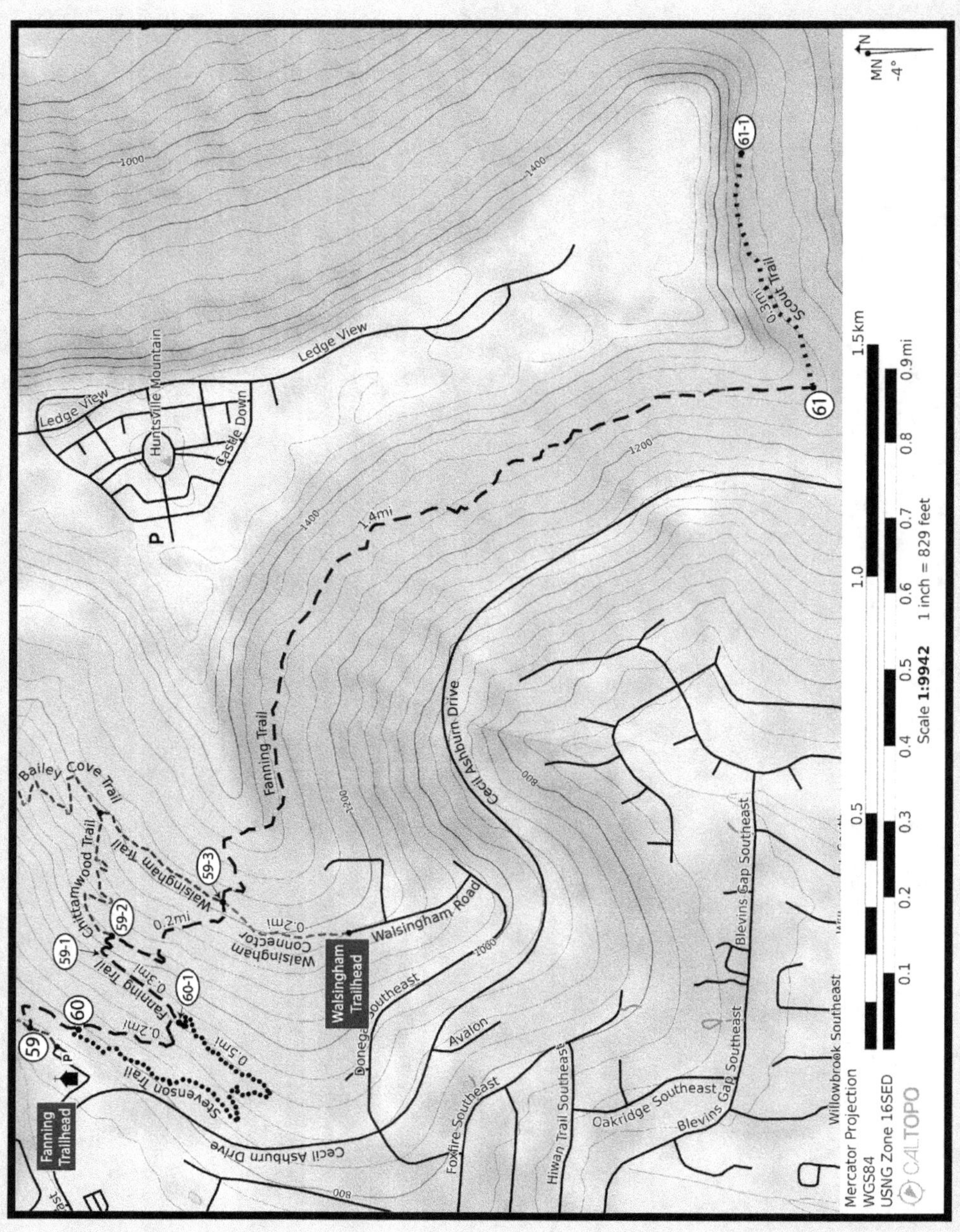

59. Fanning Trail

Stretching a little more than 2 mi., the Fanning Trail is the longest path in the Blevins Gap Preserve. If you hike the entire length, it's essentially an out-and-back trek that stretches more than 4 mi., making it a great outing for anyone wanting to hike for a few hours. When you combine the Fanning Trail's length with the elevation gain (more than 700 ft.), you'll find that it poses a modest challenge. But you're rewarded for your effort with a long walk in the quiet woods of Huntsville Mountain's western flank.

Distance: 2.1 mi.
Hiking Time: 1.5 to 2 hours
Elevation Gain/Loss: +785 ft., -247 ft.
Hiking Difficulty: Moderate to strenuous
Location: Blevins Gap Nature Preserve, 2275 Cecil Ashburn Dr. SE, Huntsville, AL 35802
Facilities: There are no restrooms and no sources of potable water at the trailhead.
Driving Directions: See page 174 and use the directions for the Fanning Trailhead.

Highlights

Bluff Views: You don't have to hike very far to enjoy nice views along the Fanning Trail. At 0.4 mi., a sign on the path points you downhill to a bench that sits at the edge of the bluff. From this comfortable spot, you can see the nearby forested ridge to the north and a green valley to the west.

Wildflowers: Within the first half-mile of the Fanning Trail, you can spy a wide variety of wildflowers in the spring, including eastern shooting star, whose white petals and yellow stamens meet to resemble tiny shooting stars. You might also spot fernleaf phacelia, which displays beautiful lavender-blue petals.

Waypoint/Mile

Trailhead (Waypoint 59) (34.67397, -86.53013) To reach the start of the Fanning Trail, begin at the northeast end of the Fanning Trailhead parking area. Enter the gravel path and cross the short wooden footbridge to follow the Jones Valley Loop Trail. Go 136 ft. to the trail kiosk, and then turn right onto the Fanning Trail, which is marked with white diamond blazes.

60 (34.67312, -86.53011) (396 ft.) The Stevenson Trail intersects on the right and goes southwest. Continue straight, climbing gradually to the south.

If you're hiking in spring, keep your eyes peeled as you make a moderate ascent on a rocky and rooted path. This is where I've often seen the lavender-colored fernleaf phacelia flowers growing in beds of moss blanketing boulders.

60-1 (34.67312, -86.53011) (0.3 mi.) The Stevenson Trail intersects on the right. To stay on the Fanning Trail, bear left and ascend to the northeast.

59-1 (34.67278, -86.52838) (0.4 mi.) You'll reach a sign marked "Overlook Bench" that points to the left. Look below and to the left to see a bench at the edge of the bluff.

Wildflowers bloom on moss-covered boulders along the Fanning Trail.

When you hike in the spring, walk a bit farther to find one of the most attractive sections of the trail. Big stacks of boulders line the path, and wildflowers bloom on small, rocky ledges covered in moss. As you continue upward, the trail gets steeper and rockier.

59-2 (34.67256, -86.52796) (0.5 mi.) As the trail bends to the right, the Chittamwood Trail intersects on the left. (The Chittamwood Trail is not marked here, so it's easy to miss it.) To stay on the Fanning Trail, keep bending to the right and continue a moderate to steep ascent on the rocky and rooted path.

59-3 (34.67029, -86.52725) (0.7 mi.) The Fanning Trail intersects the Walsingham Trail and the Walsingham Connector. At this junction, the Walsingham Trail is the farthest path on the left. The Fanning Trail is just to the right of the Walsingham Trail. As you continue on the Fanning Trail, you'll keep climbing and head northeast.

This is a pleasant part of the mountain, where boulders are scattered about the open forest floor and large hardwoods cover the slope. The path is mellow as it rises and falls easily and crosses a stream at 1.2 mi. Then the trail quickly rises and makes a long easy run across the mountain slope. In winter, look to the southwest to see slices of Jones Valley through the trees. The trail begins to rollercoaster, and several drainages snake through the forest. Keep an eye out for trillium growing among the rocks and moss-covered trees in this area.

For a brief period, the path becomes extremely rocky, and it's difficult to find the actual trail as you traverse gray and green stones. But soon it transitions back to a single-track path of packed earth.

61 (34.65938, -86.51513) (2.1 mi.) At 2.1 mi., the Fanning Trail ends at the junction with the Scout Trail, which intersects on the left and heads northeast for 0.3 mi.

Trail Facts

An Early Land Trust Supporter: The trail is named for Thomas Fanning, who donated the property to the Land Trust of North Alabama in 1988. According to the Land Trust, this was one of the first properties the organization received.

60. Stevenson Trail

Need some exercise and only have a little time to hike? Follow the half-mile Stevenson Trail for a quick jaunt through the forest that gains just enough elevation to get your blood pumping. Then loop back on the Fanning Trail for a hike that measures a little less than a mile in total.

Distance: 0.5 mi.
Hiking Time: 20 minutes
Elevation Gain/Loss: +178 ft., -39 ft.
Hiking Difficulty: Easy to moderate
Location: Blevins Gap Nature Preserve, 2275 Cecil Ashburn Dr. SE, Huntsville, AL 35802
Facilities: There are no restrooms and no sources of potable water at the trailhead.
Driving Directions: See page 174 and use the directions for the Fanning Trailhead.

Highlights

Fantastical Forest: The Stevenson Trail winds through stretches of forest that resemble something from a fantasy novel. Shafts of light beam through the boughs of old, stout trees. On the forest floor, the sun illuminates boulders covered in electric green lichen. But the cheerful scene is broken by dark shadows and deep green blankets of moss, making these woods feel mysterious.

Waypoint/Mile

Trailhead (Waypoint 60) (34.67308, -86.53023) To reach the Stevenson Trail, begin at the Fanning Trailhead and follow the Fanning Trail for almost 400 ft. to the junction with the Stevenson Trail. Turn right to take the Stevenson Trail and begin a gradual climb to the southwest.

The trail crosses a bed of stone and then climbs moderately through a jumbled landscape of boulders. To the right, Cecil Ashburn Drive is visible, and you'll likely hear traffic noise, but this is a beautiful, sunny forest with rock gardens, tall cedars, mature hardwoods and pockets of wildflowers.

60-1 (34.67112, -86.53011) (0.5 mi.) The Stevenson Trail ends at the junction with the Fanning Trail. If you turn left and descend the Fanning Trail, you'll walk about 0.3 mi. to reach the Fanning Trailhead and parking area.

Trail Facts

Where It All Began: Since the late 1980s, the Land Trust of North Alabama has preserved more than 9,000 acres of land and constructed more than 70 mi. of trails. And this is where it all began.

Wild Blue Phlox

On Dec. 22, 1988, Ed Stevenson, president of Stevenson Development Corp., donated this 16.9-acre piece of Huntsville Mountain to the Land Trust of North Alabama. It was the very first property the Land Trust acquired after it was founded in 1987 (*Source: Land Trust of North Alabama*).

61. Scout Trail

The short Scout Trail explores the southern end of Huntsville Mountain. If you're hiking the Fanning Trail, you can take the Scout Trail to extend your walk by 0.3 mi. Plus, the Scout Trail will lead you to the extreme southeastern end of this portion of the Blevins Gap Preserve (the portion that lies northeast of Cecil Ashburn Drive). Just be aware that this path is occasionally difficult to follow. In some places, beds of leaves and downed tree limbs obscure the route. Consider entering waypoints into a GPS to help you navigate the trail.

Distance: 0.3 mi.
Hiking Time: 10 minutes
Elevation Gain/Loss: +75 ft., -62 ft.
Hiking Difficulty: Easy
Location: Blevins Gap Nature Preserve, 2275 Cecil Ashburn Dr. SE, Huntsville, AL 35802

Facilities: There are no restrooms and no sources of potable water at the trailhead.
Driving Directions: See page 174 and use the directions for the Fanning Trailhead.

Highlights

Spring Wildflowers: Keep an eye out for patches of Virginia spring beauty flowers, which have five white petals bearing pink stripes.

Waypoint/Mile

Trailhead (Waypoint 61) (34.65943, -86.51508) The Scout Trail begins at the end of the Fanning Trail, which is 2.1 mi. from the Fanning Trailhead. At the junction of the Fanning Trail and Scout Trail, turn left and travel northeast. It's likely that you will see few if any blazes marking this trail.

At first, the Scout Trail crosses mostly level terrain, and then at 0.2 mi. it makes a brief, moderate climb. As you continue, scan the sky occasionally because you might spot hawks in the area. I've seen them here a few times, including a group of three soaring together. If you hike in spring, also keep an eye on the ground nearby, as you might see Virginia spring beauty flowers.

When I've hiked here after significant rain, the trail has been very wet, and at times you might struggle to see the actual path in flooded grassy areas. At 0.15 mi., you'll cross a small stream. After going about 400 more ft., you might have to scramble over the trunks of large, downed trees.

As the trail runs near the base of a rocky bluff, look to the right for a faint glimpse of Big Cove to the southeast and blue ridges on the horizon. At 0.3 mi., a large fallen tree sits near a Land Trust boundary sign. This is a good turnaround point, though the trail continues for about another 150 ft.

61-1 (34.66077, -86.50972) (0.3 mi.) After dropping to more level terrain, the path ends. But you can't really make out a path at this point—just an open forest floor covered with leaves and grass. From here, retrace your steps to return to the junction with the Fanning Trail at Waypoint 61.

Trail Facts

Honoring Boy Scouts: This trail was named to honor local Boy Scout troops that have contributed many volunteer hours to help establish Land Trust trails.

SECTION 3:
Smokerise Trail, Smokerise Connector and Sugar Tree Trail

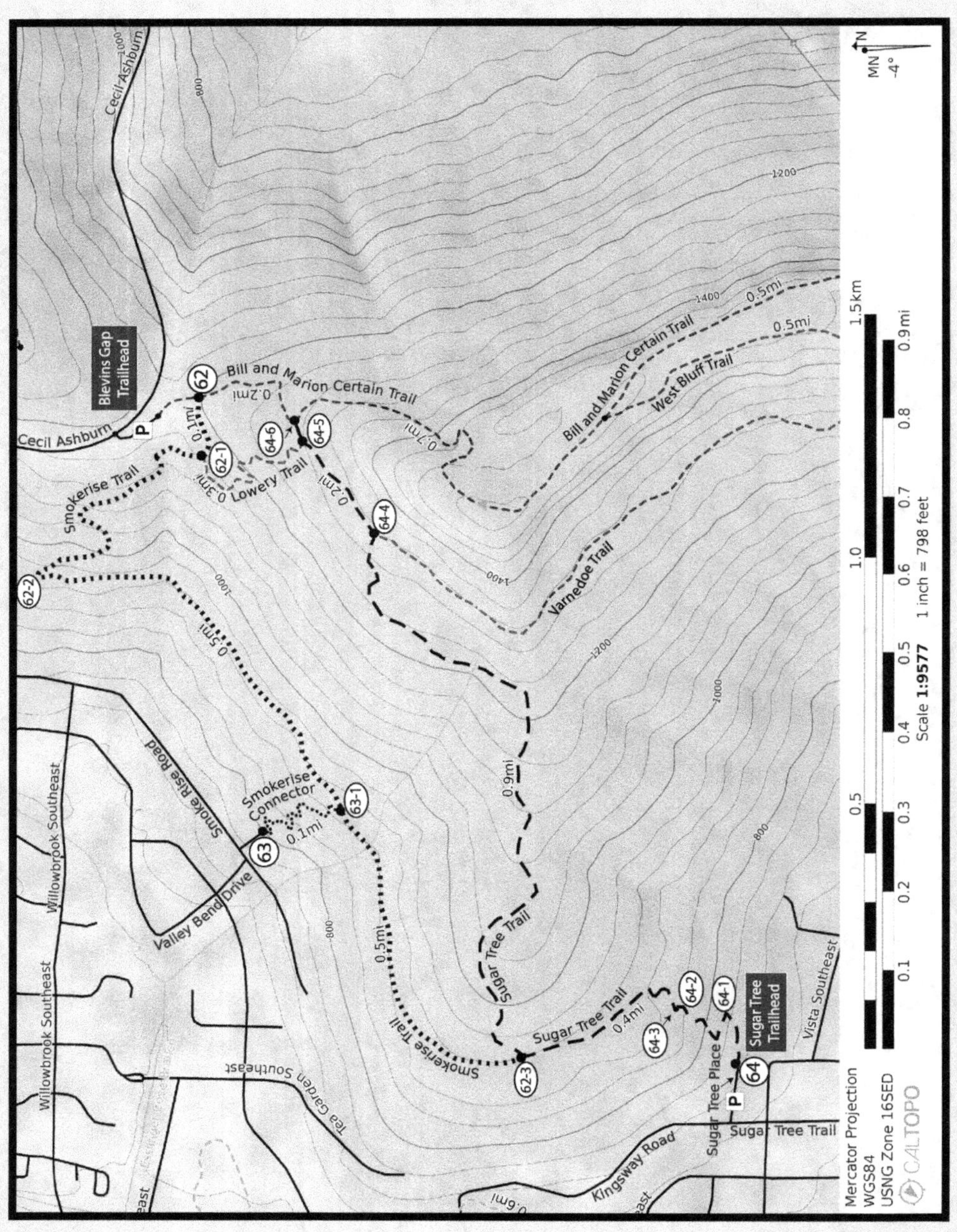

62. Smokerise Trail

After descending half a mile on an old, rugged wagon road, the Smokerise Trail leads you on a comfortable walk in beautiful woods with burbling streams and brilliant wildflowers. If you're in the mood for a moderately challenging loop, return to the trailhead via the Sugar Tree Trail and the Bill and Marion Certain Trail. That trip measures just over 2.5 mi.

Distance: 1.5 mi.
Hiking Time: 30 to 45 minutes
Elevation Gain/Loss: +125 ft., -394 ft.
Hiking Difficulty: Easy
Location: Blevins Gap Nature Preserve, 3470 Cecil Ashburn Dr. SE, Huntsville, AL 35802
Facilities: There are no restrooms and no sources of potable water at the trailhead.
Driving Directions: See page 174 and use the directions for the Blevins Gap Trailhead.

Highlights

Historic Blevins Gap Road: For hundreds of years, the Green Mountain passageway known as Blevins Gap served as the primary route for people to enter the area that Huntsville now occupies. Early settlers riding in wagons and traveling on foot crossed the mountain on the Blevins Gap Road. For the first 0.5 mi., the Smokerise Trail follows the old road, and the unusually wide trail corridor clearly signals that this was a major thoroughfare.

Attractive Woods with Wildflowers: After you descend the old wagon road, you'll take a sharp turn south and begin a comfortable stroll in beautiful woods. After spring rains, small streams meander across the forest floor, and towering hardwoods shade an open forest floor covered in golden leaves. From early spring until late summer, you'll see a variety of striking wildflowers along the path, including fire pink.

Waypoint/Mile

Trailhead (Waypoint 62) (34.65632, -86.51624) There are a few ways to reach the Smokerise Trail, but the most prominent access point is the Blevins Gap Trailhead parking area on Cecil Ashburn Drive. At the southeast end of the parking area, take the Bill and Marion Certain Trail for about 150 ft. to the junction with the Smokerise Trail (Waypoint 62 62-1). Turn right and descend to the west on the single-track path marked with diamond blazes.

62-1 (34.65620, -86.51785) (0.1 mi.) At the trail junction, the Lowry Trail intersects on the left and goes west. To continue on the Smokerise Trail, turn right and descend gradually to the northeast.

That path drops gradually through dense forest and becomes rockier. If you're hiking in spring, at about the 0.2-mi. point begin to scan the side of the trail for bright purple rose vervain flowers, as well as slender, white crow poison and deep-red fire pink. The trail eventually becomes much wider and rockier, and you'll be able to tell when you're on the old road. If you look to the side of the trail, you can see a long band of rock that was built to serve as a curb and is still somewhat recognizable.

A tree seems to defy gravity as it leans over the Smokerise Trail.

62-2 (34.65936, -86.52054) (0.5 mi.) At the end of the descent, you'll reach a sign that says, "To Sugar Tree Trail." Turn left to continue on the Smokerise Trail, which is a narrower path that runs level and heads south.

The path remains mostly level as it cruises through an attractive hardwood forest with occasionally a tree draped in thick vines. At 0.7 mi., the path crosses the first of three streams and continues through an emerald landscape of mossy rocks and trees. When you've gone a little more than a mile, be on the lookout for red trillium beside the path.

63-1 (34.65385, -86.52547) (1 mi.) To the right, the Smokerise Connector winds down the slope for 0.16 mi. and ends at the top of a steep side street off of Smoke Rise Road. To stay on the main Smokerise Trail, continue straight to the southwest.

The path is mellow and rolls along through dense forest crowded with vines and fallen trees. At 1.4 mi., the path climbs gradually, and a house is visible on the right.

62-3 (34.65046, -86.53095) (1.5 mi.) You reach the junction with the Sugar Tree Trail. If you continue straight, you can follow the Sugar Tree Trail for 0.4 mi. to the Sugar Tree Trailhead.

Rose vervain

Trail Facts

Historic Blevins Gap Road: Descriptions of the Blevins Gap Road date back to the early 1800s. Madison County maintained the road until 1875, when their attention turned to developing the Big Cove Turnpike, which went over Monte Sano Mountain. The Big Cove Turnpike was created to serve the growing number of people living on Monte Sano Mountain and those settling in areas northeast of Huntsville.

63. Smokerise Connector

This short but steep path connects the Smokerise Trail to the Willowbrook neighborhood at the western base of Huntsville Mountain and Green Mountain. The trail begins at the end of a short, steep road off Smoke Rise Road. This connector primarily serves people in the neighborhood, giving them quick access to nearby Land Trust trails. Be aware that there is no designated parking at this trailhead, and you will probably block someone's driveway if you try to park near the beginning of the trail. Find parking on a nearby street instead.

Distance: 0.16 mi.
Hiking Time: 5 to 10 minutes
Elevation Gain/Loss: +82 ft., -0 ft.
Hiking Difficulty: Moderate to strenuous
Location: Blevins Gap Nature Preserve, Smoke Rise Rd. SE, Huntsville, AL 35802
Facilities: There are no facilities or sources of potable water at the trailhead near Smoke Rise Road.
Driving Directions: From the junction of U.S. 231 (Memorial Parkway) and Whitesburg Drive, travel north on Whitesburg Dr. for 0.5 mi., and then turn right onto Lily Flagg Road. Travel east on Lily Flagg Rd. for 1.1 mi., and then turn left onto Willowbrook Drive. Travel for 1.5 mi. on Willowbrook Dr., and then turn right onto Smoke Rise Road. Track your mileage carefully and go 0.3 mi. on Smoke Rise Road. Then turn left onto the unnamed short, steep street that dead-ends at the edge of the forest. This left turn will be about 80 ft. before the junction with Valley Bend Drive. Note that there is no designated parking area at this trailhead.

Waypoint/Mile

Trailhead (Waypoint 63) (34.65502, -86.52600) The Smokerise Connector begins at the Valley Bend Trailhead, which lies at the end of a short, steep residential street off Smoke Rise Road. The trail immediately begins to wind upward through the open forest of hardwoods and cedar trees, heading south. You'll follow switchbacks on a moderate to steep ascent, and at 0.14 mi. pass a tumbling stream.

63-1 (34.65385, -86.52547) (0.16 mi.) The connector trail ends at the junction with the Smokerise Trail.

64. Sugar Tree Trail

The Sugar Tree Trail traverses the northern section of the Blevins Gap Preserve on Green Mountain. It offers hikers a moderately challenging trek, and its middle section includes a long, sustained climb measuring just over half a mile. The path serves as a link between the Sugar Tree Trailhead and the Blevins Gap Trailhead, allowing hikers to do long point-to-point treks, extended out-and-back hikes, or lengthy loops.

Distance: 1.5 mi.
Hiking Time: 1 hour
Elevation Gain/Loss: +596 ft., -62 ft.
Hiking Difficulty: Moderate to strenuous
Location: Blevins Gap Nature Preserve, Sugar Tree Place, Huntsville, AL 35802
Facilities: There are no facilities and no sources of potable water at the Sugar Tree Trailhead.
Driving Directions: From the junction of U.S. 231 (Memorial Parkway) and Weatherly Road, travel east on Weatherly Rd. for 1.9 mi. Then turn left onto Sugar Tree Trail, go 240 ft., and then turn right onto Sugar Tree Place. The trailhead is at the end of the road. While there are no designated parking spots, you can park on the side of Sugar Tree Pl.

Mayapple plants carpet the forest floor.

Highlights

Diverse Terrain: The Sugar Tree Trail will keep you engaged as it explores a wide variety of terrain. It begins in moody woods where dense tree canopy shades the forest and the path winds through a boulder garden with wildflowers. Higher up, the trail breaks into the open and broadens to be as wide as a road as it crawls up Green Mountain. Running below the summit, the trail moves through an entertaining stretch with an abandoned car (how'd it get there?), fields of mayapple, and mature woods bathed in sunshine.

Waypoint/Mile

Trailhead (Waypoint 64) (34.64665, -86.53109) At the end of Sugar Tree Place, begin at the trailhead kiosk and take the Sugar Tree Trail, which enters a shaded hardwood forest and runs through a corridor of boulders. Follow the diamond blazes marked Sugar Tree Trail.

64-1 (34.64684, -86.52988) (425 ft.) At the T junction, turn left and travel west on the level path. The trail to the right is an old route.

The Sugar Tree Trail levels out over the next 200 ft., and then the path rises gradually. Hardwoods hug the rocky and rooted trail, and wildflowers nestle against rocks, adding splashes of pink, purple and gold to the gray backdrop.

64-2 (34.64758, -86.52971) (0.2 mi.) Turn left and travel northwest to continue on the Sugar Tree Trail. Go another 384 ft. to reach Waypoint 64-3.

64-3 (34.64786, -86.53032) (0.28 mi.) To the left is a small, short rock shelter.

When you pass the shelter, you'll leave the wonderland of rocks and wildflowers and climb through dense forest. At 0.3 mi., pine needles blanket the path.

62-3 (34.65046, -86.53095) (0.4 mi.) At the Y junction, go right and ascend to the north to continue on the Sugar Tree Trail. If you go straight, you'll enter the Smokerise Trail. At this junction, the trail widens and becomes very rocky, with large flat stones serving as broad steps to carry you up the mountain. Tree limbs curl over the path to create a natural awning that provides shade.

At 0.76 mi., the long climb ends and the path levels out briefly. Soon, you're moving upward again, but the ascent is gradual as before, and the trail isn't as rugged. At 1.3 mi., you reach the oddest resident of the trail—a rusted, wrecked car. After you pass the vehicle, you curl to the right and begin a moderate ascent.

64-4 (34.65307, -86.51925) (1.3 mi.) The Varnedoe Trail intersects on the right and curls to the southwest. To continue on the Sugar Tree Trail, go straight, traveling northeast. If you hike in midspring, you may encounter large fields of mayapple, with their deep-green, umbrella-like leaves. Up ahead, the trail dives to meet the Lowry Trail.

64-5 (34.65445, -86.51730) (1.5 mi.) The Lowry Trail intersects on the left and descends to the northwest. The Sugar Tree Trail bends to the right and heads northeast.

64-6 (34.65455, -86.51671) (1.59 mi.) The Sugar Tree Trail ends at the junction with the Bill and Marion Certain Trail. If you turn left and descend on the Bill and Marion Certain Trail, you'll walk 0.2 mi. to reach the Blevins Gap Trailhead parking area on Cecil Ashburn Drive.

Trail Facts

Marvelous Mayapple: A large patch of mayapple appears to be many individual plants, but the group is actually one plant. In May, the plant produces a single fruit, which dangles beneath the umbrella-like leaves. If the fruit is ripe, you can eat it, but you'll have to get there before the turtles, as mayapple is one of their favorite foods.

SECTION 4:
Bill and Marion Certain Trail, Lowry Trail, West Bluff Trail and Varnedoe Trail

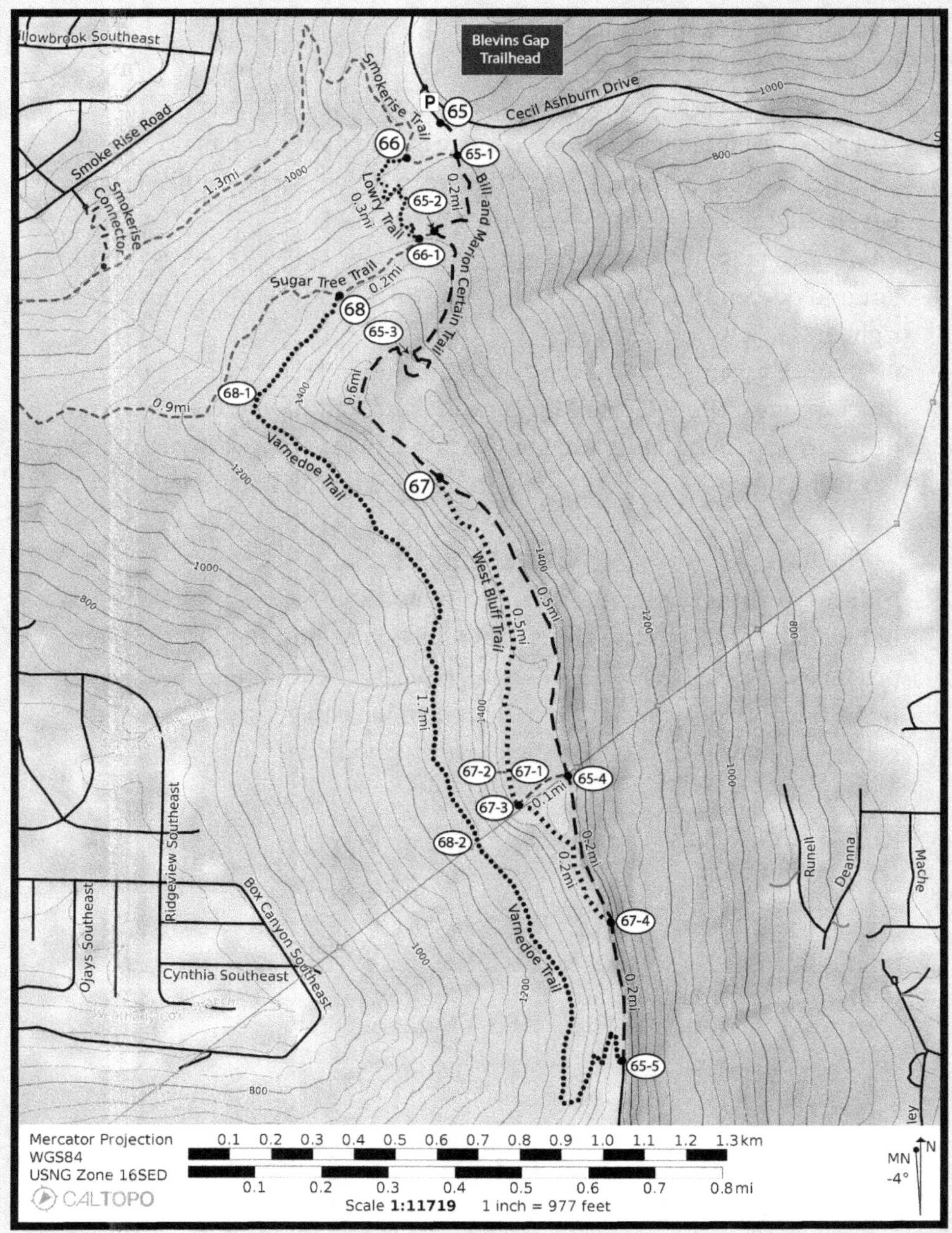

65. Bill and Marion Certain Trail

The Bill and Marion Certain Trail is one of the most popular paths in the Blevins Gap Preserve. It includes a steep but short ascent that brings hikers to an intriguing rock shelter. Then the path climbs to the top of Green Mountain to offer an easy stroll with panoramic views of the valley and distant mountains to the east.

Distance: 1.9 mi.

Hiking Time: 1 to 1.5 hours

Elevation Gain/Loss: +468 ft., -202 ft.

Hiking Difficulty: Moderate

Location: Blevins Gap Nature Preserve, 3470 Cecil Ashburn Dr. SE, Huntsville, AL 35802

Facilities: At the trailhead, there is a portable toilet but no source of potable water.

Driving Directions: See page 174 and use the directions for the Blevins Gap Trailhead.

Highlights

Rock Shelter: A little past the half-mile mark, the trail visits a natural rock shelter that offers welcome shade on a warm hiking day. A short rock ledge provides a good place to sit while you grab a snack and enjoy the soothing sounds of the nearby creek. Anyone who visits this rock formation can easily imagine that people throughout the ages have paused here to rest.

Bluff Views: About a mile in, the trail runs near the edge of the bluff on the mountain's eastern side. This affords excellent, unobstructed views of the vast valley immediately to the east. Allow time to stop for a while at a bench that sits near the edge of the bluff near the 1.7-mi. mark (just beyond Waypoint 67-4).

Fall Wildflowers: We usually associate wildflowers with spring, but several species thrive in the fall on Green Mountain. You might see the drooping, bright-yellow petals of gray-headed coneflower and the green, lacy fronds of maidenhair ferns, as well as Loomis' mountain mint, beautyberry and rabbit tobacco.

Waypoint/Mile

Trailhead (Waypoint 65) (34.65698, -86.51670) At the southeast end of the Blevins Gap Trailhead parking area, take the Bill and Marion Certain Trail, which ascends gradually to the south over rocky terrain.

65-1 (34.65624, -86.51632) (152 ft.) The Smokerise Trail intersects on the right. You'll see a prominent trail sign directing you toward the Bill and Marion Certain Trail, the Smokerise Trail, and the Sugar Tree Trail. To continue on the Bill and Marion Certain Trail, continue straight and climb, traveling southeast.

65-2 (34.65452, -86.51682) (0.2 mi.) At the junction, the Sugar Tree Trail goes right and heads southwest. Turn left to continue on the Bill and Marion Certain Trail, which soon begins a steady climb. (Note that when you leave Waypoint 65-2 and walk about 20 ft., you'll reach a junction where an old path goes downhill. Continue past this junction, bear right and head southeast.)

At 0.4 mi. you begin to climb, and the path is steep for about 0.1 mi.

65-3 (34.65163, -86.51744) (0.54 mi.) After walking for about half a mile,

A natural shelter lies along the Bill and Marion Certain Trail.

you'll reach a stream and see to the left a rock shelter. Turn left to reach the shelter. When you're done exploring the rock formation, go to the left side of the shelter and make a short climb. The path crosses back over the top of the rock shelter and turns right to head southwest. After a short distance, the trail bends to the north.

At 0.6 mi., you'll see on the right a path that leads back to the shelter. Continue past this junction, climbing to the northwest. The trail climbs steeply and at 0.67 mi. reaches a bench. From this point, the path rises to run level and crosses the crest of Green Mountain. If you walk this trail in midspring, you'll encounter large swaths of mayapple plants.

67 (34.64903, -86.51678) (0.9 mi.) The West Bluff Trail intersects on the right and runs southeast. Bear left and continue to the southeast on a path that widens and offers expansive views of Little Mountain and distant green hills to the east.

65-4 (34.64254, -86.51331) (1.4 mi.) At the powerline, you'll have a sweeping view of the Big Cove Valley from the north to the east, as well as Little Mountain to the east. When you enter the powerline break, you'll see on the right a connector trail that runs for 0.1 mi. to intersect with the West Bluff Trail, which offers more great views.

67-4 (34.63914, -86.51213) (1.7 mi.) The West Bluff Trail intersects on the right and heads northwest. Continue straight, traveling south. After walking about 50 ft., you'll reach a bench that sits just off the left side of the trail. This is the perfect spot to rest and refuel while soaking in the sweeping view of Big Cove.

65-5 (34.63615, -86.51187) (1.9 mi.) The Bill and Marion Certain Trail ends at a junction with the Varnedoe Trail, which intersects on the right and drops steeply down the western side of the mountain.

Trail Facts

Bill and Marion Certain: The trail is named for the Certain family, who sold this property to Forever Wild, which is the state of Alabama's land trust organization. The Land Trust of North Alabama and Forever Wild worked together to preserve this part of the mountain because it is an important part of the Blevins Gap Nature Preserve (*Source: Land Trust of North Alabama.*)

66. Lowry Trail

The brief and steep Lowry Trail connects the Smokerise Trail and the Sugar Tree Trail near the Blevins Gap Trailhead. Hikers who begin at the Blevins Gap Trailhead can take the Lowry Trail if they want a more challenging (and slightly more appealing) route to reach the Sugar Tree Trail and higher-elevation portions of the Bill and Marion Certain Trail.

Distance: 0.3 mi.
Hiking Time: 10 minutes
Elevation Gain/Loss: +137 ft., -12 ft.
Hiking Difficulty: Moderate to strenuous
Location: Blevins Gap Nature Preserve, 3470 Cecil Ashburn Dr. SE, Huntsville, AL 35802
Facilities: At the trailhead, there is a portable toilet but no source of potable water.
Driving Directions: See page 174 and use the directions for the Blevins Gap Trailhead.

Highlights

A Rewarding Challenge: The Lowry Trail might leave you winded, but it runs through a beautifully rugged stretch of forest. While you're climbing, you'll have a clear view of the slope above. This is a mature section of woods with healthy hardwoods dispersed widely across open ground. The route includes switchbacks that wind among jagged rocks draped in rich green moss and splotched with pale lichen.

Waypoint/Mile

Trailhead (Waypoint 66) (34.65617, -86.51768) To reach the Lowry Trail, begin at the Blevins Gap Trailhead parking area on Cecil Ashburn Drive. Enter the Bill and Marion Certain Trail and walk 0.1 mi. to the junction with the Smokerise Trail. Turn right onto the Smokerise Trail and walk 0.1 mi. to the junction with the Lowry Trail, which intersects on the left at Waypoint 66.

The path soon becomes steeper and snakes its way up the mountain.

After a little more than 0.1 mi., the trail levels out briefly on the boulder-strewn slope. But soon you resume a steady climb on the rocky and rooted path, which follows a series of switchbacks.

66-1 (34.65445, -86.51730) (0.3 mi.) The Lowry Trail ends at the junction with the Sugar Tree Trail. If you turn left onto the Sugar Tree Trail, you'll travel east, head back toward the Bill and Marion Certain Trail, and reach the trailhead. The other option is to turn right onto the Sugar Tree Trail and begin one of several possible long loop hikes.

Trail Facts

Land Trust Donors: The trail is named for the Lowry family, which donated a portion of the land that makes up the Blevins Gap Preserve.

67. West Bluff Trail

The West Bluff Trail is one of the most popular destinations for people hiking the Blevins Gap Preserve. The path hugs the bluff on the west side of the mountain to offer stellar views of south Huntsville and Redstone Arsenal. Rock outcrops along the trail make perfect spots to take photos with an impressive backdrop.

Distance: 0.8 mi.

Hiking Time: 20 to 25 minutes

Elevation Gain/Loss: +69 ft., -170 ft.

Hiking Difficulty: Easy

Location: Blevins Gap Nature Preserve, 3470 Cecil Ashburn Dr. SE, Huntsville, AL 35802

Facilities: At the trailhead, there is a portable toilet but no source of potable water.

Driving Directions: See page 174 and use the directions for the Blevins Gap Trailhead.

Highlights

Bluff Views and Great Photo Ops: Be sure to bring your phone or other camera for this hike. A small rock outcrop at 0.4 mi. and a large outcrop at 0.57 mi. are ideal places to take great photos from the high bluff overlooking south Huntsville.

Waypoint/Mile

Trailhead (Waypoint 67) (34.64903, -86.51678) To reach the West Bluff Trail, begin at the Blevins Gap Trailhead parking area on Cecil Ashburn Drive. Follow the Bill and Marion Certain Trail for 0.9 mi., and you'll reach the junction with the West Bluff Trail on the right. Turn right onto the West Bluff Trail, traveling southeast.

The path moves to the edge of the bluff, allowing you to get your first decent views to the west. The trail drops gradually, crosses a stream, and then climbs steeply for about 80 ft. to level off.

67-1 (34.64277, -86.51482) (0.4 mi.) On the right, a 90-ft. path leads to an overlook with a bench.

67-2 (34.64271, -86.51535) (0.43 mi.) This outcrop offers a bird's-eye view of the valley. Tall pines hugging the bluff frame a picture before you: Filling the foreground are houses and other buildings nestled among the trees. Far in the distance, a vast tract of wooded land runs to the horizon.

At 0.57 mi., you get another opportunity to take some great photos, as a rock outcrop provides another panoramic view. Go 50 ft. more to reach Waypoint 67-3.

67-3 (34.64171, -86.51467) (0.57 mi.) On the left, a connector trail runs northeast through the powerline break for 0.1 mi. to meet the Bill and Marion Certain Trail. Continue straight to head southeast on the West Bluff Trail. You'll pass through high grass and at 0.6 mi. leave the powerline break and descend.

67-4 (34.63914, -86.51213) (0.8 mi.) The West Bluff Trail ends at a junction with the Bill and Marion Certain Trail.

Trail Facts

Sprawling Redstone Arsenal: The West Bluff Trail offers one of the best chances to see the vast size of Redstone Arsenal, which covers nearly 60 square miles.

The West Bluff Trail offers sweeping views of the Tennessee Valley.

68. Varnedoe Trail

Compared to the West Bluff Trail and Bill and Marion Certain Trail, the Varnedoe Trail offers a bit more solitude and draws fewer hikers. That's because the Varnedoe Trail doesn't traverse the top of the mountain, so it offers fewer views. But trail runners and hikers seeking fairly level terrain will appreciate the Varnedoe Trail. It has a 1.6-mi. section that gains and loses very little elevation. That gives you plenty of time to stride out and enjoy your zen mode before you end the trip with a steep climb that stretches almost 0.3 mi.

Distance: 1.8 mi.

Hiking Time: 1 hour

Elevation Gain/Loss: +424 ft., -278 ft.

Hiking Difficulty: First 1.6 mi., easy; last 0.28 mi., strenuous

Location: Blevins Gap Nature Preserve, 3470 Cecil Ashburn Dr. SE, Huntsville, AL 35802

Facilities: At the trailhead, there is a portable toilet but no source of potable water.

Driving Directions: See page 174 and use the directions for the Blevins Gap Trailhead.

Highlights

A Good Trail for Running: Local trail runners often use the Varnedoe Trail to train for races. The path offers a long stretch that's relatively level, which allows runners to work on their speed while also negotiating a bit of rocky terrain. On the final leg of the route, runners face a steep climb that helps build their strength and stamina.

Impressive Tennessee Valley View: No, the Varnedoe Trail doesn't boast the number of stellar overlooks you encounter on the top of the mountain. However, at 1.1 mi. the trail crosses a powerline break, where you're greeted by a very nice western view. As you look down the wide forest break, a spur of Green Mountain a half-mile away forms a great slope that dominates the scene. Beyond this slope, Weatherly Mountain rolls like a cresting wave. Beyond that, the Tennessee River forms a wide crescent slicing across the green countryside, and even farther out, long mountain ridges form a hazy wall of green and blue on the horizon.

Waypoint/Mile

Trailhead (Waypoint 68) (34.65306, -86.51933) The Varnedoe Trail can be accessed via the Sugar Tree Trail and the Bill and Marion Certain

tain Trail. If you're looking for a long hike, you can begin at the Sugar Tree Trailhead and follow the Sugar Tree Trail for 1.4 mi. to its junction with the Varnedoe Trail.

The hike described in this book follows a somewhat shorter route to access the Varnedoe Trail. The trip begins at the Blevins Gap Trailhead parking area on Cecil Ashburn Drive. Take the Bill and Marion Certain Trail 0.2 mi. to the Sugar Tree Trail. Then take the Sugar Tree Trail 0.2 mi. to the junction with the Varnedoe Trail. Turn left onto the Varnedoe Trail and travel southwest.

The narrow, leaf-covered path begins by running level through a landscape of high boulders and some very tall and stout hardwood trees.

68-1 (34.65076, -86.52151) (0.2 mi.) The trail skirts a small rock shelter and then takes a decisive turn to the left to head southeast. As you continue down the level path, you can look to the southwest to see distant ridges through the treetops.

At 0.9 mi., the trail weaves up and down the slope to go around downed trees. For the next 0.1 mi., the path remains relatively level, but there are a few rocky areas where runners will need to pay attention.

68-2 (34.64111, -86.51580) (1.1 mi.) As you cross a powerline break, enjoy a long view of the Tennessee Valley to the west.

Over the next half-mile, the path rollercoasters and alternates between sections with packed earth and spots that are rocky and rooted. In the spring, you might encounter eastern redbud trees, whose pink and purple blossoms pop amidst the greens, grays and browns of the forest. At 1.6 mi., the path begins a steep climb up a wide, rocky path.

65-5 (34.63608, -86.51187) (1.88 mi.) The Varnedoe Trail ends at the junction with the Bill and Marion Certain Trail. At the trail junction at the top of the ridge, turn left and follow the wide treadway north. After walking 30 ft., you'll see on the left the trail marker for the Bill and Marion Certain Trail.

To return to the Blevins Gap Trailhead, I recommend that you take the Bill and Marion Certain Trail. This 1.9-mi. walk covers mostly easy terrain, and you'll have excellent bluff views as you traverse a high ridge on Green Mountain.

Trail Facts

The Varnedoes: The trail is named for Bill and Louise Varnedoe, long-time residents of Green Mountain and well-known members of the local caving and hiking communities. Louise, who passed away in 2020 at the age of 90, earned a degree in physics from Maryville College in Tennessee and worked for the Atomic Energy Commission in Oak Ridge. She also worked as an engineer at the U.S. Army Ballistic Missile Agency on the Redstone Missile Program. Later, she worked at Dynetics in Huntsville.

Louise and Bill founded the Green Mountain Fire Department, and Bill was the first chief of the Huntsville Cave Rescue Unit. During World War II, Bill flew on combat missions as a B-17 navigator. He later graduated from Georgia Tech as an electrical engineer and worked at NASA, contributing to the Apollo and Saturn programs (*Sources: Land Trust of North Alabama and the Vietnam Veterans of America Chapter 1088 Facebook group.*)

Green Mountain Preserve

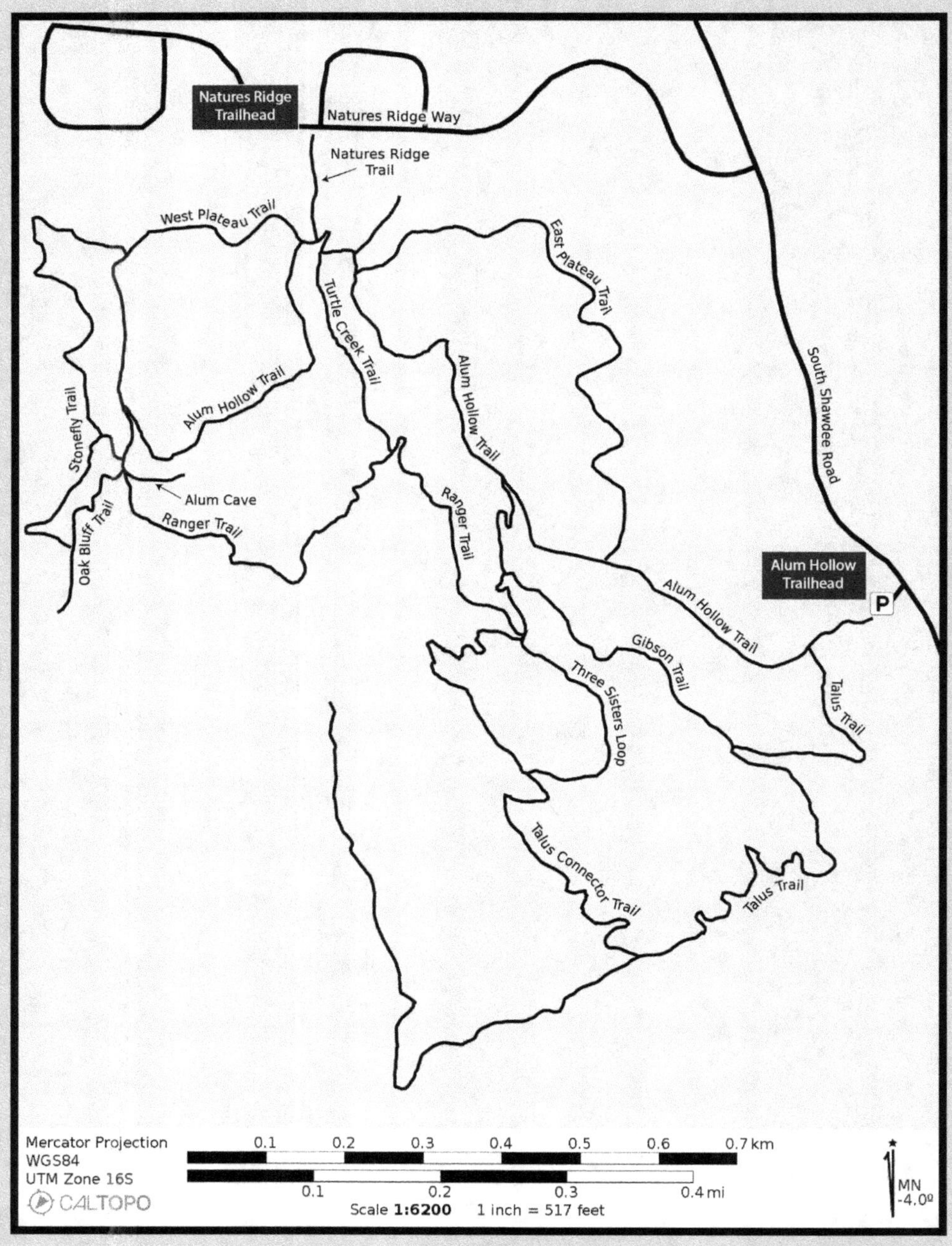

CHAPTER 6

Green Mountain Nature Preserve

In 2016, Robert and Susan Kuehlthau donated 122 acres of Green Mountain land to the Land Trust of North Alabama to establish the Green Mountain Nature Preserve. Then, in 2021, the couple donated an additional 248 acres. Over time, this preserve has become a favorite destination for local hikers who appreciate the area's rugged beauty and natural features, including waterfalls, rock shelters, wildflowers and excellent bluff views.

Located on the southeastern border of Huntsville, Green Mountain stretches for seven miles and rises to an elevation of 1,450 feet. The nature preserve lies in the heart of the mountain, and it includes at least 13 trails with a combined distance of more than six miles. Many of the trails explore the plateau at the top of the mountain, while others explore the slopes and base of Alum Cave Hollow, a small valley that's more than 500 feet deep.

The most popular path in the preserve is probably the Alum Hollow Trail. Much of this path runs along the top of a plateau, and the level terrain and bluff views appeal to a wide range of people, including parents hiking with their kids, trail runners, and regular visitors walking for exercise. But its main appeal is that it leads to Alum Cave (a rock shelter once used by Native Americans) and a neighboring creek with waterfalls.

While trails on the plateau offer easy terrain, the paths that explore Alum Cave Hollow offer moderate to strenuous treks for adventurous hikers. A highlight is the Ranger Trail, which makes a steep dive from the plateau and visits a lively creek in the lower elevations of the hollow. It then scrambles over rocky terrain and climbs to Alum Cave.

General Information

Location: 13800 South Shawdee Rd., Huntsville, AL 35803

Hours: Dawn to dusk

Primary trail activities allowed: Hiking, biking

Pets: Leashed pets allowed.

Fees: There are no fees to use the trails. At the trailhead there is a donation box for the Land Trust of North Alabama.

Facilities: There are no facilities and no sources of potable water at the Alum Hollow Trailhead and the Natures Ridge Trailhead.

Information: (256) 534-5263; www.landtrustnal.org/properties/green-mountain-preserve/; questions@landtrustnal.org

Driving Directions

Alum Hollow Trailhead

From the junction of U.S. 231 (Memorial Parkway) and Weatherly Road, travel east on Weatherly Rd. for 1.5 mi., and then turn right onto Bailey Cove Road. Travel 171 ft., take a slight right to continue on Bailey Cove Rd., and travel another 1.2 mi. Then turn left onto Green Mountain Road, travel 1.8 mi., and turn right onto South Shawdee Road. Go 2 mi., and then turn right into the parking area for the Alum Hollow Trailhead.

Natures Ridge Trailhead

From the junction of U.S. 231 (Memorial Parkway) and Weatherly Road, travel east on Weatherly Rd. for 1.5 mi., and then turn right onto Bailey Cove Road. Travel 171 ft., take a slight right to continue on Bailey Cove Rd., and travel another 1.2 mi. Turn left onto Green Mountain Road, travel 1.8 mi., and then turn right onto South Shawdee Road. Go 1.6 mi., and then turn right onto Natures Ridge Way. Travel 0.4 mi. to the trailhead information sign, which is on the left.

SECTION 1:
Alum Hollow Trail, East Plateau Trail, Ranger Trail, Natures Ridge Trail and Gibson Trail

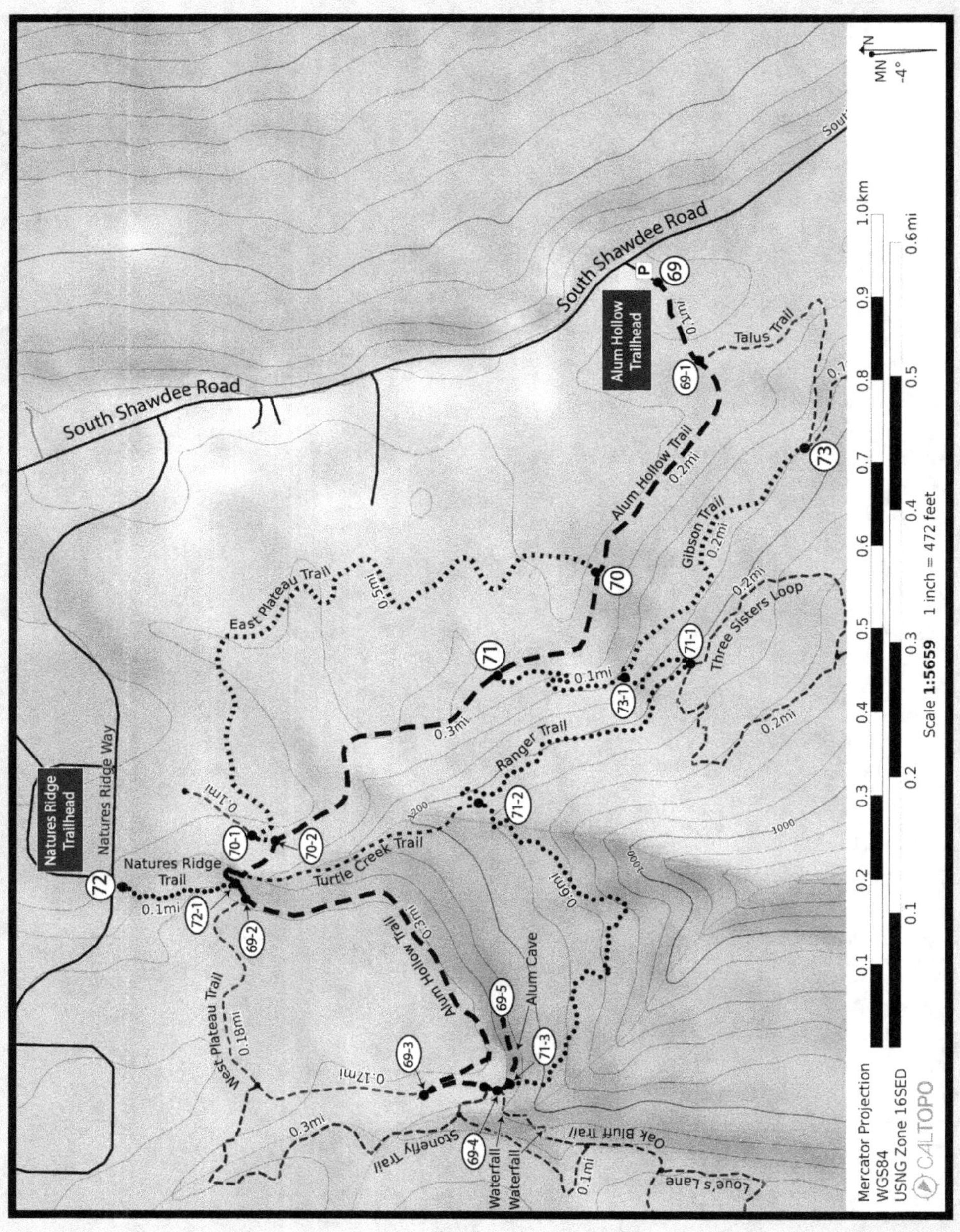

69. Alum Hollow Trail

This is the most popular path in the Green Mountain Nature Preserve. For the most part, the trail is easy, it boasts dramatic views, and it ends at an impressive rock shelter. Also, near the end of the path you can descend a short distance to reach a stream and waterfalls. While the first mile of the hike is mostly flat, the final portion includes a short but steep descent to reach Alum Cave.

Distance: 1.1 mi.

Hiking Time: 30 to 40 minutes

Elevation Gain/Loss: +83 ft., -168 ft.

Hiking Difficulty: Easy (with one moderate section near the end)

Location: Green Mountain Nature Preserve, 13800 South Shawdee Rd. SE, Huntsville, AL 35803

Driving Directions: See page 216 and use the directions for the Alum Hollow Trailhead.

Highlights

Alum Cave: The trail's most notable feature isn't really a cave, but rather a large undercut rock that forms a natural shelter with a vast low roof. Whenever I duck into the cool shade of this shelter, I'm fascinated by the idea that people have visited this site for more than 10,000 years. As a trail interpretive sign notes, "Caves on the mountainsides served as temporary shelters for hunting bands or final resting places for the dead."

Great Views and Rugged Scenery: The Alum Hollow Trail gives you the feeling of being in a remote mountain wilderness. For most of the way, the path skirts the edge of the bluff, so you enjoy lofty views of a broad, deep valley and towering ridge. You really feel the sense of being at a high elevation. The mature oaks and the cedars and rock outcrops along the dusty path resemble a walk in the high mountains. When you descend to Alum Cave, the scenery is equally impressive, as the rock shelter looks out over a deep draw and a nearby stream crashes down a steep drainage.

Waypoint/Mile

Trailhead (Waypoint 69) (34.58942, -86.51000) Begin at the kiosk at the southwestern end of the Alum Hollow Trailhead parking area. From the kiosk, take the marked Alum Hollow Trail, traveling north on a wide path of packed earth.

69-1 (34.58914, -86.51092) (354 ft.) The Talus Trail intersects on the left and heads southeast. Continue straight and gradually descend to the southwest.

Take the footbridge across a stream to reach higher ground and get your first view of Alum Cave Hollow, which is the valley to the west. The path levels out and continues along the edge of the bluff.

70 (34.59028, -86.51379) (0.2 mi.) At the Y junction, go left to continue on the Alum Hollow Trail, which runs level to the west. The path to the right is the East Plateau Trail, which rises gradually to the north.

The path continues through stands of pines, cedars and old hardwoods as it skirts the bluff. A forested ridge dominates your view to the west.

71 (34.59130, -86.51512) (0.4 mi.) The Ranger Trail intersects on the left and drops down the steep slope. To stay on the Alum Hollow Trail, go straight, traveling northwest.

After you walk another 315 feet, you'll reach a bench sitting on a rocky point. This is a great place to relax and enjoy the scenery. Just beyond the half-mile mark, the path begins to follow a stream, and at 0.6 mi. the sound of the rushing water blends with the whoosh of wind blowing up from the hollow.

70-2 (34.59380, -86.51718) (0.6 mi.) The East Plateau Trail intersects on the right and heads northeast. To continue on the Alum Hollow Trail, bear left and descend toward the creek.

A quick descent to the creek brings you to a wide, 20-ft.-long footbridge. Once you've crossed the stream, turn right and head north toward a nearby neighborhood. After a short distance, the trail hooks left and goes southwest.

72-1 (34.59399, -86.51784) (0.71 mi.) The Natures Ridge trail intersects on the right and runs north. Continue straight, heading southwest.

69-2 (34.59401, -86.51810) (0.73 mi.) The West Plateau Trail intersects on the right and bends to the northwest. To follow the Alum Hollow Trail, go left and travel south.

69-3 (34.59203, -86.52055) (1.02 mi.) The Alum Hollow Trail intersects with the West Plateau Trail. To continue on the Alum Hollow Trail, turn left and travel south.

69-4 (34.59125, -86.52054) (1.07 mi.) To the right, the Oak Bluff Trail drops down to the creek and a set of falls. To explore Alum Cave, bear left and hug the rock wall, which soon becomes a deep and broad natural shelter with a low roof.

Alum Cave was used as a shelter during the Middle Woodland period (1AD – 500AD)

71-3 (34.59115, -86.52045) (1.1 mi.) The Ranger Trail intersects and makes a steep drop. Continue along the rock shelter, which stretches about 200 feet.

69-5 (34.59122, -86.51961) (1.2 mi.) You reach the eastern end of the rock shelter.

Trail Facts

Native Americans and Alum Cave: Stone tools and potsherds found in and around Alum Cave indicate that hunters and gatherers visited the rock shelter for at least 10,000 years. An interpretive sign near the trailhead explains that Native Americans sought out such places at high elevation so they could more easily spot herds of game as well as the fires of "interloping bands" of hunters. Also, Native Americans couldn't find certain resources in the lower elevations of the Tennessee Valley. So, they ventured into the mountainous areas to gather important foods and medicinal plants like potato beans and ginseng.

70. East Plateau Trail

Looking for a pleasant hike on a level trail? Curling through the northeast section of the Green Mountain Preserve, the East Plateau Trail does just what the name implies—it crosses the mountain plateau and gains and loses little elevation. Along the way, residential homes are visible, so this isn't really a remote trail, but the open and airy pine and hardwood forest is inviting. At the end of the East Plateau Trail, you can take the Alum Hollow Trail back to the trailhead for a trip that totals 1.4 mi. and includes nice bluff views.

Distance: 0.6 mi.
Hiking Time: 15 to 20 minutes
Elevation Gain/Loss: +52 ft., -94 ft.
Hiking Difficulty: Easy
Location: Green Mountain Nature Preserve, 13800 South Shawdee Rd. SE, Huntsville, AL 35803
Driving Directions: See page 216 and use the directions for the Alum Hollow Trailhead.

Highlights

Terrain for Beginning Trail Runners: The East Plateau Trail is a perfect option for beginning trail runners. It crosses flat and rolling terrain that is largely free of rocks and roots. If you're new to the sport, it's wise to begin with relatively level trails that don't include a lot of obstacles or steep terrain. It generally takes longer and requires more effort to run a trail than a paved road or a track of equal distance. By easing into trail running, you can dial in your pace, work on your technique, and test gear without getting injured or worn out. To reach the East Plateau Trail, follow the Alum Hollow Trail, which traverses similar terrain, but also includes some nice views. You can combine these two routes for an awesome run.

Waypoint/Mile

Trailhead (Waypoint 70) (34.59012, -86.51365) Begin at the kiosk at the southwestern end of the Alum Hollow Trailhead parking area. Take the Alum Hollow Trail for 0.2 mi. to the junction with the East Plateau Trail, which intersects on the right. Turn right onto the East Plateau Trail and climb gradually to the north on a single-track path.

The trail begins in dense forest dominated by pines. At 175 ft., the trail nears a fence line for private property, and soon the woods become a mix of mature pines and oaks. The trail rolls along comfortably, passes homes and nears a backyard before turning left to move downhill to the northwest. At 0.4 mi., you cross a stream on a 65-ft.-long wooden footbridge. On a hill ahead, more houses come into view.

70-1 (34.5937, -86.5172) (0.6 mi.) The East Plateau Trail intersects with an unofficial trail that stretches for 262 ft. and ends at the Land Trust boundary near homes. To continue on the East Plateau Trail, take a sharp left turn to head southwest.

The East Plateau Trail goes about another 100 feet and ends at a junction with the Alum Hollow Trail.

70-2 (34.5934, -86.5173) (0.6 mi.) The East Plateau Trail ends at the junction with the Alum Hollow Trail.

Trail Facts

The Wardlaw Bridge: At 0.4 mi., you cross a stream on a 65-ft.-long wood footbridge built in memory of John W. Wardlaw, who passed away in 2016. Wardlaw was a resident of Green Mountain and an engineer at McDonnell Douglas/Boeing. He was active in the community, serving as safety chairman of the Green Mountain Civic League, which works to protect the Green Mountain environment and the mountain's residents.

71. Ranger Trail

The Ranger Trail explores a creek deep in Alum Cave Hollow and offers a more rugged and challenging way to reach Alum Cave. Beginning on the edge of the plateau, the trail dives into the hollow and crosses a tumbling stream. It then makes a long, steady climb over rocky ground to end at the cave.

Distance: 0.8 mi.
Hiking Time: 30 to 40 minutes
Elevation Gain/Loss: +256 ft., -315 ft.

Hiking Difficulty: Strenuous
Location: Green Mountain Nature Preserve, 13800 South Shawdee Rd. SE, Huntsville, AL 35803
Driving Directions: See page 216 and use the directions for the Alum Hollow Trailhead.

Highlights

Alum Cave: The Ranger Trail ends at the western end of Alum Cave, which is actually a wide and deep natural shelter rather than a cave. The rock formation stretches about 200 ft. and offers a lofty view of the hollow, making it one of the primary attractions in the Green Mountain Nature Preserve. Artifacts discovered at the site indicate that people have been visiting this shelter for more than 10,000 years.

Creek Crossings: Near the half-mile mark, the trail explores a creek deep in the hollow. If you hike within a few days of a good rain, you'll find a lively, rushing stream with miniature falls and chutes and pools of cool, clear water.

Waypoint/Mile

Trailhead (Waypoint 71) (34.59128, -86.51511) To reach the Ranger Trail, begin at the kiosk at the southwestern end of the Alum Hollow Trailhead parking area. From the kiosk, walk 0.4 mi. on the Alum Hollow Trail to where the Ranger Trail intersects on the left. Turn left onto the Ranger Trail and travel southwest, descending into Alum Cave Hollow.

The hike begins with a descent that is occasionally very steep and stretches a little more than 0.1 mi.

73-1 (34.58977, -86.51533) (0.13 mi.) The Gibson Trail intersects on the left. The Ranger Trail turns right and descends gradually.

After you've walked another 90 ft., you begin another short but very steep descent. The path then reaches ground that is much more level and descends gradually along the base of a bluff.

71-1 (34.58930, -86.51490) (0.2 mi.) The Three Sisters Loop Trail intersects on the left. To continue on the Ranger Trail, turn right to travel northwest.

The path is pretty mellow until about 0.3 mi., when it becomes very

A lively stream rushes through Alum Cave Hollow.

rocky. After another 0.1 mi., the trail reaches a stream.

71-2 (34.59106, -86.51708) (0.49 mi.) You cross an attractive section of the creek where the stream rushes into a small pool. When the creek is running strong, you can encounter a couple of larger pools. On warm spring days, these are good spots to enjoy a soak.

When the path moves away from the creek, it becomes rocky again, and you'll cross a point of land with impressive towering pines. The route then requires you to traverse fields of large rocks and boulders. It can be a challenge to identify the actual trail in this stony landscape, but there are white diamond blazes marking the way. Plus, you'll see round markers with a white arrow on a green background. If you're seeking a good workout, you'll get it here on a steady, steep climb. At 0.76 mi., the trail passes the wreckage of an old truck.

71-3 (34.59116, -86.52046) (0.8 mi.) After a long, steady climb, the Ranger Trail ends at the junction with the Alum Cave near the west end of the cave.

Trail Facts

Trail Ranger: You might think this rugged path is named in honor of forest rangers or U.S. Army Rangers. But it's actually named for the remains of a Ford Ranger truck that sit just below Alum Cave.

The wrecked remains of a Ford Ranger truck

225

72. Natures Ridge Trail

This short path connects the Green Mountain Nature Preserve trails and a nearby neighborhood.

Distance: 0.09 mi.
Hiking Time: 3 minutes
Elevation Gain/Loss: +19 ft., -27 ft.
Hiking Difficulty: Easy
Location: Green Mountain Nature Preserve, Natures Ridge Way, Huntsville, AL 35803
Fees: There are no fees to use this trail.
Facilities: There are no facilities and no water sources at the trailhead.
Driving Directions: See page 216 and use the directions for the Natures Ridge Trailhead.

Highlights

Quick Access to Miles of Trails: Some Land Trust trails are designed to provide people in certain neighborhoods easy access to nearby nature preserves. In this case, people living near the Natures Ridge Trail can walk a few minutes on this path to access the 366-acre Green Mountain Nature Preserve and its more than 5 miles of trails.

Waypoint/Mile

Trailhead (Waypoint 72) (34.59519, -86.51789) From the information kiosk beside Natures Ridge Way, head south on the Natures Ridge Trail. (**Note that you can also access the Natures Ridge Trail from the Alum Hollow Trailhead parking area. If you choose this option, take the Alum Hollow Trail for 0.71 mi. to the junction with the Natures Ridge Trail, which intersects on the right. Turn right onto the Natures Ridge Trail and travel north.)

From the trailhead on Natures Ridge Way, walk south for about 150 ft. and cross a wooden footbridge. The trail passes a house, crosses a powerline corridor and enters the woods.

72-1 (0.09 mi.) (34.59399, -86.51784) The Natures Ridge Trail ends at the junction with the Alum Hollow Trail.

Trail Facts

Natures Ridge Name: This trail is named for the nearby road Natures Ridge Way. This trail is an example of the Land Trust's efforts to make trail systems easily accessible for people who live nearby.

73. Gibson Trail

This short interior trail links the Talus Trail and the Ranger Trail. If you begin on the Talus Trail, you can use the Gibson Trail to very quickly and easily cut over to the Ranger Trail and head down into the hollow. The Gibson Trail also allows hikers to do a variety of different loops. For example, you can combine the Talus, Gibson, Ranger, and Alum Hollow Trails for a 1-mi. loop that's moderately challenging (there's a short, steep climb) and offers good bluff views.

Distance: 0.23 mi.
Hiking Time: 10 minutes
Elevation Gain/Loss: +63 ft., -13 ft.
Hiking Difficulty: Easy
Location: Green Mountain Nature Preserve, 13800 South Shawdee Rd. SE, Huntsville, AL 35803
Driving Directions: See page 216 and use the directions for the Alum Hollow Trailhead.

Highlights

Bluff Line Walk: When you've walked about 0.1 mi., you'll begin a really nice section of the Gibson Trail. The path passes through corridors of boulders and hugs the edge of a bluff, where you'll enjoy a clear view of the forest below.

Waypoint/Mile

Trailhead (Waypoint 73) (34.58810, -86.51215) To reach the beginning of the Gibson Trail, begin at the Alum Hollow Trailhead parking area. Follow the Alum Hollow Trail 354 ft. to the junction with the Talus

Trail. Travel 0.2 mi. on the Talus Trail to reach the junction with the Gibson Trail, which intersects on the right. Turn right onto the narrow Gibson Trail and follow the white diamond blazes.

The mostly level path winds through a very shaded forest of mature hardwoods. After about 400 ft., the trail becomes much rockier as you traverse a boulder-strewn slope. After walking 0.1 mi., you'll skirt the rocky edge of a bluff and walk between high boulders. At 0.14 mi., the trail begins a gradual climb to meet the Ranger Trail.

73-1 (34.59005, -86.51505) (0.23 mi.) The Gibson Trail ends at the junction with the Ranger Trail. If you turn right onto the Ranger Trail, you'll ascend 0.15 mi. to reach the mountain plateau. If you turn left onto the Ranger Trail, you'll descend into the hollow.

Trail Facts

Phill Gibson: The trail is named for Phill Gibson, a longtime supporter of the Land Trust of North Alabama who has served as a trail care partner and helped in many ways to develop the infrastructure of the Land Trust trail system.

SECTION 2:
Talus Trail, Talus Connector and Three Sisters Loop Trail

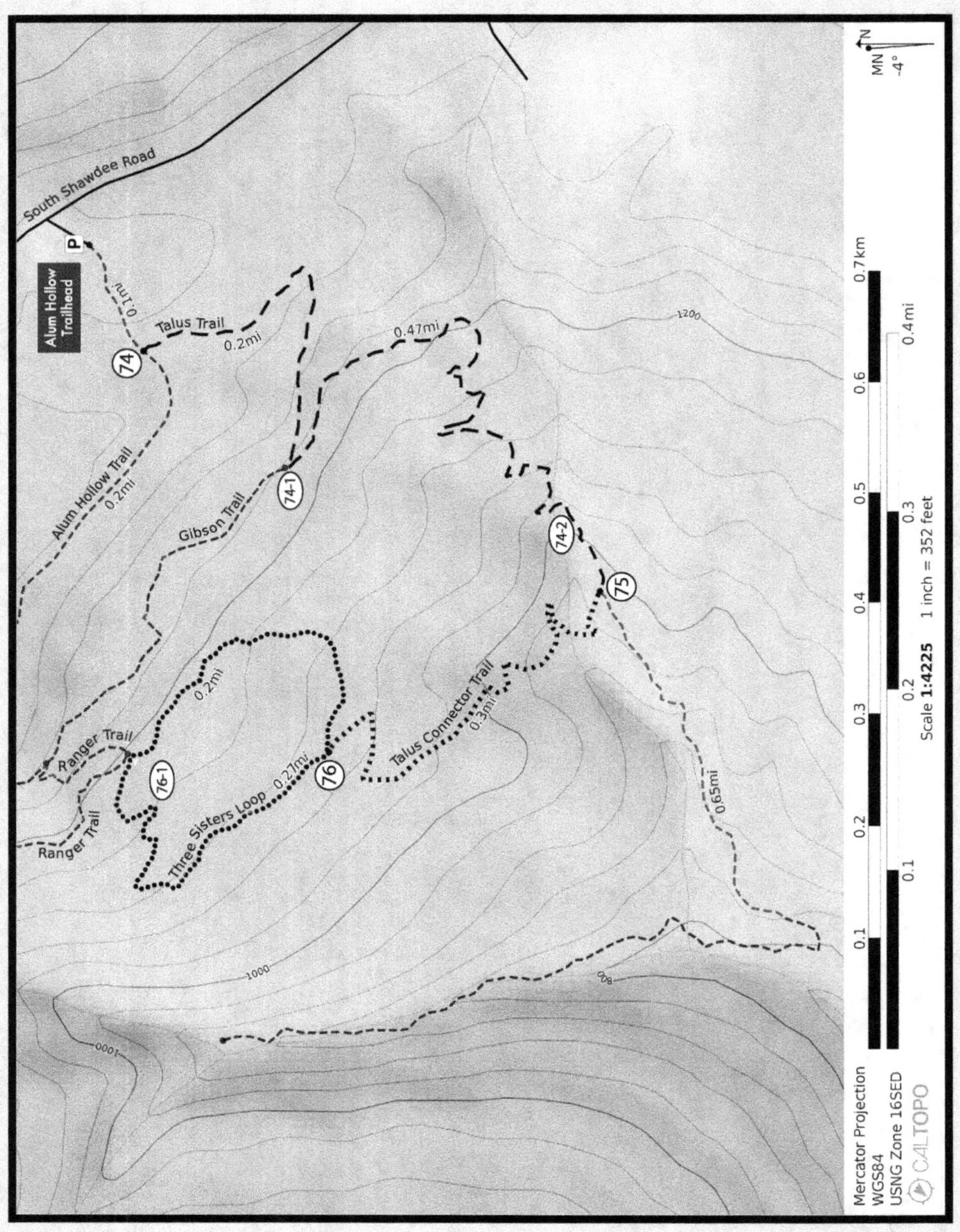

74. Talus Trail

From its junction with the Alum Hollow Trail, the Talus Trail takes you deeper into the hollow on a long, steady, comfortable descent. At the 0.67-mi. mark, an obvious path continues, but portions of this extension trail are unofficial and not marked on some maps. This unofficial trail (marked with red dotted lines on the map) goes to the base of the hollow. Parts of the trail are very rocky and difficult to navigate, so it's recommended for experienced hikers only.

Distance: 0.67 mi.; Talus Trail + unofficial trail, 1.3 mi.
Hiking Time: 30 minutes; Talus Trail + unofficial trail, 1 hour
Elevation Gain/Loss: +23 ft., -405 ft.; Talus Trail + unofficial trail, +156 ft., -598 ft.
Hiking Difficulty: Easy to moderate; Talus Trail + unofficial trail, moderate to strenuous
Location: Green Mountain Nature Preserve, 13800 South Shawdee Rd. SE, Huntsville, AL 35803
Driving Directions: See page 216 and use the directions for the Alum Hollow Trailhead.

Highlights

Stream Emerging from Rocks: When you've walked a little more than 0.6 mi. on the official Talus Trail, look left to see a large rock formation with an alcove. After periods of rain, you might see a stream that flows through a small opening in the rocks and tumbles down small steps. Granted, it's not a huge water feature, but it's a real surprise to see this hidden stream seemingly appear from nowhere.

Waypoint/Mile

Trailhead (Waypoint 74) (34.58919, -86.51099) Begin at the kiosk at the southwestern end of the Alum Hollow Trailhead parking area. From the kiosk, take the marked Alum Hollow Trail for 354 ft. to the junction with the Talus Trail, which intersects on the left. Turn left onto the Talus Trail and travel south on the level path.

The narrow path bends to the east, cuts across the upper portion of a slope, and descends gradually.

74-1 (34.58810, -86.51215) (0.2 mi.) The Gibson Trail intersects on the right and goes northwest. Bear left to make a hairpin turn and head back toward the southeast. Near 0.3 mi., the trail drops a little more aggressively. Not far beyond 0.5 mi., the path makes a steep drop as it skirts a prominent creek drainage.

74-2 (34.58582, -86.51280) (0.63 mi.) Look left to see the rocky alcove where water emerges from a small cave-like opening.

75 (34.58563, -86.51333) (0.67 mi.) The Talus Connector intersects on the right and descends northwest toward the creek drainage. You can also continue straight to take an unofficial trail that drops into the base of the hollow.

The unofficial trail makes a moderate to steep descent through an open hardwood forest. At 0.95 mi. (from the trailhead at Waypoint 74), the path turns right to go down to the base of the hollow. Not far beyond 0.1 mi., you'll cross the dry rocky drainage that's about 40 ft. wide. The trail then parallels the drainage heading north. At 1.2 mi. from the beginning of the Talus Trail, you'll encounter on the left a massive rock overhang. At 1.3 mi., the discernible trail ends at the junction of two large drainages.

Trail Facts

Anatomy of a Trail: This trail was really named in jest. Because the path is rocky, hikers risk twisting an ankle. With a nod and a wink to this, the trail is named for the talus, a small bone that sits between the lower leg and the heel bone. So watch your step, and don't hurt your talus.

75. Talus Connector

The Talus Connector links the Talus Trail and the Three Sisters Trail. This is a popular side trip for people hiking the Talus Trail, as it explores a peaceful pocket of woods where a rock bluff forms a natural amphitheater in a flat stream basin. Hikers on the Talus Trail can also use this connector to access interior trails and explore deeper into the hollow.

Distance: 0.3 mi.
Hiking Time: 15 to 20 minutes
Elevation Gain/Loss: +186 ft., -47 ft.
Hiking Difficulty: Easy
Location: Green Mountain Nature Preserve, 13800 South Shawdee Rd. SE, Huntsville, AL 35803
Driving Directions: See page 216 and use the directions for the Alum Hollow Trailhead.

Highlights

Peaceful Pocket of Woods: At 0.2 mi. the trail drops into a wide flat area in a creek drainage. In this shaded, remote section of the forest, a large rock formation forms a sort of headwall to make the area feel like a natural amphitheater.

Waypoint/Mile

Trailhead (Waypoint 75) (34.58563, -86.51333) To reach the beginning of the Talus Connector, begin at the Alum Hollow Trailhead and follow the Alum Hollow Trail for 354 ft. Then turn onto the Talus Trail and follow it 0.67 mi. to the junction with the Talus Connector. Turn right onto the Talus Connector and travel northwest, descending toward the creek drainage.

After a little more than 200 ft., you'll reach the flat basin of the creek drainage. From here, the trail makes a horseshoe bend to the left and climbs out of the drainage. The terrain ahead is rocky and sliced by smaller drainages. As you continue up the slope, you'll wind among stands of cedars.

76 (34.58771, -86.51493) (0.3 mi.) The Talus Connector intersects with the Three Sisters Loop Trail, which you can follow to the east or west to reach the Ranger Trail.

76. Three Sisters Loop Trail

You'll feel far away from the city as you loop through remote woods tucked between high ridges. While this trail is peaceful, it's also functional, allowing hikers to move between the Talus Trail and other paths in the northern part of the preserve.

Distance: 0.47 mi.
Hiking Time: 15 to 20 minutes
Elevation Gain/Loss: +105 ft., -105 ft.
Hiking Difficulty: Easy
Location: Green Mountain Nature Preserve, 13800 South Shawdee Rd. SE, Huntsville, AL 35803
Driving Directions: See page 216 and use the directions for the Alum Hollow Trailhead.

Highlights

Open Forest and Ridge Views: The wonderful thing about this trail is it gives you the sense that you're deep within wilderness. Because the hardwoods here are widely spaced, you get clear views of surrounding peaks and ridges that rise hundreds of feet. As you gaze at the string of high, forested hills, it feels like the streets and homes of Green Mountain are a world away.

Waypoint/Mile

Trailhead (Waypoint 76) (34.58771, -86.51493) This interior trail can be reached via the Talus Connector or the Ranger Trail. For this book, I've used the Talus Trail route, so you'll begin at the Alum Hollow Trailhead parking area, walk 354 ft. on the Alum Hollow Trail, and then take the Talus Trail to the Talus Connector. On the Talus Connector, travel 0.3 mi. to the junction with the Three Sisters Loop. Turn left onto the Three Sisters Loop and travel northwest.

The leaf-covered path climbs gradually. Look to the southwest, where winter trees will reveal a distant ridge that forms a blue bar on the horizon. When you've walked a little more than 0.1 mi., the immediate ridge across the hollow to the west comes into clearer view. But soon the path hooks right to turn away from the ridge and climb gradually to the north on switchbacks.

76-1 (34.58930, -86.51490) (0.27 mi.) The Ranger Trail intersects on the left. If you reach this junction during a spring hike, you'll likely see a good number of wildflowers in the area, including jack-in-the-pulpit, hairy phlox and golden ragwort. To continue on the Three Sisters Loop, bear right to take the gently rolling path in open, sunny woods dotted with cedars. A short rocky bluff rises on the left, while the woods to the right offer views of a nearby ridge. At around 300 ft., the narrow trail starts to descend gradually, and sweet gum trees join the mix of hardwoods.

The path rollercoasters for a bit and then drops moderately to steeply, with the ridge to the south looming in the distance. At 0.47 mi., you return to Waypoint 76 and the junction with the Talus Connector.

Trail Facts

Who Were the Three Sisters? The Three Sisters Trail is named for three large boulders that lie along the trail.

SECTION 3:
West Plateau Trail, Stonefly Trail and Oak Bluff Trail

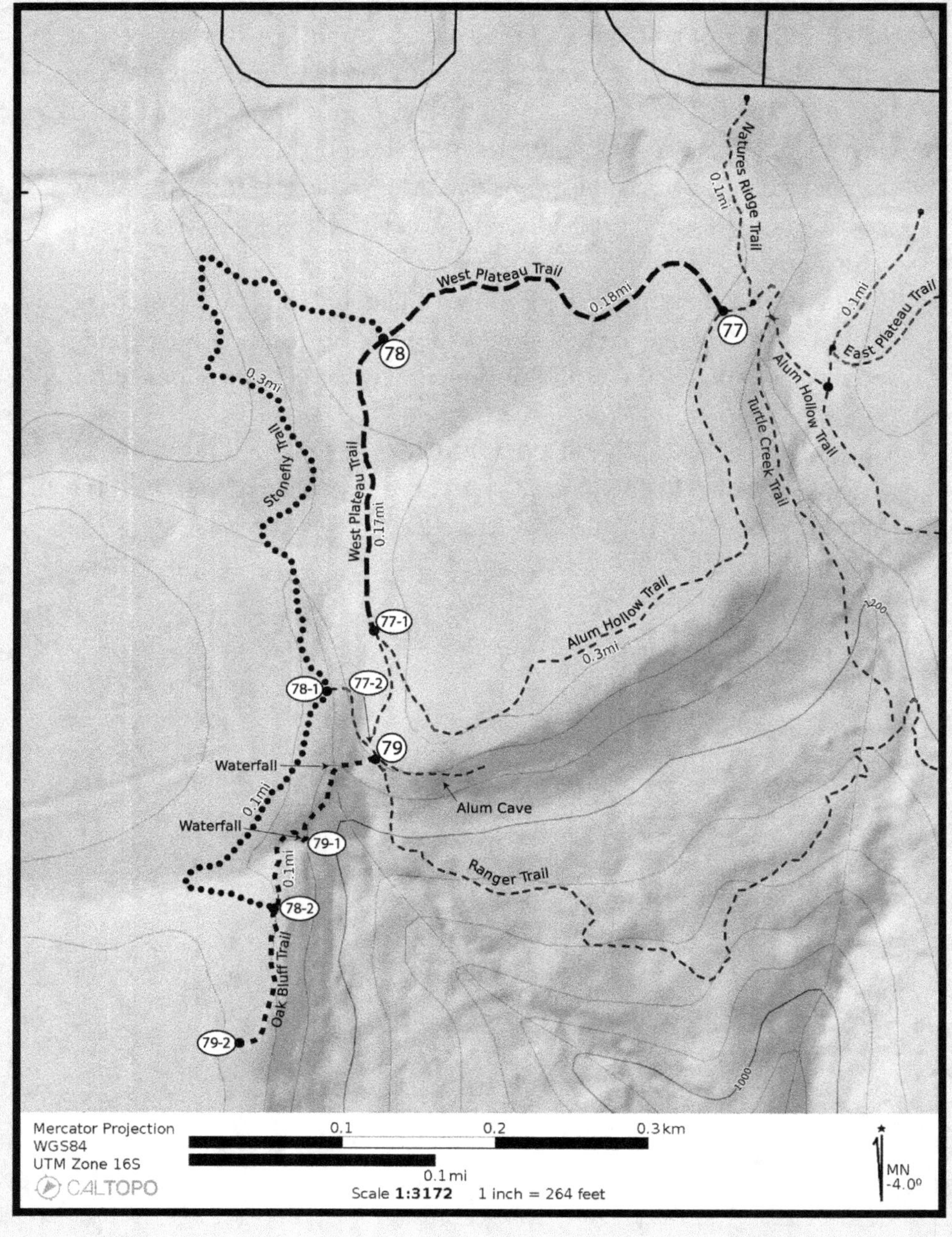

77. West Plateau Trail

The West Plateau offers an alternate route to reach Alum Cave. The path runs through pines and avoids bluffs, so it's not as scenic as the Alum Hollow Trail. But the West Plateau Trail does provide a change of scenery for those who typically walk along the bluff to reach the cave. Also, if you're a beginning trail runner trying to improve your skills, the West Plateau Trail covers ground that's a bit more challenging than the neighboring East Plateau Trail.

Distance: 0.3 mi.
Hiking Time: 10 to 15 minutes
Elevation Gain/Loss: +29 ft., -52 ft.
Hiking Difficulty: Easy to moderate (with one steep descent)
Location: Green Mountain Nature Preserve, 13800 South Shawdee Rd. SE, Huntsville, AL 35803
Driving Directions: See page 216 and use the directions for the Alum Hollow Trailhead.

Highlights

Alum Cave and Waterfall: The West Plateau Trail ends at Alum Cave, the large natural rock shelter that is the most popular destination in the Green Mountain Nature Preserve. From the end of the West Plateau Trail, you can also make a short descent to the nearby rushing creek and a waterfall.

Waypoint/Mile

Trailhead (Waypoint 77) (34.59398, -86.51813) The West Plateau Trail explores the northwestern portion of the Green Mountain Nature Preserve. To reach it, begin at the Alum Hollow Trailhead parking area. Take the Alum Hollow Trail 0.7 mi. to the junction with the West Plateau Trail, which intersects on the right. Turn right onto the West Plateau Trail and head northwest in a stand of pines.

The trail enters dense forest, with a neighborhood street and power-line corridor visible. At 170 ft., you reach a Y junction. Bear left to take the West Plateau Trail. (The path to the right goes beyond the Land

Trust boundary and ends near houses.) The West Plateau Trail bends back to the south and rises gradually, passing through tall pines as well as sweet gum trees and other hardwoods.

78 (34.59376, -86.52045) (0.18 mi.) The Stonefly Trail intersects on the right and goes northwest. To stay on the West Plateau Trail, continue straight and descend to the southwest.

The trail parallels a drainage and then rollercoasters through the forest about another 0.1 mi. The path then begins a steep descent.

77-1 (34.59203, -86.52055) (0.3 mi.) The West Plateau Trail ends at the junction with the Alum Hollow Trail.

Trail Facts

Important Land Donation: In 2016, Robert and Susan Kuehlthau donated to the Land Trust of North Alabama 122 acres of land on Green Mountain, including Alum Cave and the nearby creek and waterfalls.

78. Stonefly Trail

The Stonefly Trail explores the northwest corner of the Green Mountain Nature Preserve, running between the West Plateau and Oak Bluff trails. This tranquil path runs beside burbling streams and finishes with an inspiring view at the edge of a bluff.

Distance: 0.4 mi.
Hiking Time: 15 minutes
Elevation Gain/Loss: +51 ft., -107 ft.
Hiking Difficulty: Easy
Location: Green Mountain Nature Preserve, 13800 South Shawdee Rd. SE, Huntsville, AL 35803
Driving Directions: See page 216 and use the directions for the Alum Hollow Trailhead.

Highlights

Quiet Forest and Peaceful Streams: As you're walking the Stonefly Trail, you'll briefly see nearby houses, but the majority of the patch feels remote and tranquil. As the trail rolls easily and heads south, it visits two modest-sized streams, and a connector trail will take you down to the bank of the main creek.

Bluff View: The trail ends at the junction with the Oak Bluff Trail, which—as the name implies—follows the edge of the mountain plateau. From the bluff you can gaze out over the deep, forested hollow to the east.

Waypoint/Mile

Trailhead (Waypoint 78) (34.59376, -86.52045) The Stonefly Trail lies on the western edge of the Green Mountain Nature Preserve. To access it, begin at the kiosk at the Alum Hollow Trailhead parking area. Follow the Alum Hollow Trail 0.7 mi. to the junction with the West Plateau Trail. Then travel 0.19 mi. on the West Plateau Trail to the junction with the Stonefly Trail. Turn left onto the Stonefly Trail and descend, heading west.

In this corner of the preserve, mature trees dot the land, and you get long views across a clear forest floor. The path drops immediately and at 335 ft. crosses a creek. As the trail rises from the creek, it turns sharply south. When you've walked 0.1 mi., you'll cross a hill and see houses adjacent to the preserve. Ahead, the path rises and falls gently and at 0.2 mi. arrives at the confluence of two creeks. Hop across the small stream that flows in from the west, and then continue to amble across rolling terrain.

78-1 (34.59167, -86.52094) (0.3 mi.) A connector trail intersects on the left. The path measures about 150 ft. and drops down to meet the creek. To continue on the Stonefly Trail, go straight and head southwest.

At 0.4 mi., the path takes a sharp turn left to run east toward the bluff.

78-2 (34.59167, -86.52094) (0.4 mi.) The Stonefly Trail ends at the junction with the Oak Bluff Trail near the edge of the bluff.

Trail Facts

The Stonefly Name: Phill Gibson, a trail care partner with the Land Trust of North Alabama, said that when he was young, he frequently visited the creek that runs near the Stonefly Trail. "I was real keen on identifying insects, so I was aware that you could find stonefly larvae in that creek," Gibson said in a report on the Land Trust website (www.landtrustnal.org). "I had not found them in any other creek up there. Those are the same stoneflies that fly fishermen pattern so many of their hand-tied lures after. I doubt they can still be found there, due to all the settlement we have there now."

79. Oak Bluff Trail

The Oak Bluff Trail visits several of the best natural features in the preserve, including Alum Cave, a couple of waterfalls, and high bluffs with views of Alum Cave Hollow. Be aware that the first part of the hike includes a scramble up a short but steep rocky section. But once you reach the top of the plateau, you'll enjoy an easy walk across the forested plateau.

Distance: 0.17 mi.
Hiking Time: 5 to 10 minutes
Elevation Gain/Loss: +71 ft., -0 ft.
Hiking Difficulty: Moderate
Location: Green Mountain Nature Preserve, 13800 South Shawdee Rd. SE, Huntsville, AL 35803
Driving Directions: See page 216 and use the directions for the Alum Hollow Trailhead.

Highlights

Alum Cave: The Oak Bluff Trail begins near the western end of Alum Cave, the most popular destination in the Green Mountain Nature Preserve. Though it's really a rock shelter and not a cave, it's still impressive. Alum Cave has a wide opening like a massive mouth, and a broad, deep dirt floor that sits beneath a low stone ceiling.

Waterfalls: After walking about 50 ft., you'll reach the first waterfall, where a tongue of water drops into a small pool. Just 200 ft. farther down the trail, the path runs beneath a curtain of water that falls from the lip of a rocky alcove.

Bluff Views: After less than 0.1 mi., the path crawls to the top of the plateau and runs along the edge of the bluff, where hikers can gaze out over the deep forest cut known as Alum Cave Hollow.

Waypoint/Mile

Trailhead (Waypoint 79) (34.59118, -86.52058) The Oak Bluff Trail begins on the western side of the Green Mountain Nature Preserve. To reach the trail, begin at the Alum Hollow Trailhead parking area. Follow the Alum Hollow Trail for 1.1 mi. to reach the junction

The Oak Bluff Trail passes a narrow curtain of water.

with the Oak Bluff Trail and Ranger Trail. Turn right onto the Oak Bluff Trail, which heads west and descends to the creek.

After dropping about 50 ft., you reach the creek and base of a waterfall. Cross the creek and walk along the base of the bluff.

79-1 (34.59075, -86.52101) (255 ft.) The path passes beneath a waterfall that drops like a narrow curtain. Just past the waterfall, the trail turns right to ascend the slope to the left of the waterfall. When you reach the top of the bluff, the trail turns left to move south along the bluff.

78-2 (34.59032, -86.52128) (0.1 mi.) The Stonefly Trail intersects on the right and soon drops to the northwest. To continue on the Oak Bluff Trail, go straight and head south to walk along the edge of the bluff.

79-2 (34.58942, -86.52155) (0.17 mi.) The Oak Bluff Trail ends at the Land Trust boundary. The land beyond this point is private property, so turn around here and retrace your steps.

Madison County Nature Trail

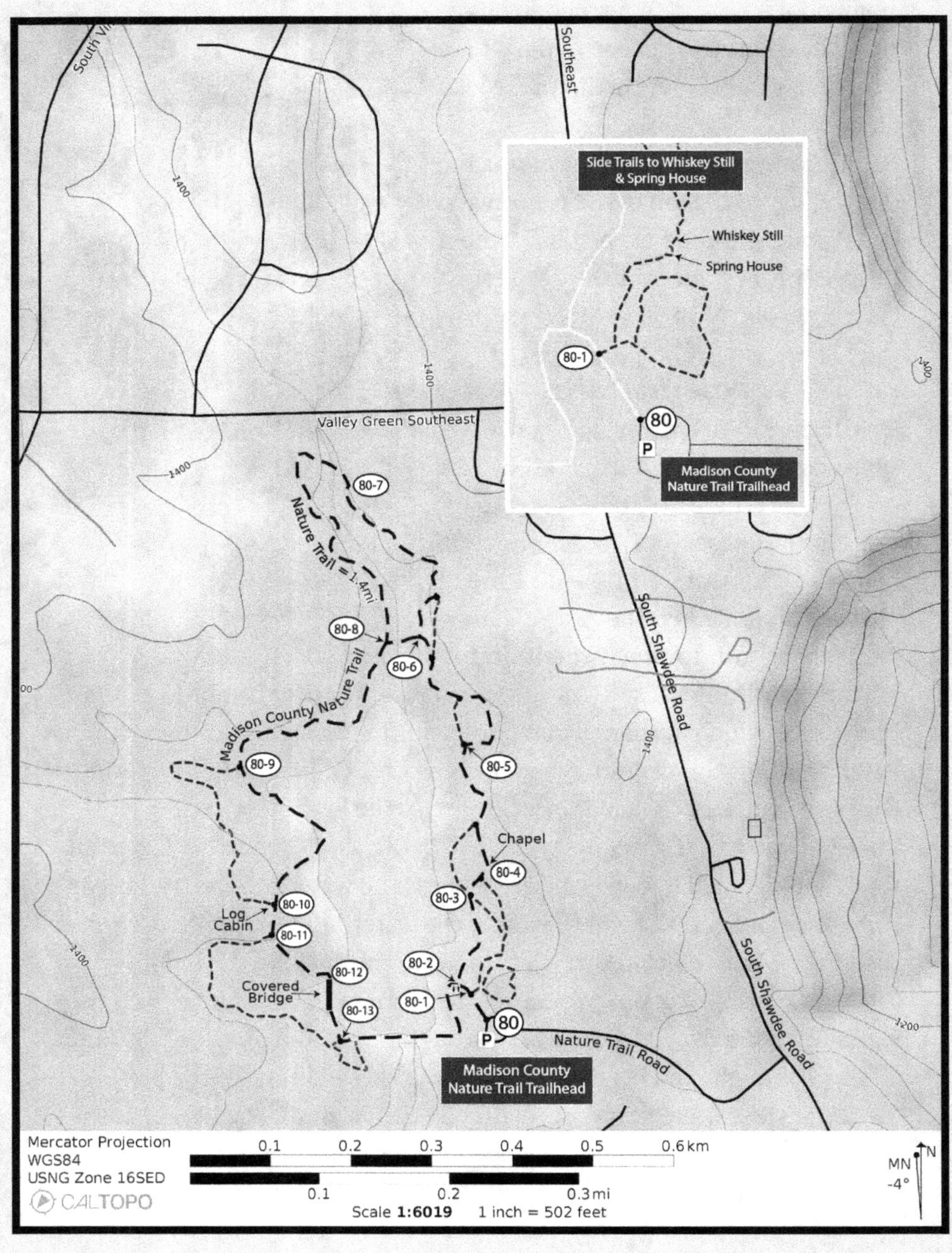

CHAPTER 7

Madison County Nature Trail
(aka Green Mountain Nature Trail)

Looping around a lake atop Green Mountain, the Madison County Nature Trail is a popular destination for families. Open free to the public each day (except Christmas Day and New Year's Day) from 7 a.m. until 30 minutes prior to sunset, the nature trail is a wide, well-marked, mostly level path that is perfect for kids, beginning hikers and people seeking comfortable terrain. Some parts of the trail are dirt, while some sections are gravel or pavement.

Completed in 1975, the 1.5-mile Nature Trail and several side trails run through a 72-acre park that includes restrooms, a covered pavilion, picnic tables, and drink vending machines. The centerpiece of the park is 17-acre Sky Lake, where fishing is allowed for kids under 16 and adults over 60.

As it circles through an attractive hardwood forest, the Nature Trail visits several interesting features, including a small A-frame chapel, a restored log cabin and a rustic covered bridge. Not far from the park entrance, side trails lead to a replica of a moonshine still.

With its high-quality trail system, historic structures and family-friendly amenities, the Madison County Nature Trail is the perfect place to educate and entertain kids or simply relax in the great outdoors.

General Information

Location: 5000 Nature Trail Rd. SE, Huntsville, AL 35803

Hours: 7 a.m. to 30 minutes before sunset

Primary trail activities allowed: Hiking, biking

Pets: Leashed pets allowed.

Fees: There is no fee to use the trail. Fishing is allowed for kids under 16 years old and adults over 60 Monday through Friday with a $3 charge. Veterans are allowed to fish for free with veteran's ID.

Facilities: The picnic pavilion includes several tables, plus restrooms, drink vending machines and a water fountain. There is also a porch where you can sit in chairs that overlook the lake. In addition, there is a large outdoor picnic area with tables and benches.

Information: (256) 883-9501; www.madisoncountyal.gov/services/
green-mountain-nature-trail-1594

Driving Directions

From the junction of U.S. 231 (Memorial Parkway) and Weatherly Road, travel east on Weatherly Rd. for 1.5 mi. Then turn right onto Bailey Cove Road and travel south for 1.2 mi. Next, turn left onto Green Mountain Road and travel 1.8 mi. Then turn right on South Shawdee Road, drive 1.4 mi., and turn right onto Nature Trail Road to enter the park.

80. Madison County Nature Trail

The Madison County Nature Trail is the ideal place for a family outing. Kids and adults will enjoy exploring the well-marked nature trail, which is fairly level and loops around Sky Lake. The trail surface ranges from gravel to dirt to some paved sections. Along the way, you'll encounter plenty of interesting things, such as a reconstructed log cabin and a covered bridge. Near the trailhead, a pavilion and picnic tables provide good spots for a picnic. Also, this is the only Braille trail in Alabama, and a half-mile of the path includes descriptive plaques written only in Braille.

Distance: 1.5 mi.
Hiking Time: 40 to 50 minutes
Elevation Gain/Loss: +174 ft., -187 ft.
Hiking Difficulty: Easy

Highlights

Sky Lake: Sky Lake provides an attractive backdrop as you hike the Nature Trail. When you visit, there's a good chance you'll see ducks and geese cruising across the still water. Plus, a pier and numerous side paths give you access to the edge of the lake, where kids under 16 and adults over 60 can fish.

Log Cabin: On the western side of the lake, the Nature Trail runs near a reconstructed log cabin and a replica well. While the cabin did not occupy this land during pioneer days, it was constructed with

The Madison County Nature Trail runs through the Cambron Covered Bridge.

authentic logs that were hewn around 1810. When you step inside the cabin, you'll see a fireplace and mantle, plus stairs leading to a loft.

Chapel: This wooden A-frame chapel is used for church services, weddings and memorials. A pulpit and some short pews are tucked into the structure, while another couple of rows of benches sit outside the building.

Covered Bridge: If you're into photography, be sure to bring your camera when you cross the Cambron Covered Bridge. Measuring about 113 ft., the rustic wooden structure crosses a southwestern inlet of the lake. At the southern end, the bridge touches the edge of the forest, and the tree canopy creates moody shadows. For another great photo of the bridge, visit in the fall when the leaves change color. From the eastern side of the lake, you can see the full length of the bridge surrounded by brilliant red, gold and orange foliage. On a clear day, you can capture the bridge and the fall colors reflecting in the water.

***The following hike description goes counterclockwise around the lake.*

Waypoint/Mile

Trailhead (Waypoint 80) (34.59780, -86.51717) In the northwest corner of the parking area, take the gravel path that runs to the right of the office and passes through a breezeway.

80-1 (34.59809, -86.51732) (50 ft.) A path covered in pine needles intersects on the right. Go straight, continuing to descend, and then bear left to reach the main Nature Trail. (If you turn right onto the path at Waypoint 80-1, you can hike a short distance to see a historic springhouse

A small outdoor chapel lies along the Madison County Nature Trail.

and moonshine still display. For directions, look below under "Historic Features on Side Trails" and see the inset map.)

80-2 (34.59826, -86.51752) (150 ft.) Turn right onto the main Nature Trail and travel north. After about another 150 ft., you'll pass a picnic table and a trail that descends to a pier.

80-3 (34.59925, -86.51748) (0.1 mi.) At the Y junction, bear to the right and head to the northeast. Go about 260 ft. to Waypoint 80-4.

80-4 (34.59977, -86.51728) (0.15 mi.) The trail reaches the chapel. After you pass the chapel, you'll reach another trail junction. Go right and continue north.

80-5 (34.60086, -86.51743) (0.25 mi.) At the trail junction, turn right to continue on the main Nature Trail.

After walking another 226 ft., you can see on the left a narrow path that descends to the south. This path just connects back to Waypoint 80-5, so continue straight and descend to the northwest. Not far ahead, at 0.33 mi., bear left at a Y junction to continue on the main Nature Trail.

80-6 (34.60227, -86.51802) (0.38 mi.) At the trail junction, turn right to extend your hike and explore the northern portion of the Nature Trail. To shorten your hike, turn left to take a connector path that leads to a wooden footbridge on the Nature Trail.

80-7 (34.60397, -86.51893) (0.56 mi.) To the right is a shelter.

80-8 (34.60205, -86.51852) (0.8 mi.) The wooden footbridge intersects on the left and stretches about 120 ft. Continue straight and begin to climb south.

80-9 (34.60065, -86.52059) (0.98 mi.) A path intersects on the left and continues 0.2 mi. to the log cabin. To continue on the main Nature Trail, go straight and head south.

80-10 (34.59911, -86.52007) (1.1 mi.) The trail passes the log cabin.

80-11 (34.59880, -86.52013) (1.16 mi.) A trail intersects on the right and winds through the western side of the property. (If you take this route, you can walk 0.2 mi. and loop back to the Nature Trail near Waypoint 80-13.) To continue on the Nature Trail, bear left and head southeast toward the water.

80-12 (34.59826, -86.51923) (1.22 mi.) Cross the covered bridge, heading south.

80-13 (34.59758, -86.51920) (1.27 mi.) Turn left to take the gravel path that traverses the dam on the southern end of the lake. At the east side of the lake, the path turns north and ends at Waypoint 80-2 at 1.5 mi.

Historic Features on Side Trails

(See Inset Map)

To see additional historic features near the Nature Trail, begin at the trailhead and proceed to Waypoint 80-1. Turn right onto a side trail and immediately bear left. You'll walk about 200 ft. to reach the Spring House.

Spring House: This is an example of the typical springhouse used by pioneers to store food and other perishable supplies before refrigeration was invented. The house would be built around a natural spring that fed water into the structure and kept the interior at a constantly cool temperature. From the Spring House, continue descending to the north to reach a moonshine still display.

Moonshine Still: This is a replica of a "groundhog still," which was the most common type of still used in Alabama. An interpretive sign explains how the tank, burner and tubing were used to transform corn mash into moonshine.

From the still, you can retrace your steps to access the main nature trail or continue north 14 ft. to a Y junction. From the junction, the trail to the left goes 220 ft. to the northwest to meet the main Nature Trail at Waypoint 80-3, while the path to the right goes about 350 ft. to the northwest to meet the main Nature Trail at Waypoint 80-4.

Trail Facts

Cambron Bridge: The covered bridge is named for Joe E. Cambron, who was the Madison County bridge foreman from 1958 to 1974.

Hikes By Theme

History

North Plateau Loop Trail
William Arthur Wells CCC
  Memorial Trail
Hotel Basin Trail
Toll Gate Trail
Old Railroad Bed Trail
Fagan Springs Trail
Sink Hole Trail
Alms House Trail
Three Caves Loop Trail
Waterline Trail
Wagon Trail
Arrowhead Trail
Trough Springs Trail
Bushwhacker Johnston Trail
Burritt on the Mountain
Big Cove Turnpike Trail
Alum Hollow Trail
Madison County Nature Trail

Hikes for Kids

North Plateau Loop
Fire Tower Trail
Bog Trail
Bucca Family Bike Trail
South Plateau Loop Trail
Stone Cuts Trail
Bluff Line Trail
Old Railroad Bed Trail
Fagan Springs Trail
Wildflower Trail
Cold Spring Trail

Bankhead Parkway
Rock Bluff Trail
Jones Valley Loop Trail
Alum Hollow Trail
Oak Bluff Trail
Madison County Nature Trail

Streams, Ponds and Lakes

North Plateau Loop
Bog Trail
McKay Hollow Trail
Flat Rock Trail
Keith Trail
Bluff Line Trail
High Trail
Old Railroad Bed Trail
Fagan Springs Trail
Wildflower Trail
Wagon Trail
Young-Kennedy Trail
Cold Spring Trail
Arrowhead Trail
Natural Well Trail
Trough Springs Trail
Jones Valley Loop Trail
Smokerise Trail
Smokerise Connector Trail
Bill and Marion Certain Trail
Alum Hollow Trail
Ranger Trail
Talus Trail
Talus Connector Trail
Stonefly Trail

Hikes By Theme *continued*

Oak Bluff Trail
Madison County Nature Trail

Running Trails

North Plateau Loop Trail
Fire Tower Trail
South Plateau Loop Trail
Mountain Mist Trail
Keith Trail
Bluff Line Trail
Toll Gate Trail
High Trail
Gaslight Trail
Watts Trail
Fagan Springs Trail
Wildflower Trail
Bankhead Trail
Oak Park Trail
Cold Spring Trail
Arrowhead Trail
Natural Well Trail
Bankhead Parkway
Warpath Ridge Trail
Jones Valley Loop Trail
Stevenson Trail
Sugar Tree Trail
Smokerise Trail
Bill and Marion Certain Trail
West Bluff Trail
Varnedoe Trail
Alum Hollow Trail

East Plateau Trail
Talus Trail
Talus Connector Trail
3 Sisters Loop Trail
West Plateau Trail
Stonefly Trail
Madison County Nature Trail

Great Views

North Plateau Loop
South Plateau Loop
Panther Knob Trail
Three Caves Loop Trail
Cold Spring Trail
Warpath Ridge Trail
Burritt on the Mountain
Bill and Marion Certain Trail
West Bluff Trail
Alum Hollow Trail
Oak Bluff Trail

Waterfalls

Flat Rock Trail
Jones Valley Loop Trail
Oak Bluff Trail

Wildflowers

Sinks Trail
Bluff Line Trail
Fagan Springs Trail
Wildflower Trail
Bill and Marion Certain Trail

Index

A.

Alabama Birding Trails 159
Alabama snow-wreath 90, 92
Alabama State Parks Division xii
Alms House Trail 78, 79, 83-85, 89, 94-99, 103, 110, 249
Alum Cave 215, 219-221, 223-225, 237, 238, 240, 241
Alum Cave Hollow 215, 220, 223- 225, 240, 241
Alum Hollow Trail xi, 215, 218- 227, 231, 233, 234, 237-239, 241, 249, 250
Alum Hollow Trailhead 216, 219, 220, 222-224, 226, 227, 231, 233, 234, 237-241
amphibians xx
anemones xviii, 90
Appalachian Mountains xv, xvi
armadillo xix
Arrowhead Trail 132-139, 143, 145, 249, 250
Audubon-led hikes 159

B.

Bailey Cove 180
Bailey Cove Branch stream 173, 177, 178, 179, 182, 184
Bailey Cove Trail 176-182, 184
Bankhead Parkway Blockade Trailhead 55, 57, 59, 70, 149
Bankhead Parkway (Closed Section) 7, 31, 32, 55-57, 60, 114, 127, 128, 148-151, 249, 250
Bankhead Trail 112, 115, 116, 121, 123, 124, 250
Bankhead Trailhead (Land Trust Nature Preserve) 65, 67, 72, 75, 78, 81, 82, 84, 85, 97, 107, 110, 113, 115, 119
barred owl xix, xx
barn owl xx
beavers xix
Belue Trail 80, 83, 84, 85, 99,
Big Cat Hill Bypass 132, 133, 136,
Big Cove Turnpike Trail 159, 160, 165-170, 249
Big Spring xi
Big Spring Creek 22
birding 63, 159
birds xix, 93
Biker's Trailhead 2, 3, 5, 14, 15, 17, 18, 26, 29, 32, 34, 36-39, 43-51, 59, 60
Bill and Marion Certain Trail 173, 195, 196, 201-211, 249, 250,
Blevins Gap Nature Preserve 173, 175, 177, 179, 181, 183, 187, 190, 191, 195, 198, 199, 203, 205, 206, 207, 209,
Blevins Gap Road 170, 195, 197,
Blevins Gap Trailhead 173, 174, 195, 196, 198, 201, 203, 204, 206-211
Blossomwood 89
Blue Spring Creek 23
Bluff Line Trail 66-70, 82, 85, 98, 103, 109, 249, 250
bobcats xviii
Bog Trail 10, 13-16, 18, 27, 249

boots xii, xxvi, xxx, 24
Boy Scouts 155, 170, 193
Bucca Family Bike Trail 10, 13, 14, 16-19, 28, 29, 249
Burritt hiking parking area 160, 162, 165-169
Burritt on the Mountain xxxiii, 158-161, 163- 165, 168, 170, 249, 250
Bushwhacker Johnston 135, 136, 144, 145, 147
Bushwhacker Johnston Trail 142-144, 146, 249
Buzzards Roost Trail 118, 121-123

C.

Chestnut Knob 35
children, hikes for xiii, 160, 249
Chittamwood Trail 176, 182-184, 189,
Cincinnati Arch xv, xvi
Civil War 135, 144, 145
Civilian Conservation Corps (CCC) 7, 8, 34, 42, 44, 50-52, 249
Cleermont Trailhead 64, 87, 110,
climate xiv
clothing xxii, xxvi-xxviii
Cold Spring Trail 8, 32, 126, 127, 128, 129, 150, 249, 250
Cold Spring Trailhead 65, 75, 77, 127
copperhead xx, xxiii
cottonmouth xx, xxiii
Cumberland Plateau xv, xvi

D.

Dallas Branch Creek 121, 122, 124
Dallas Branch Trail 116, 118, 122, 123, 124
deer xviii
Discovery Trail 144, 159, 160, 162, 165-168, 170
distances xxxvii
Dummy Line Trail 71, 77, 112-115

E.

East Plateau Trail 218, 220, 222, 223, 237, 250
eastern chipmunk xix
eastern cottontail rabbits xix
eastern diamondback rattlesnake xx, xxiii
eastern milk snake xx
eastern hognose snake xx
eastern red cedars xvii
eastern redbud trees 211
Edwards, Chad vii

F.

Fagan Creek xviii, xxi, 67, 68, 70, 71, 83, 86-90, 92, 95, 98
Fagan Creek xviii, xxi, 67, 68, 70, 71, 83, 86-90, 92, 95, 98, 111
Fagan Springs 93, 95
Fagan Springs Trail 85, 86, 88, 89, 95, 98, 108, 122, 249, 250
Fanning Trailhead 173, 174, 177-184, 187, 188, 190-192

Fire Tower xii, 11, 13, 14, 18, 26. 28
Fire Tower Trail 7, 8, 10-16, 18, 19, 27, 28, 154, 249
first-aid kit xxix
Flat Rock Connector 54, 58
Flat Rock Trail 30, 36-40, 58, 155, 249, 250
flycatchers xix
footwear xxvi, xxvii, 75,
Ford Ranger 225
forests xiii, xvii, xviii, xix, xx, 82, 93

G.

Gaslight Trail 74, 76, 78, 79, 98, 250
geography xv, xviii, 159
geology xv, 159
Gibson Trail 218, 224, 227, 228, 232
Goat Rock 31, 33, 36
Goat Trail 30, 33-37, 39, 44, 50, 51, 154
Goat Trail-Flat Rock Connector 30, 35, 37, 39,
Gore-Tex xvii
gray foxes xviii
Green Mountain xi, xvi-xviii, xxvi, 6, 139, 166, 170,
173, 195, 197, 198, 200, 203, 205, 210-212, 214, 215,
216, 219, 222-224, 234, 238, 243
Green Mountain Nature Preserve 215, 219, 222, 224,
226, 227, 231, 233, 234, 237-241
Green Mountain Nature Trail 243, 244
greenways vii, xiii, xxiv
Gurley xi

H.

Hampton Cove 154
Hazel Green xi
High Trail 66, 67, 69, 70, 71, 73, 77, 103, 113, 114, 249,
250
Hiker's Trailhead 3, 15, 16, 24-27, 29, 36-39, 153, 154
Historic Springhouse 97, 99
Hoksbergen, Ben vii, xv
Hotel Basin Trail 66, 70, 71, 72, 249
Hotel Monte Sano xi, 8, 11, 14, 15, 27, 29, 69, 70-73,
81, 84, 114,
Hunt, John xi
Huntsville Area Mountain Bike Riders (HAMR) vii,
xii, 68, 113
Huntsville Mountain 173, 187, 191, 197
Huntsville Times 161
Huntsville Track Club 116

I.

Indian pink xviii, 22, 90, 92
indigo buntings xix,
International Mountain Bicycling Association
(IMBA) 25

J.

Joe B. Shirley Fire Tower 26
Johnston, Rev. Milus E. "Bushwhacker" 135, 136, 144,
145, 147
Jones Valley 189
Jones Valley Farm 179

Jones Valley Loop Trail 173, 176-178, 180-184, 188,
249, 250

K.

Keith Trail 42, 44, 49, 50, 52, 57, 58, 249, 250
kids, hikes for xvii, xxxiv, 1, 5, 16, 17, 45, 46, 63, 67, 87,
89, 127, 159, 160-162, 173, 177, 215, 243, 244, 249

L.

Land Trust of North Alabama vii, xiii, xxxiii, xxxv,
33, 67, 72, 75, 78, 81, 84, 85, 87, 89, 94, 97, 100-102,
107, 110, 111, 113, 115, 119, 121, 123, 125, 127, 133, 137,
143, 145, 156, 173, 183, 189, 191, 205, 212, 215, 216,
228, 238, 240
Little Chalybeate Spring 27, 29
loblolly pine xvii
Logan Point 32, 55, 56, 58-61, 150, 151
Logan Point Alternate Trail 47, 54, 56-58, 61
Logan Point Trail 44, 47, 50, 54-58, 60, 61
Lowry Trail 196, 201, 202, 206, 207

M.

Madison County Nature Trail xxxiii, 242-246, 249,
250
Madison Limestone Company 100
mammals xviii
map and compass xxviii, xxix
Maple Hill Cemetery 75
Marshall Space Flight Center xii
mayapple xviii, 91, 128, 199-201, 205
McCurdy Barnyard 159
McKay Hollow 5, 6, 17, 21, 22, 26, 27, 33, 133, 134, 137-
139, 153, 154, 164
McKay Hollow Trail xxv, xxxiv, 1, 6, 20-24, 28, 133,
136, 137, 139, 249
Mills Hollow 26
Monte Sano Lodge 5, 7, 8
Monte Sano Mountain ix, xi, xvi-xviii, 33, 48, 51, 63,
69, 94, 107, 133, 135, 149, 151, 154, 159, 164, 169, 179,
197, 251
Monte Sano Preserve Bankhead Parking Lot 65, 68,
72, 76, 78, 85, 98, 107, 108, 113, 115
Monte Sano Railroad Company 14
Monte Sano Railway xi, 11, 12, 14, 81, 82, 84, 114
Monte Sano Railway Dummy Line 81, 114
Monte Sano State Park xii, xiii, xxi, xxxiii, xxxv, xxx-
viii, 1-5, 11, 14, 15, 17, 19, 21, 24-26, 31-34, 36- 38, 43,
45, 46, 48, 49, 51, 55, 57, 59, 77, 116, 125, 128, 133,
137, 139, 149, 151, 153, 155, 156, 166, 170
Mountain Mist 50K 1, 31
Mountain Mist Trail 28, 30-34, 36, 44, 45, 47, 55, 57,
60, 128, 150, 250
mosquitoes xxi, xxii, 16

N.

Nashville Dome xv, xvi
Natural Well 137-140
Natural Well Trail xxxvi, 132-139, 143, 249, 250
Natures Ridge Trail 226

Natures Ridge Trailhead 216
North Alabama Japanese Garden 11, 12
North Plateau Loop xii, 1, 4-8, 12, 13, 32, 129, 249, 250

O.

Oak Park Parking Area 65, 119
Oak Park Trail 116, 118-123, 250
Oak Park Trailhead 65, 122, 123
Oak Tree Trail 160, 163, 164, 165
Old Bluff Line Trail 66, 68, 69, 82,
Old Railroad Bed Trail xi, 11, 63, 68, 76, 80-86, 98, 108, 114, 249
O'Shaughnessy, James 13
O'Shaughnessy Point 17, 19, 25, 27, 153
orchids xviii, 90
Owens Cross Roads xi

P.

Panther Knob 61
Panther Knob Trail 47, 54-56, 58-61, 73, 76, 250
planetarium xii, 8
plants xviii, xix, xiv, xxv, xxxi, 12, 82, 90-93, 127, 128, 159, 199, 201, 205, 221
poison ivy xviii, xxiv, xxv
poison oak xviii, xxiv, xxv
poison sumac xviii, xxiv, xxv
Polaris Industries 116
pump house 104

R.

red foxes xviii
Red Lizard Trail 152, 153, 155, 156, 157,
red-shouldered hawks xix
Redstone Arsenal xii, 207, 208,
red-tailed hawks xix
reptiles xx
Rock Bluff Trail 159, 160, 162-168, 170, 249
Rocket City Astronomical Association 8
Rocky Nightmare Trail 20, 23-25, 154
rodents xviii
Round Top Mountain 159, 163-166, 168
running xxiii, 1, 31, 32, 33, 63, 222, 250

S.

safety xxi, xxx
salamanders xx
Shoals, The xvi
shoes xxvi, xxvii, xxx, 24,
shortleaf pine xvii
sinkholes 45, 48, 94, 95,
Sink Hole Trail 80, 91, 93, 94, 97, 99, 110, 249
Sinks Trail xviii, 32, 34, 36, 42-48, 50, 51, 55-57, 60, 61, 150, 250
Smith-Williams House 164
Smokerise Connector 194, 197, 198, 249
Smokerise Trail 173, 194-198, 200, 204, 206, 249, 250
snakes ix, xx, xxiii, xxiv, 69, 121, 206
Solomon's seals 90
SORBA Huntsville 116

South Monte Sano Trailhead 64, 69, 70, 133, 134, 137, 138, 143-146
South Plateau Loop Trail 13, 15, 16, 20, 23, 25, 27, 28, 33, 153, 154, 249, 250
Southeast Church of the Nazarene 173, 174
Southern Off-Road Bicycle Association (SORBA) 19
southern red oaks xvii
southern shagbark hickory xvii
space shuttle 140, 166
Space Walk Trail 139, 140, 166, 170
spicebush 128
spiders ix, xxi, xxiii, xxiv
spring beauties xviii, 90
springhouse 27, 97, 245, 247
Sputnik xii, 14
Saint John's wort 92
Stone Cuts Trail 42, 44-50, 57, 58, 60, 61, 249
succession forest xvii
Sugar Tree Trail 173, 175, 194-201, 204, 206, 207, 210, 250
Sugar Tree Trailhead 173, 175, 197, 198, 199

T.

Talus Connector 230, 232-235, 249, 250
Talus Trail 220, 227, 228, 231-235, 249, 250
Tennessee River xvi, 145, 210
Tennessee Valley xiv, xvi, 140, 209, 210, 211, 221
Three Benches Area 44
Three Caves Loop Trail 96, 100-103, 249, 250
Three Caves Quarry 97, 100, 102, 104
Three Caves Trailhead 64, 103, 110
Toll Gate Road 75-77, 86
Toll Gate Trail xxvi, 67, 71, 73-79, 83, 85, 86, 108, 113, 114, 116, 249, 250
trail etiquette xxxi
trail running xxiii, 1, 31, 32, 33, 63, Bailey 222, 250,
Trough Springs xxxvi, 134, 136, 144, 145, 146
Trough Springs Trail xxvi, 138, 142-144, 146, 165, 167, 249
trout lilies 90
trillium 91, 189, 196
turkey vultures xix

U.

University of Alabama in Huntsville vii, xv
U.S. Army Aviation and Missile Command xii
U.S. Space & Rocket Center 98, 102

V.

Varnedoe Trail 173, 201, 202, 205, 209-211, 250
Valley Bend shopping center 180
Valley Bend Trailhead 198
Viduta Pike Trail 166, 169
violets xviii, 90
Virginia bluebells xviii, 90, 91,
Virginia pines xvii
vireos xix

W.

Wagon Trail 68, 83, 85, 86, 88, 92, 93, 95, 99, 103,
106-109, 111, 249
Weatherly Mountain 210
Walsingham Connector 176, 180-182, 189
Walsingham Trail 176, 180-184, 189
warblers xix
Warpath Ridge Trail 25, 28, 35, 152-157, 250
water and food xxviii
waterfall(s) xxxv, 1, 36-40, 63, 103, 121, 122, 140, 177,
178, 215, 219, 237, 238, 240, 241, 250
Waterline Trail 67, 69, 70, 96, 97, 99, 101-103, 107,
109, 111, 249
Watts Trail 80, 85, 86, 88, 92, 108, 250
weather xiv, xv, xxi, xxii, xxvi, xxvii, xxviii, 7, 89
weathering 48
Weber, Soos vii
Weninegar, Lynne vii
Wernher von Braun xii, 5, 8
Wernher von Braun Planetarium 5, 8
West Bluff Trail 173, 202, 205, 207-209, 250
wildflowers xviii, xxii, 43, 63, 89-92, 178, 187, 188, 190,
192, 195, 200, 203, 215, 235, 250

Y.

Young Adult Conservation Corps (YACC) 29
Young-Kennedy Trail 99, 103, 106-111, 249

About the Author

Marcus Woolf has worked as an editor and writer for outdoor adventure magazines and other media for more than 25 years. His writing has appeared in publications such as *Outside* magazine and *Backpacker*. As a native of Huntsville, Marcus grew up on Monte Sano Mountain, where he discovered his love for hiking. After living in California for eight years, he returned to Huntsville to be closer to family and Alabama football. In 2009, Wilderness Press published his first hiking guidebook, *Afoot & Afield: Atlanta*. When he isn't mapping trails for books, Marcus enjoys backpacking, canoeing and kayaking with his wife, Wendy.